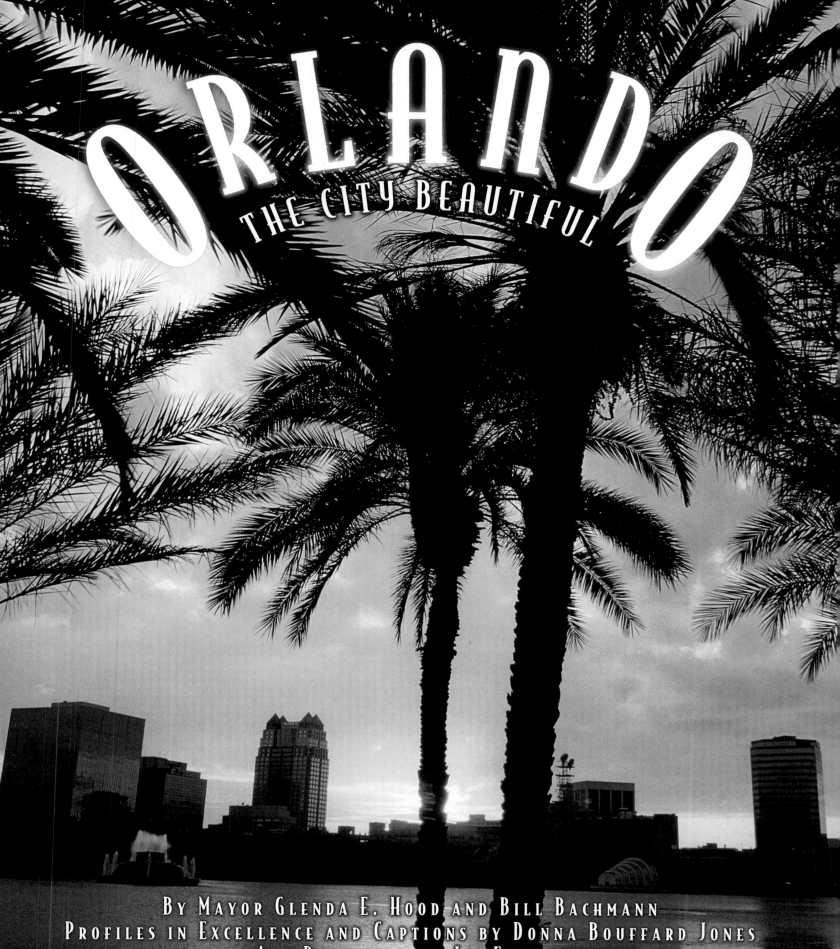

ORLANDO
THE CITY BEAUTIFUL

By Mayor Glenda E. Hood and Bill Bachmann
Profiles in Excellence and Captions by Donna Bouffard Jones
Art Direction by Jil Foutch
Sponsored by the Greater Orlando Chamber of Commerce

LIBRARY OF CONGRESS CATALOGING-IN-PUBLICATION DATA

Hood, Glenda E. (Glenda Evans), 1950-
    Orlando : the city beautiful / by Glenda E. Hood and Bill Bachmann
; profiles in excellence and captions by Donna Bouffard Jones.
      p.   cm.
    Includes index.
    ISBN 1-881096-46-7 (alk. paper)
    1. Orlando (Fla.)—Civilization. 2. Orlando (Fla.)—Pictorial
works. 3. Orlando (Fla.)—Economic conditions. 4. Business
enterprises—Florida—Orlando. I. Bachmann, Bill. II. Jones,
Donna Bouffard, 1963- . III. Title.
F319.07H66 1997
975.9'24—dc21
              97-35678

URBAN
TAPESTRY
SERIES
TOWERY
PUBLISHING, INC.

TOWERY PUBLISHING, INC., 1835 UNION AVENUE, MEMPHIS, TN 38104

PUBLISHER: *J. Robert Towery*
EXECUTIVE PUBLISHER: *Jenny McDowell*
NATIONAL SALES MANAGER: *Stephen Hung*
MARKETING DIRECTOR: *Carol Culpepper*
PROJECT DIRECTORS: *Tamera "Tee"
  Nielsen-Pritchard, Thomas P. Smith*
EXECUTIVE EDITOR: *David B. Dawson*
MANAGING EDITOR: *Michael C. James*
SENIOR EDITORS: *Lynn Conlee, Carlisle
  Hacker*
EDITORS/PROJECT MANAGERS: *Mary Jane
  Adams, Lori Bond*
STAFF EDITORS: *Jana Files, Susan Hesson,
  Brian Johnston*

ASSISTANT EDITORS: *Pat McRaven,
  Jennifer C. Pyron, Allison Ring*
EDITORIAL CONSULTANT: *Joseph A. Mittiga*
CREATIVE DIRECTOR: *Brian Groppe*
PROFILE DESIGNERS: *Laurie Lewis, Kelley
  Pratt, Ann Ward*
DIGITAL COLOR SUPERVISOR: *Brenda Pattat*
PRODUCTION RESOURCES MANAGER: *Dave
  Dunlap Jr.*
PRODUCTION ASSISTANTS: *Geoffrey Ellis,
  Enrique Espinosa, Robin McGehee*
PHOTOGRAPHY EDITOR ASSISTANT: *Lisa
  Donahou*
PRINT COORDINATOR: *Beverly Thompson*

EVERETT & SOULÉ

CONTENTS

Legend describes a common scenario in the Central Florida of the early 1800s.

Swept along on a current of panic created by a report that local natives were

preparing to attack, settlers huddled in a cramped farmhouse—muskets

loaded, ready for battle. On this day, a young woman appeared in a clearing near the

settlers' makeshift fort, hysterically recounting her story of a daring escape from a group

Although Orlando today is far different

of Indians intent on running the settlers out of the area. But an attack never came.

from the city that greeted settlers in

Only days later did the settlers learn the real cause of the young woman's anguish.

the late 1800s, it still holds the perfect

Her story of ambush was fabricated in hopes that the "realities" of life in the harsh

blend of economic prosperity and qual-

Central Florida frontier would convince her parents to return to their native Georgia—

ity of life.

and cure her lingering case of homesickness.

Good Roads ✦ VISIT ✦ Pure Water.
Orlando Fla
No INSECTS.   RICH LANDS.

B Y   M A Y O R   G L E N D A   E .   H O O D

It was against this backdrop that my great-grandfather, Charles Goodlow Evans, moved his family to Central Florida in the 1850s. For him, the family from Georgia, and many others, life in Central Florida came with considerable risk, but it also offered wonderful opportunities, including good weather and plenty of water for growing citrus crops, as well as enough wide-open space to make raising cattle a profitable venture in this new frontier.

Like the rest of those early settlers, my great-grandfather carved his orange grove and pasture out of the palmetto scrub and pine trees that would become his new hometown.

Would he, or any of them, have ever dared to dream that this fledgling community—a frontier crossroads of citrus and cattle in sparsely populated 19th-century Florida—was destined to become a city of international trade and world prominence? Never.

In his lifetime, my great-grandfather witnessed a remarkable growth of technology, from homemade tallow candles to the electric light. And if he could share the front-row seat I've had for the past four and a half decades, he would be just as amazed at the civic transformation Orlando has made during *my* lifetime—a transformation I consider no less remarkable than the advent of the electric light. And we're not finished yet!

Strawberries have been a leading agricultural commodity in Central Florida for many generations, and some fans of the fruit will do almost anything for a taste of sweet success. Here, a group of kids vie for the best oversized strawberry shortcake at Nickelodeon Studios.

As cities go, Orlando is relatively young, an adolescent so to speak. From the chaos of the Second Seminole Indian War, a settlers' outpost took root in 1842 near an abandoned U.S. Army facility called Fort Gatlin. The tiny community was named Jernigan, after Aaron Jernigan, who established the area's first trading post. As the frontier of Central Florida opened, the town grew rapidly. A post office followed in 1850, and seven years later, the community was renamed Orlando.

Why Orlando? There are plenty of theories. One says the city took its name from Orlando Reeves, a soldier killed in a Seminole raid and buried along the shore of what is today known as Lake Eola. Another claims the person in the grave was not a soldier, but a wealthy landowner named Orlando Rees, who also died in a Seminole attack. Either way, the theories

Orlando Wilderness Park, a man-made wetland east of the city, features towering pine and cypress trees (BELOW). Today totaling more than 36,000, Florida's Seminole population honors the traditions of its ancestors (OPPOSITE).

▲ STEVE VAUGHN

claim that settlers called the area "Orlando's Grave," later dropping the word "grave" to enhance the image of their bustling new town.

Another theory is far more imaginative. In the 1850s, one of the most influential local citizens was Judge J.G. Speer. (In fact, it was Speer's political manipulations that helped Jernigan become the county seat.) The theory says that Speer, who had a great love for William Shakespeare, wanted to pay tribute to the bard by naming the community Orlando after the character in *As You Like It*.

The story of how Orlando became The City Beautiful is not nearly as well known as the tradition it has inspired. By 1908, Orlandoans declared to all who would listen that theirs was The Phenomenal City, a belief bolstered by an attempt to stage a World's Fair here.

However, Mayor William H. Jewell and the City Aldermen, as the City Council was then called, had a different agenda and began a program to beautify the community.

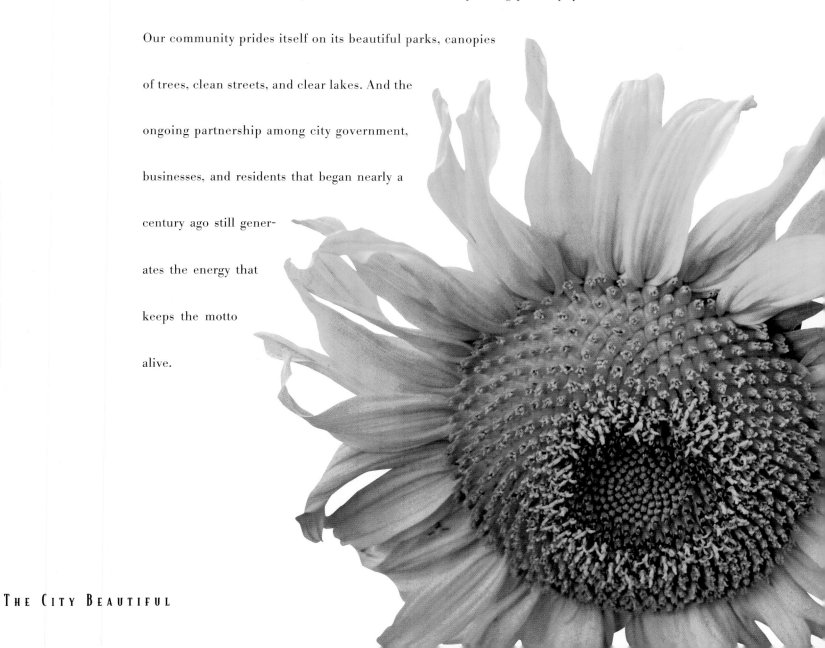

City workers planted trees, flowers, and shrubs, and encouraged business owners and

residents to do the same.

Jewell's beautification efforts were so popular that people forgot all about the World's

Fair and convinced the mayor that the city needed a new, more fitting motto. And so, a

contest was organized. The winning entry was, appropriately, The City Beautiful.

Not only has the motto stuck, but so has the tradition of beautification. Over the years,

the concept behind The City Beautiful has become an operating philosophy for Orlando.

Our community prides itself on its beautiful parks, canopies

of trees, clean streets, and clear lakes. And the

ongoing partnership among city government,

businesses, and residents that began nearly a

century ago still gener-

ates the energy that

keeps the motto

alive.

Sunshine takes on many forms in Central

Florida, from the famed citrus crops that are

more precious than gold to the bright orange

and yellow hues of a large sunflower.

ORLANDO

names and mottoes aside, the forces that shaped the Orlando we know today began churning in the mid-1950s. America was entering the space age and Orlando was on the leading edge. The Martin Company, a successful aircraft manufacturer, chose to build a plant here to develop its fledgling aerospace business. The company eventually became Martin Marietta and is now known as Lockheed Martin.

Lockheed Martin has been important for several reasons. Besides being Orlando's largest manufacturer, the company has been the seed for the city's bumper crop of high-technology manufacturing. Over the past decade, for example, employment in high-technology industries in and around Orlando has increased by more than 100 percent. And since 1980, some 79 percent of the total manufacturing growth in the area has been in high-tech industries.

Lockheed Martin's impact on our educational system has been just as marked because in order to grow, the company needed a steady supply of engineers. To fill the need, a group of civic leaders teamed with company officials and convinced the State Board of Regents to establish an engineering university in Orlando. Opening its doors in 1968, Florida Technological University, as the school was first chartered, is now the University of Central Florida (UCF). UCF excels in many disciplines, but its engineering program remains

Always striving to reach new heights, Central Florida is a community pulsing with new energies, whether it's another exciting space shuttle launch or a crowd-pleasing dolphin at Sea World.

one of the university's greatest strengths and its engineering graduates provide a pool of ready

talent for Lockheed Martin's research, development, and manufacturing activities in Orlando.

In the footsteps of Lockheed Martin came the National Aeronautics and Space

Administration (NASA). Backed by President John F. Kennedy's promise to safely send

an American to the moon and back, Cape Canaveral, located due east of Orlando on

Florida's Atlantic coast, became the pad from which all Americans have been launched

into space since Alan Shepard's inaugural flight in 1961. From my backyard, 50 miles away

in Orlando, my family and I witnessed history as we watched first the *Mercury*, then

the *Gemini*, and then the *Apollo* rockets climb columns of fire into the Florida sky.

Cape Canaveral was chosen because of geography. Not only was it on the water and largely

Since opening in 1971, Walt Disney World has been one of Orlando's largest employers and tourist draws. More than 50,000 cast members capture the imagination of 20 million visitors each year.

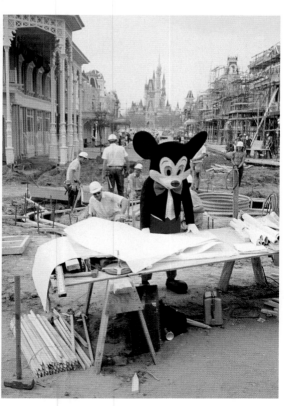

unpopulated, but it was also close to the equator, making it easier

for a rocket to reach orbit. The Cape's remoteness meant that

many of the thousands of highly paid engineers and technicians

involved in the space program would live in Orlando.

Geography also played a critical role in Walt Disney's decision

to build his biggest and best theme park in Orlando. There was

plenty of land to buy, reasoned Disney, and from its position in

the center of the state, Orlando offered easy access to the inter-

state highways on Florida's east and west coasts.

I remember vividly the months before the Disney announcement. Orlando knew something big was brewing. Community leaders were aware someone was buying land—some 28,000 acres of it—but no one was able to pinpoint who. Walt Disney veiled his plans for Central Florida in such secrecy that just days before he made his official announcement, those Orlandoans supposedly in the know were convinced the land in question was going to be the site of an automobile manufacturing plant. Yet, on November 15, 1965, Walt Disney charted a new course for Orlando, and the rest, as they say, is history.

Today, spurred by a $15 billion-a-year tourism industry, Orlando is the world's premier travel destination and one of the fastest-growing metropolitan areas in the United States. Revenue generated by the 37 million tourists who visit the area annually is the cornerstone of our local economy.

Tourism has provided the community with another commodity—a rapidly rising international profile. Slowly, visitors from around the world have found Orlando to be a place for something other than vacations. The city's can-do attitude and rapid rate of growth create an ideal mix for generating international business opportunities.

Theme parks such as Universal Studios Florida make it possible for visitors to get up close and personal with Orlando's growing film and television industries.

O rlando is unique in Florida, and a glance at a map quickly reveals why: It's the

only major inland city in the state. While all of Florida's other metropolitan

areas have first been seaports, Orlando's gateway is through the air.

Orlando International Airport is world class in every regard. Like the city itself, it has

Alligators are so much a part of Florida life

emerged from humble beginnings as a U.S Air Force base to become the second-fastest-

that they seem to show up just about every-

growing airport in the world, handling more than 25 million passengers a year. It is our

where. Gatorland, located south of the city,

gateway for business and investment, and provides easy transportation of goods for trading

has paid homage to the great lizards since

partners around the globe. Although international commerce has traditionally been con-

1949 (BELOW).

fined to our large hometown corporations, many small businesses now find it important

to venture into the world marketplace to keep pace with the competition. Orlando's remark-

Orlando's commitment to the arts can be

able ease of access to these markets through its international airport makes this possible.

seen on the grounds of downtown's Bob

I think even my great-grandfather would agree that this city has it all: As the premier tourist

Carr Performing Arts Centre and in the

destination in the world, a hub of international investment and trade, and a leader in con-

many other statues that pepper the city.

ventions and corporate meetings, Orlando also offers a high quality of life for its residents.

I am a third-generation Orlandoan. My elementary school was located on East Pine Street

across from Lake Eola Park on a site now occupied by a high-rise office building. My high

school graduation ceremony was held in the old Municipal Auditorium before it was re-

modeled and renamed the Bob Carr Performing Arts Centre.

As a young girl, I considered downtown Orlando a special place. My grandmother and I

often took the bus from my house for a Saturday afternoon lunch and a movie at the Beacham

Theatre. I remember watching people in their Sunday best walking through the richly

decorated lobbies of the Angebuilt Hotel on Orange Avenue or the San Juan Hotel just up the

street. For young people like me, it was exciting to window-shop outside the department

stores and the five-and-dimes. Downtown sidewalks were filled with workers and shoppers,

and you could sense the pulse of the city.

More vivid still are the childhood memories of my neighborhood. It was a haven of safety in a hustle-bustle world. People knew each other and cared for each other. Children played together outside, even in the sweltering heat of the Orlando summer. We rode our bikes and learned to swim and water-ski on the neighborhood lakes.

A golden cherub trumpets the fun to be had at Church Street Station, an enormous entertainment complex that offers plenty of shopping, dining, and live music.

In a very real sense, my neighborhood was an extended family. People walked, visited each

In Orlando, water has a way of bringing

other, and took food to those who were ill. We were proud of where we lived. I remember

friends and neighbors together. For local

several times when my parents joined other parents in the neighborhood for a weekend

youngsters, the most popular spots include

beautification project.

nearby water rides, natural springs, and

These are my roots and, as mayor of Orlando, this is the character of my stewardship.

lakes located throughout the area.

As our community continues to grow, we must never waver from the belief that a thriv-

ing central city with livable residential neighborhoods is the key to the quality of life we expect for our families. Over the years, Orlando has created a pattern of well-managed

growth in our culturally diverse city.

While downtown remains a center of business, culture, and entertainment, our residen-

Horace Grant, forward-center for the

tial neighborhoods—steeped in the Central Florida frontier tradition of people caring

Orlando Magic, consistently shows die-

about people—are insulated from the pressures exerted by one of the most dynamic local

hard fans that he has the right stuff.

▲ GLENN JAMES/NBA PHOTOS

economies in the nation. We have been

careful to include parks and green space

in our growing urban landscape—a testa-

ment that our commitment to the beautifi-

cation of our public spaces has evolved

from Mayor Jewell's simple, public initia-

tive into today's working philosophy of

civic responsibility.

o be sure, things have changed dramatically since the days when my great-

grandfather tended his groves and his cattle. But the quality of life he sought

for his family—which existed as a dim flicker of light in his rough frontier

community—now burns as brightly as the Florida sun in this city of ours. Today, we

enjoy opportunities for education, cultural enrichment, employment, recreation, and

health care that my father—let alone my

great-grandfather—could never have

imagined. We enjoy these opportunities not

by chance, but because we have built a

consensus within our community to bring

them about.

Despite the changes technology has

created over the past century and a half, close

examination reveals that Orlando largely

remains the same kind of community that my

When birds of a feather opt not to stay together, you might find them resting atop an alligator island (RIGHT) or enjoying a bird's-eye view from the signature swan boats at Lake Eola Park (OPPOSITE).

great-grandfather found so attractive. It has been quite a while since we have had a Satur-

day morning barn raising, as my great-grandfather did. But we *have* built houses on a

weekend through Habitat for Humanity. The citizen's militia—organized to fend off frontier

bandits—is also gone, replaced by Citizens for Neighborhood Watch. We are a community

that offers the opportunity to work and raise a family, a community where residents care

about each other, a community where neighbors still gather to staff and fund community

service and improvement projects.

This is Orlando—my hometown. It is rewarding to see neighbors

working together with business and government to keep our economy

strong, our streets safe, and our families secure in their role

as nurturing environments in which to raise children

and build strong ties. It is my greatest wish that

all who visit or choose to live here feel at home

in our City Beautiful. ✳

Symbols of friendship abound in Orlando, where youngsters are quick to show their fondness for Mickey. In 1988, Dr. Nelson Ying, originally from China, gave the city this Chinese Ting, located in Lake Eola Park (OPPOSITE).

THE FOURTH OF JULY FIREWORKS show at downtown's Lake Eola Park is an established tradition, attracting thousands of people who arrive early with blankets, chairs, picnic baskets, and cameras for an evening of good music, food, and fun.

Lᴀᴋᴇ Eᴏʟᴀ Pᴀʀᴋ ʜᴀs ʙᴇᴇɴ ᴀ popular destination for more than 80 years. Many natives of both the two-legged and four-legged variety take full advantage of the park's central location.

Some of the area's web-footed visitors enjoy the tranquillity of a morning swim, but for those who prefer dry land, there's plenty of space for a power walk, gatherings with friends, or a weekend retreat.

f LORIDA'S TRADEMARK SUNSETS—
among the most photographed
in the world—signal the end of
another beautiful day in Orlando.

Downtown's waterways reflect the changing face of the skyline as businesses prepare for nightlife in the big city (PAGES 34 AND 35).

THE CITY BEAUTIFUL

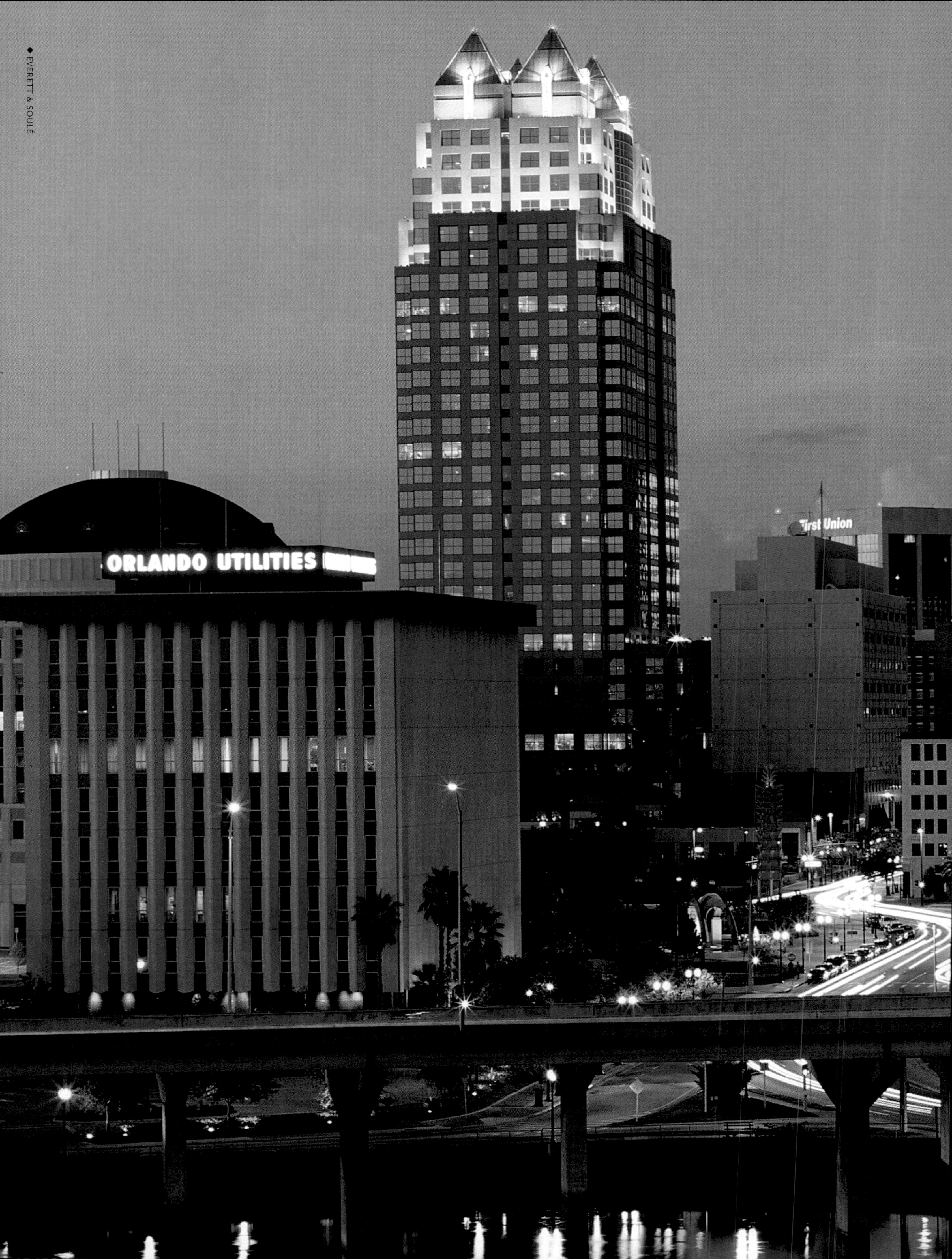
ORLANDO UTILITIES
First Union
◆ EVERETT & SOULÉ

VISITORS LOOKING NORTH INTO THE city are greeted by the dramatic downtown skyline. Dominating the scene is the 35-story Sun Trust Center, a modern-day sentinel of the new Orlando. In the foreground, the East-West Expressway, one of the city's major people movers, cuts a quick path across town.

ATTENDING TO THE NEEDS OF more than 30 million annual visitors and nearly 200,000 city residents takes a fair amount of experience and commitment. Getting an early jump on the day, workers at City Hall (OPPOSITE) are greeted by Ed Carpenter's Tower of Light, a contemporary work of art that has been compared to everything from a stalk of celery and a very tall pineapple to a large kitchen tool (LEFT).

A LTHOUGH MOST PROFESSIONALS climb the corporate ladder *inside* Orlando's high-rises, others have found a faster way to reach the top.

A GOOD CLEANING HELPS KEEP
the brand-new Orange County
Courthouse looking hot (LEFT),
while city firefighters use *their*
ladders and hoses to cool things
down at a local nightclub (RIGHT).

ORLANDO

Patterns of daily life can be seen just about anywhere you look in Orlando. From downtown's Barnett Bank (opposite) to the stair-stepped crown of First Union Bank (top) to a colorful wall at the old Orange County Courthouse (bottom), area architecture is truly a feast for the eyes.

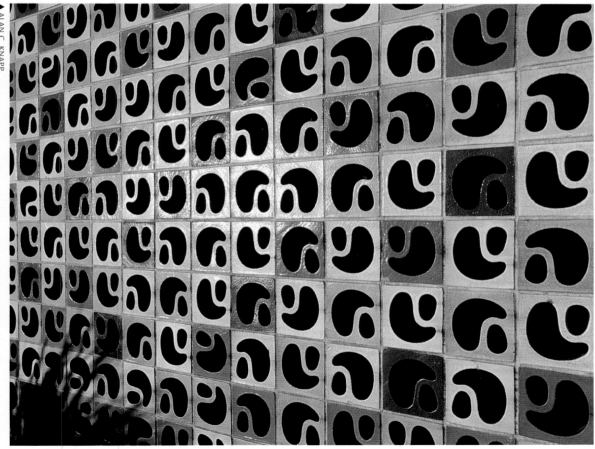

AS EVIDENCED BY ORLANDO'S burgeoning business district, the City Beautiful is an attractive place for companies to start up, expand, or relocate. The metropolis boasts a thriving economy and one of the lowest state and local tax burdens in the nation. Nearly 50,000 employees work within the city limits, most in close proximity to the region's top business and government groups, as well as consulates, international trade organizations, and professional associations.

B EAUTIFUL LANDSCAPES AREN'T the only reason tourists come to town in droves; Orlando/Orange County attracts its fair share of conventioneers, thanks to its ranking among the nation's top five destinations for convention facilities. To accommodate the more than 2.6 million people who annually attend nearly 18,000 meetings and trade shows in the area, the Orange County Convention Center (OPPOSITE) expanded recently to become one of the largest facilities of its kind in the United States.

ORLANDO SCIENCE

Orlando's Loch Haven Park—a place where science, art, and theater embrace—has been called a haven for the body, mind, and soul. Located within the park is the Orlando Museum of Art, which holds a growing permanent collection of 19th- and 20th-century American art, pre-Columbian artifacts, and African objects, in addition to hands-on and traveling exhibits (ABOVE). Nearby, the $40 million Orlando Science Center has become the largest state-of-the-art science showcase in the Southeast, featuring everything from intriguing laser shows to a voyage through the human body (OPPOSITE).

f OR MORE THAN 50 YEARS, THE Florida Citrus Bowl stadium has brought the wide world of championship sports to Orlando (OPPOSITE). With permanent seat- ing for more than 70,000 fans, the stadium has become an interna- tional destination for the ultimate in sports face-offs, including such top-notch events as World Cup Soccer. Neighboring Tinker Field is home to the Class-AA Orlando Rays, a farm club of Major League Baseball's Tampa Bay Devil Rays (ABOVE).

H EY BATTER, BATTER!" IS THE
shout heard 'round Orlando
just about any time of year, thanks
in part to its minor-league teams—
the Class-AA Orlando Rays and
the Class-A Kissimmee Cobras.

ORLANDO

AN AVERAGE YEAR-ROUND TEMPER-
ature of 72 degrees invites locals
to enjoy life outdoors to the fullest
extent. For some of the area's youth, the neighborhood playground is a home away from home
for tumbling or just hanging out.

Mᴇᴛʀᴏ Oʀʟᴀɴᴅᴏ ɪs ʀɪᴄʜ ɪɴ history and heritage, and each year, communities come together to celebrate the triumph of the human spirit. In Eatonville, the nation's oldest incorporated African-American township, hundreds of residents gather for reflection, expression, music, and dance at the annual tribute to slain civil rights leader Dr. Martin Luther King Jr.

Pʟᴀʏᴇʀs ᴘᴀsᴛ ᴀɴᴅ ᴘʀᴇsᴇɴᴛ ᴄᴏɴ-tribute to Orlando's growing love for music. Jacqueline Jones, the city's high priestess of jazz, tunes up body and voice back-stage before one of her unforget-table performances (ᴏᴘᴘᴏsɪᴛᴇ).

Other luminaries include new Orlando resident and worldwide jazz great Sam Rivers (ʟᴇғᴛ), not to mention writer, composer, actor, singer, and big band leader Michael Andrews (ʀɪɢʜᴛ).

THE ARTS TAKE CENTER STAGE IN Orlando, where local cultural icons such as the Orlando Opera, the Civic Theatre of Central Florida, and the Bob Carr Performing Arts Centre provide year-round enrichment. At the annual Orlando-UCF Shakespeare Festival, Artistic Director Jim Helsinger (TOP) produces two of the bard's works at the Walt Disney Amphitheater in Lake Eola Park. Leading the next generation of theater greats is local actor Roger Floyd, who's also penned several original plays (BOTTOM).

ARTISTIC DIRECTOR CHRIS JORIE keeps performances in check at the Civic Theatre of Central Florida (TOP). For several years, John DiDonna (BOTTOM, AT LEFT) has directed the action at Eola Theatre, while local playwright Patrick Scott Barnes has written and produced cutting-edge works (BOTTOM, AT RIGHT).

Beacham Theatre Wed-Thurs-Fri
Lawrence **NEW** Grace
Tibbett **MOON** Moore

NO PARKING   NO PARKING 11AM-

THE CITY'S ORIGINAL ARTS AND entertainment centerpiece, Beacham Theatre was formally opened to the public on December 9, 1921. Built by Orlando businessman and Georgia native Braxton Beacham Sr. on the grounds of the old county jail downtown, the playhouse has been drawing long lines of patrons ever since.

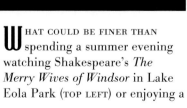

WHAT COULD BE FINER THAN spending a summer evening watching Shakespeare's *The Merry Wives of Windsor* in Lake Eola Park (TOP LEFT) or enjoying a concert by the talented Orlando Opera at the Bob Carr Performing Arts Centre (TOP RIGHT)? Indeed, the possibilities seem endless, from rising stars at the Annie Russell Theatre on the campus of Rollins College (BOTTOM LEFT) to the beauty and grace of Orlando's own Southern Ballet Theatre (BOTTOM RIGHT).

Local artist Linda P. Schapper has been creating tapestries and quilts for more than two decades. "The Family of Christ," a 19-by-55-foot quilt made up of 12,000 pieces of cloth, is possibly her most famous work, having been displayed behind Pope John Paul II when he visited New York City's Central Park in 1995.

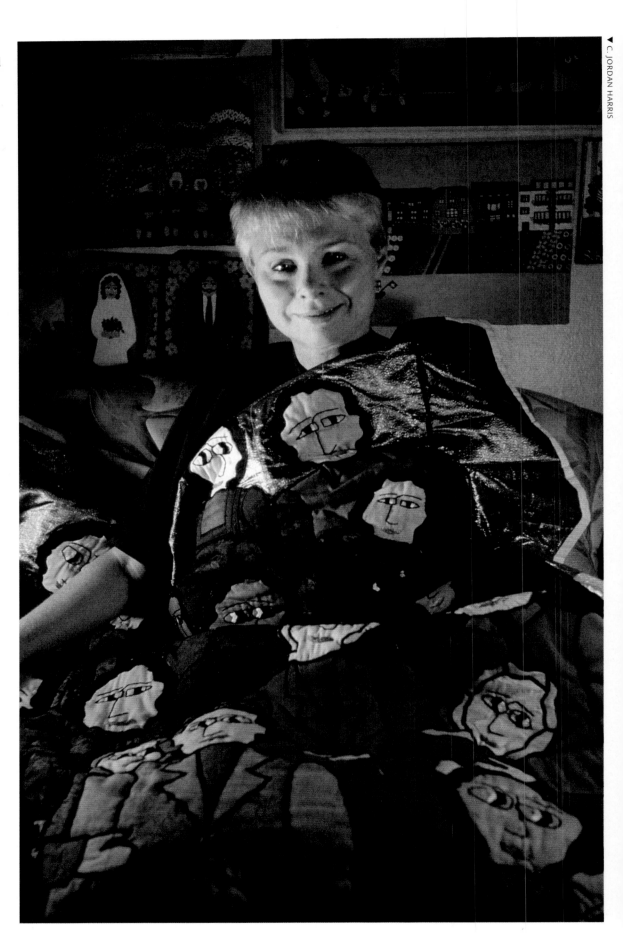

ORLANDO

N ATIONAL ARTIST AND LONG-time Orlando resident Keith "Scramble" Campbell (TOP), a former vice president of the Orlando Museum of Art, travels across the country on a campaign to make public art a part of every-day life. His cartoon surrealism style, also called Scramble Vision, has appeared at Woodstock '94 and on national billboards, ply-wood fences, and the walls of many local businesses.

Orlando artist Victor Bokas (BOTTOM) is known for his Greek symbolism and his alter ego Biff, a symbolic dog that appears in unusual places within the artist's work. One of Bokas' better-known creations is *The Visual Journey*, a singular artistic story told through 100 separate pieces.

T HE ART CENTER OF MAITLAND IS
a masterpiece unto itself, with
unique architecture and attractive
grounds that offer a stimulating,
creative setting for anyone with
brush and paints in hand. The
center promotes American art and
artists through changing exhibits
of contemporary works, as well
as special instruction by local
masters in the facility's central
studios.

64

Central Florida has become a canvas of colors as professional and amateur artists from across the country and across town leave their marks on the area's streets, sidewalks, and galleries.

A FREE OUTDOOR GALLERY OF WALL art sends a colorfully painted reminder to look for the beauty in everything you see, whether it's a construction fence or a well-worn barn.

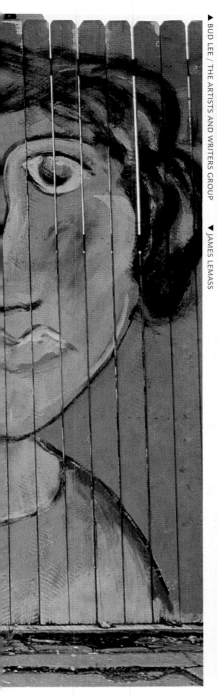

THE CITY BEAUTIFUL

Tʜᴇ Oʀʟᴀɴᴅᴏ ᴀʀᴇᴀ ʙᴏᴀsᴛs sᴏᴍᴇ of the most beautiful hidden sculpture gardens in the nation. These secluded treasures are home to many stone, terra-cotta, and bronze pieces, which have been preserved and placed among beds of native plants and flowers.

CAPTURING THE IMAGINATION OF all who look upon it, Donald DeLue's *Rocket Thrower* stands at the entrance of Loch Haven Park. The figure was purchased in 1987 by the City of Orlando as part of its public arts program.

IMAGINE SPENDING YOUR DAYS just marveling at the wondrous sky. That's what these 48-foot-high, stainless steel statues do to pass the time. Called *At the Airport*, the work was created by New York artist William King, who donated the pieces to the Orlando International Airport in 1983.

THERE'S MORE TO THE ORLANDO International Airport than take-offs and landings. The nearly 26 million passengers who arrive daily are greeted by an elegant hotel, colorful shops, restaurants, and unique exhibits—not to mention a few familiar faces. The airport's more than 36 airlines schedule some 1,000 flights per day to more than 100 cities world-wide. Indeed, you couldn't get around better if you had wings, a wand, and pixie dust!

THE CITY BEAUTIFUL

S TEP BACK IN TIME UNDER THE wide archways and rounded parapets of downtown Orlando's beautifully restored train station. A reminder of a gentler age of travel, the station opened in 1927 to accommodate passengers of the Atlantic Coast Line. The traditional red tile roof, false bell towers, and stucco walls are typical of the Mission Revival-style buildings and homes of this earlier time.

O RLANDO'S COLORFUL FLEET OF LYNX buses takes a lighthearted view of the hustle and bustle of a city on the move. A larger-than-life approach to commercial and public service advertising, the one-of-a-kind rolling billboards have become a citywide novelty, as well as a great way to get around.

ORLANDO'S HERITAGE IS TRULY reflected in its relationship with the water. In the 1800s, pleasure boating was a welcome concept on the quiet currents of Lake Concord near the heart of the city. Today, old traditions still abound on the city's waterways, where a gentle canoe ride down a lazy river is a great way to spend the day.

IN HIS POEM "FOUR POPLARS," Nobel laureate Octavio Paz might have been dreaming of Florida's rich landscapes and waterways when he wrote, "Yellow slips into pink, / night insinuates itself in the violet. / Between the sky and the water / there is a blue and green band; / sun and aquatic plants, / a calligraphy of flames / written by the wind. / It is a reflection suspended in another."

THE CITY BEAUTIFUL

In Greater Orlando, contemporary art is hardly limited to a traditional canvas, as local artists give new life to the city's outdoor walls, stairwells, fences, and walkways.

THE RISING SUN PROVIDES A brilliant backdrop for a fishing boat as it embarks on a new day of work.

Y OU'RE NEVER FAR FROM THE water in Orlando, a geographic blessing that many residents use to full advantage. Some prefer the swift tranquillity of an afternoon of rowing with the countryside in view. But for those who crave a more exhilarating freshwater spray, a jet ski will satisfy the need for speed.

A WATER-SKIER TAKES ADVANTAGE of the last moments of daylight on Lake Ivanhoe, just north of downtown Orlando.

AUTHOR MARJORIE KINNAN Rawlings had plenty of inspiration when she described a Florida river as "a movement of green and gold expanse that reaches from sky to sky." Sunrise over the St. Johns River near Orlando is no exception (PAGES 92 AND 93). A mecca for paddleboaters in the 1800s, the unique St. Johns flows northward from its source, an inland estuary created by a series of lakes.

Much of Hunter's Creek, a master-planned community approximately 20 miles south of Orlando, appears just as it did when ancestors of the Timucuan Indians first camped along the water's edge of what is now called Shingle Creek.

H OLDING BOTH MYSTERY AND magic for young explorers, the crystal clear waters of the area's natural springs are a miracle of complex geology, featuring nearly every plant community found in Central Florida. In areas such as Rock Springs, Blue Springs, and Wekiva Springs, the warm pools are part of continuous parkland reserves with miles of nature trails, bike paths, and campsites.

THE CITY BEAUTIFUL

W HETHER THEIR PLATFORM IS A concrete bridge or a towering cypress, area youngsters eagerly jump, swing, and dive into deep waters.

I N 1943, A GROUP OF LOCAL WATER-
skiers gathered to entertain troops
visiting the botanical wonderland
called Cypress Gardens. Since

then, the theme park has thrilled
thousands of visitors with its signature shows, featuring stunts by
championship skiers.

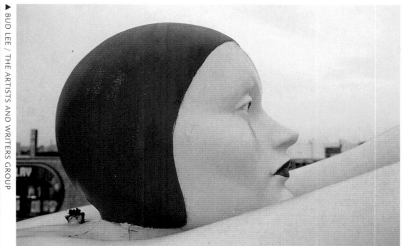

Ａpproximately 60 miles from downtown Orlando is Daytona Beach, considered by many to be the world's most famous "sandbox." There, such pop culture mainstays as the one-piece swimsuit seem frozen in time atop the Jantzen Swimwear store (LEFT AND TOP RIGHT), and local antique dealers take a similarly nostalgic look at beach life (BOTTOM RIGHT).

URF'S UP! LIKE A RELIGIOUS ICON, the figure atop the Ron Jon Surf Shop in Cocoa Beach (OPPOSITE) draws Floridians and others by the thousands. Here, a group of surfers and their boards stand ready to hang 10 at Ormond Beach just north of Daytona (ABOVE).

MUSIC PLAYS A LARGE PART IN Orlando, where recording studio owners Thomas Reich and Mario Alayon (TOP) do their part to foster the industry's next generation of artists. Plenty of local nightspots offer a range of recorded and live music to get your feet movin', including local favorite Janie Lanes, who thrills the crowd at the Sunset Strip (BOTTOM).

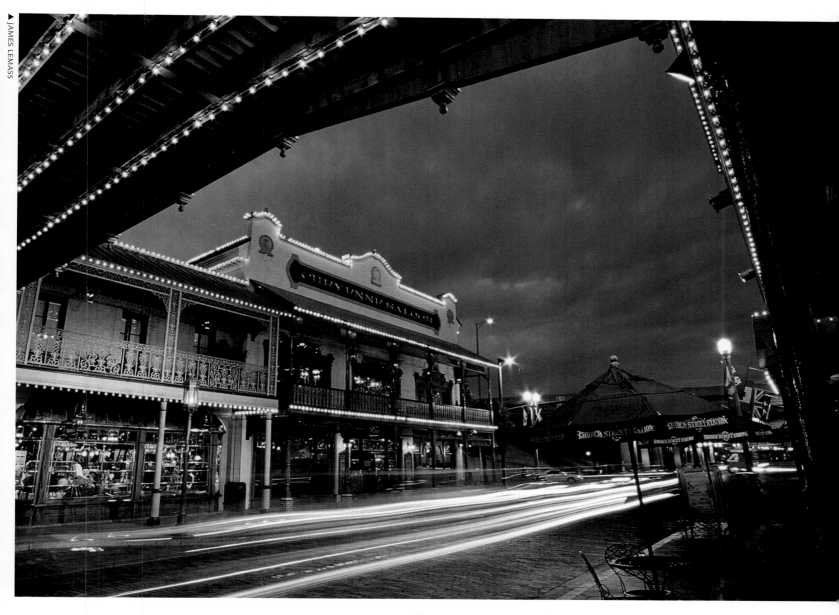

Reminiscent of the city's earlier days, replicas of ornate gaslights and delicately trimmed balconies give Church Street Station added flair. An old railroad depot, the entertainment and shopping complex—with its cobblestoned streets, re-created storefronts, and lavish Victorian interiors—was the catalyst for the 1970s renovation and restoration of downtown.

Church Street Station's elaborate decor perfectly complements its exciting entertainment options. As downtown's main attraction, the venue offers everything from dance hall shows to country and Top 40 tunes. The Exchange (opposite) features video games and a model train track suspended from the ceiling. Nearby, Rosie O'Grady's (bottom left) serves up creative cuisine along with healthy portions of cool jazz.

CIRCLES OF LIFE ARE PRESERVED with great care at the Orange County Historical Society and Museum. Open year-round, the facility presents regional artifacts dating from the Stone Age, as well as from 19th-century pioneer and early 20th-century industrial times.

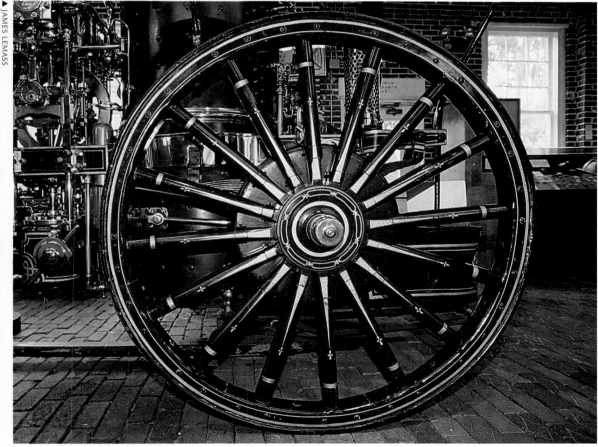

THE CITY BEAUTIFUL

f LORIDA HAS BEEN CALLED THE "grow anything" state. Thanks to the perfect blend of rich soil, year-round sunshine, and tropical rains, generations of Central Florida farmers have yielded millions of dollars in bumper crops.

A GRIBUSINESS—PARTICULARLY citrus, strawberry, and other crop production—has long been a major moneymaker in Central Florida. It all started in the 1800s when the newly completed Florida Railway opened up a wider market for the region's untapped agricultural gold mines.

AN ORANGE BLOSSOM IS A WELCOME sight to grove owners. Citrus continues to reign as one of the area's primary industries, and such food-related companies as Golden Gem Growers, Southern Fruit Distributors, T.G. Lee Foods, and A. Duda & Sons remain on the cutting edge of agribusiness.

A'TOES

IF BIRDS OF A FEATHER FLOCK together, then why's this watermelon posing as a tomato? Fruits and vegetables of just about every size, shape, and color make their way from Central Florida farms to grocery stores and tables nationwide.

THE CITY BEAUTIFUL

T HE LOCAL ASIAN COMMUNITY IS a major part of Orlando's charm. Old ways endure and ancient cultures prevail in the popular restaurants and shops of the city's Vietnamese, Chinese, Thai, and Japanese communities.

N O CRAVING IS TOO GREAT FOR Orlando's more than 3,000 restaurants and world-renowned chefs. From pizza and pasta to sushi, steak, and seafood, Central Florida offers a broad range of ambiences and menus.

WHETHER YOUR GOAL IS AN evening of family fun or an intimate dinner for two, Orlando can accommodate. The Bubble Room, a full-service restaurant known for its gigantic portions and larger-than-life desserts, offers zany memorabilia and a Tunnel of Love (LEFT). On the other end of the spectrum, candlelight and haute cuisine await visitors to the Mobil four-star, AAA three-diamond Chalet Suzanne on Lake Wales (RIGHT).

ƒINE DINING IS A WAY OF LIFE IN Orlando, where award-winning favorites include (CLOCKWISE FROM TOP LEFT) Le Coq au Vin, Siam Orchid, La Coquina at the Hyatt Regency Grand Cypress, and Enzo's on the Lake Restaurant.

ON SATURDAY MORNINGS, SMART shoppers and bargain hunters head for the open fruit and produce bins of Orlando's Farmers Market, located beneath the overpass near Church Street Station. The market is a family-friendly place where patrons can purchase anything from carrots and candy to peas, pasta, and plants.

THE ORANGE HAS LONG BEEN A local icon, reminding visitors and residents that Florida is king of the citrus hill.

THERE'S NOTHING QUITE LIKE A moment of solitude accompanied by your favorite thinking cap.

DISNEY'S FORT WILDERNESS Resort not only gives children plenty to see and do, but also provides parents with time to relax and reflect on the day's adventures.

IT HAS BEEN SAID THAT FLORIDA'S VAST AND inexpensive land, growth potential, and year-round balmy weather are what lured Walter E. Disney to locate his theme park near Orlando. Now situated on more than 30,000 acres of pristine land (twice the size of Manhattan), the Walt Disney World Resort is a draw unto itself. Since its 1971 opening, the expansive complex has hosted more than 500 million guests at its three major theme parks: the Magic Kingdom, Epcot, and Disney-MGM Studios.

ORLANDO

A MURAL HONORING THE PARK'S CREATOR and namesake welcomes visitors to Walt Disney World. Although Disney succumbed to cancer in 1966, some five years before opening day, his dream lives on in the hearts and minds of all who gather here. Today, the resort features parades, the Swan Hotel, MGM Studios, a new sports complex, hands-on exhibits, and thrills and excitement at every turn.

THE CITY BEAUTIFUL

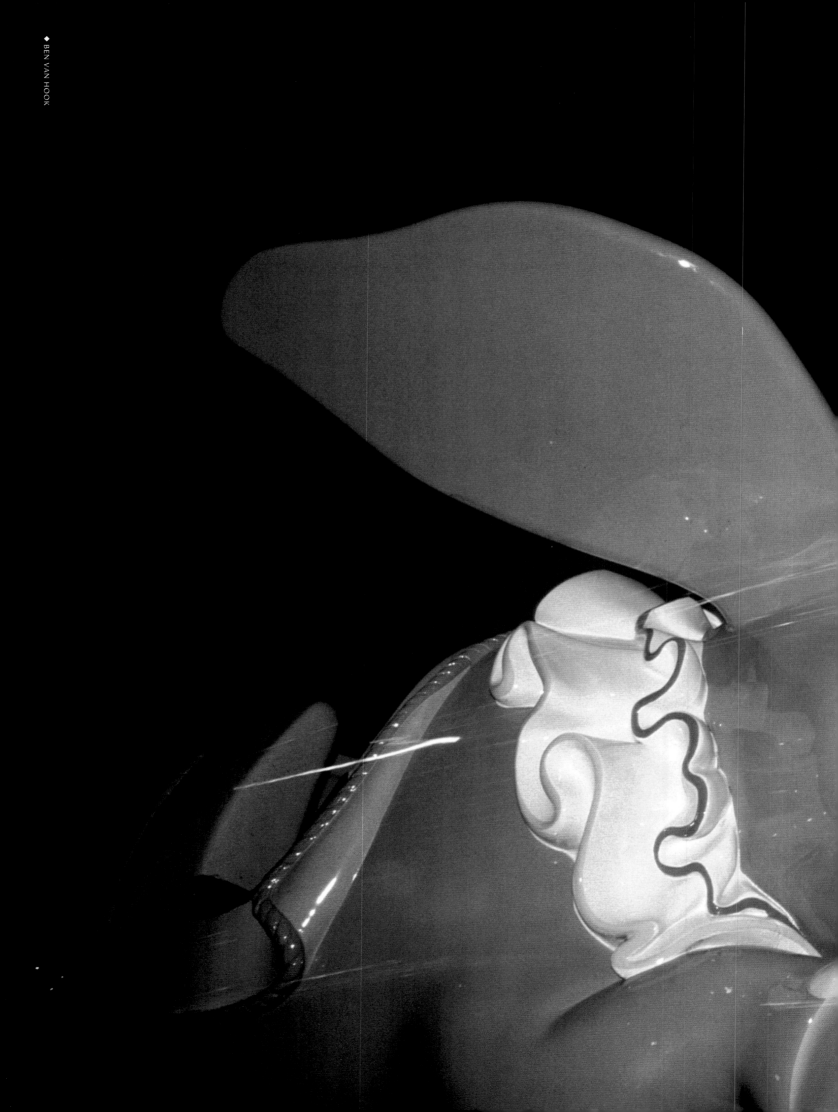

WALT DISNEY WORLD IS A LAND where contrasting images challenge both mind and spirit. As the giant sundial in the atrium of the Team Disney building demonstrates the ancient art of timekeeping (PAGE 135), palm trees near the 180-foot-high Spaceship Earth at Epcot beckon the sun for their own purposes (PAGE 134).

A REA THEME PARKS BRING TOGETH-er diverse people from around the world, offering a brand of excitement to thrill just about everyone.

A REPLICA OF THE UNIVERSAL STUDIOS trademark globe rotates at the entrance to Universal Studios Florida. The 444-acre theme park and working studio offer visitors a chance to "ride the movies" at attractions based on popular films and television shows.

ORLANDO

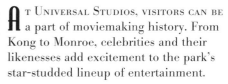

At Universal Studios, visitors can be a part of moviemaking history. From Kong to Monroe, celebrities and their likenesses add excitement to the park's star-studded lineup of entertainment.

A PERENNIAL SEA WORLD FAVORITE, Mother Nature's mermaids, otherwise known as bottle-nosed dolphins, frolick in the park's community pool (PAGES 140 AND 141).

For those who want to do some splashing of their own, the Wet 'n Wild water park is the place to go. The 25-plus-acre facility features plenty of twisting slides, games, and other diversions to satisfy adventure-seeking swimmers and sunbathers.

Ṣea World's 200-acre commercial marine zoological park combines entertainment and education in its many animal shows, aquariums, and touch pools. Dolphins leap as high as 18 feet to demonstrate their skills for eager audiences, while other colorful creatures present the calmer side to sea life in a 160,000-gallon aquarium, home to more than 15 marine habitats and 7,000 sea creatures.

ORLANDO

WHETHER THEY'RE PERFORMING, POSING, or just passing the time, the animals are always the stars of the show at Sea World. The park's wide representation of marine life ranges from tropical reefs to the wild arctic, gentle manatees to terrors of the deep, and brightly colored birds to beckoning sea lions. Among its most famous residents are Shamu, a four-ton orca; Baby Shamu; and Baby Namu.

▲ JAMES LEMASS

ORLANDO

FLAMINGOS ARE A FAMILIAR SIGHT at Sea World and other parks throughout the state. Although the native flamingo has been extinct since the 19th century, its Caribbean cousin today makes a good understudy for this true Florida icon.

WHILE TODAY'S STATE LAWS AND regulations limit captures to specific areas and seasons, alligators were once fair game for local hunters. A good prize, like this 1930s "hood ornament," could fetch hundreds of dollars in exchange for its leathery skin and exotic meat.

MANY AREA THEME PARKS AND fish camps promote a friendlier image of the oft-maligned alligator. One such hot spot is Gatorland, home to more than 5,000 of these recalcitrant reptiles (RIGHT). In addition to educating the public and preserving the species, the park harvests 1,000 of its gators each year, selling the meat and skins to the public. Samples of the meat are available on-site at Pearl's Smokehouse for those willing to give the delicacy a try.

ORLANDO

f OR THOSE WHO APPRECIATE MORE
than the average, everyday
challenge, Gatorland's wrestling
demonstrations give visitors an
opportunity to learn more about
the park's namesake residents
(OPPOSITE). Equally exciting is
a round of steer wrestling, one
of many events at the Kissimmee
Rodeo, held every Friday at the
Kissimmee Sports Arena (ABOVE).

Central Florida loves its cattle, and locals find plenty of ways to express their devotion. Some of the largest ranches in the world are located in the Kissimmee area, and cattle production is one of the state's top-grossing industries.

154

Tʜᴇ Kɪssɪᴍᴍᴇᴇ Rᴏᴅᴇᴏ ᴅʀᴀᴡs hundreds of urban cowpokes eager to watch the real folks sharpen their skills. It's not the age that counts, some say, but the spirit beneath the hat.

NATHANIEL BUTLER / NBA PHOTOS

FERNANDO MEDINA / NBA PHOTOS

ANDREW BERNSTEIN / NBA PHOTOS

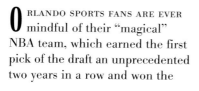

ORLANDO SPORTS FANS ARE EVER mindful of their "magical" NBA team, which earned the first pick of the draft an unprecedented two years in a row and won the Eastern Conference championship after only six years of existence. Fans consistently fill the more than 17,000 seats at the Orlando Arena—called the O-rena by die-hard fanatics—to see superstars (CLOCKWISE FROM TOP RIGHT) Dennis Scott, Anfernee "Penny" Hardaway, and Rony Seikaly strut their stuff.

THE CITY BEAUTIFUL

F OR THE ARDENT SPORTS ENTHUSIAST, there's nothing like that winning connection between ball and player.

MORE THAN SURF AND SAND, AREA sporting events encompass mountain and dirt biking, ice hockey, arena football, motocross, horse racing, lawn bowling, rowing, and hiking. But Central Florida's fastest-growing sport is soccer, which has swept the fields in popularity among young, amateur, and professional athletes alike. Programs such as Legacy Soccer, which began after the city hosted the 1994 World Cup games, work to teach children of all ages and abilities that soccer is for everyone.

THE CITY BEAUTIFUL

WOMEN—OR THE MEN WHO impersonate them—are often the stars of the show in Orlando. In December 1995, American Gladiators Orlando Live! opened three miles from Disney World. The 1,600-seat dinner theater allows the audience to cheer as contestants pit their athletic skills against such well-known warriors as Dallas, Raven, and the rest of the regular crew (OPPOSITE). Miss Sammy exhibited "her" feminine wiles on the cover of *Orlando Weekly*'s 1997 "Best of Orlando" issue (LEFT).

CELEBRATION AVE

JONATHAN M. HAYT

EVERETT & SOULÉ

Central Florida's newest town, aptly named Celebration, was incorporated in 1994 and is the realized vision of The Celebration Company, a Walt Disney subsidiary. With a traditional retail and business district—modeled after the variety of architectural styles found in small American towns—Celebration is anything but old-fashioned, providing residents with state-of-the-art information networks, schools, health care facilities, and plenty of recreational amenities.

BUD LEE / THE ARTISTS AND WRITERS GROUP

THE DONNELLY HOUSE IS JUST ONE of the treats that abound in nearby Mount Dora, a short 25 miles from Orlando. Built in the Victorian Gothic style, the landmark was opened in 1893 and is listed on the National Register of Historic Places.

A TOUCH OF NEW ENGLAND FLAVOR greets visitors to the well-manicured Winter Park, located approximately 15 minutes north of Orlando. Founded in 1885 by affluent Congregationalists who wanted to escape harsh northern winters, the quaint town is set on one of six connected lakes and is home to the state's oldest recognized college, Rollins. Bordering Central Park, a center-city oasis complete with flowering plants and flowing fountains year-round, are an Amtrak rail line and Park Avenue's attractive cafés, gourmet restaurants, and elegant boutiques.

L ITTLE HAS CHANGED ABOUT THE look of Winter Park's grand ol' Alabama Hotel, which has long lured the rich and famous with its warm Florida sunshine and soothing area lakes. Converted to condominiums in 1981, the 19th-century, Mediterranean-style structure remains a centerpiece for those eager to remember the days of yesteryear.

The great outdoors has long been a lure for Central Floridians. In the 1920s, guests of the Wyoming Hotel often joined together in a friendly game of croquet (TOP), a sport that remains popular in Orlando decades later. Today, residents of Mount Dora enjoy the Florida sunshine while matching wits in an energetic shuffleboard contest (BOTTOM).

Downtown Mount Dora is a storybook collection of Victorian-style homes, antique shops, restaurants, bakeries, barbershops, and tree-lined streets. The railroad originally brought people to the area, which sits 184 feet above sea level (a virtual mountain by Florida standards). Today, that same small-town feel—along with antique boat shows, art festivals, bike races, and holiday parades—keeps visitors coming back year after year.

The City Beautiful

PURE ROMANCE ABOUNDS IN THESE dream homes, where Grand Traditional and Palm Beach-style architecture become larger than life. Graced by arched windows and doorways, open floor plans, and lush landscaping, these delightful domiciles deserve equally dashing dwellers.

No details escape Orlando designers. Pools, ponds, and gardens have evolved into a balance of comfort and elegance designed to blend with area homes and the warm, tropical climate. With the goal of preserving the state's natural beauty, Florida builders are required to leave as much original vegetation as possible.

THE CITY BEAUTIFUL

GREATER ORLANDO'S LUXURIANT natural habitats lure thousands to walk through the canopies of tall oaks, sweet gums, magnolias, and palms. An oasis of abundant greenery, Blue Spring State Park (OPPOSITE) attracts its share of visitors and provides an ideal wintertime retreat for the endangered manatee, which thrives in the park's continuously warm, 72-degree springwater. Similarly, local waterways draw hundreds of pleasure boaters out to enjoy the wind in their hair on a warm Florida day (PAGES 184 AND 185).

With its fine cypress swamps, hardwood hammocks, pines, sand hills, lakes, and streams, Lake Louisa State Park is 1,790 acres of pure wilderness in the heart of Florida (PAGES 186 AND 187). Swimming, fishing, canoeing, and nature studies are popular activities at the park.

ORLANDO

WATER LILIES, WILDFLOWERS, AND other colorful flora are common in and around Central Florida's pristine lakes and freshwater marshes. Located only three miles from downtown, Dickson Azalea Park features spectacular displays of its namesake bloom (TOP). Tiger lilies burst forth at Leu Botanical Gardens, situated along the southern shore of Lake Rowena (BOTTOM). Donated to the city in 1961 by Orlando businessman and exotic plant collector Harry P. Leu, the reserve boasts more than 2,000 camellias and the state's largest formal rose garden, with 1,000 bushes representing some 250 varieties.

ORLANDO

ALTHOUGH THESE EXAMPLES OF Mother Nature's bounty could be mistaken for close-ups of microscopic life forms, they're really views of a prickly cactus (OPPOSITE) and an ornamental greenhouse plant (ABOVE), both common to the area.

◆ EVERETT & SOULÉ

O RLANDO RESIDENTS HAVE countless opportunities to bask in the simple pleasures that city life doesn't often afford.

R IDES AND LIVE PERFORMANCES
sometimes take a backseat to
floral displays at the Cypress Gardens theme park, which features
some 8,000 plant varieties from
90 countries.

O NCE A 16-ACRE CYPRESS SWAMP, Cypress Gardens was transformed by businessman Dick Pope and his wife, Julie, into one of the most popular destinations of its kind. Opened in 1936, the park features daring performances by adventuresome water-skiers, holiday displays that illuminate the picturesque grounds, and boats that journey through the lush surroundings.

FROM DESERT PYRAMIDS TO A replica of the Great Wall of China, the Wonders of the World are within reach at several of Orlando's unique attractions.

MODELED AFTER A SIMILAR PARK in Hong Kong, Splendid China brings the beauty of the Far East to Orlando, complete with some 10,000 bonsai and depictions of more than 60 of China's best-known monuments and cultural sites. Approximately 150 prominent Chinese artisans traveled to Central Florida to work on the park's exhibits, which feature replicas of the Great Wall, the Temple of Confucius, and the Imperial Palace. Authentic performances featuring ceremonial costumes round out the experience.

ORLANDO HAS ITS SHARE OF THE BIG and tall, from the larger-than-life wheels of a monster truck display on International Drive to the statuesque rockets at the Kennedy Space Center.

THE CITY BEAUTIFUL

WHETHER CRUISING OUTER SPACE on the wings of the shuttle *Atlantis* or watching the moon from the comfort of planet Earth, people have long held a fascination for the heavens. Each year since 1966, more than 3 million "starstruck" visitors have toured the Kennedy Space Center to get a glimpse of man's continued quest to conquer the final frontier.

AREA RESIDENTS HAVE BROUGHT their love of space down to Earth in the form of "otherworldly" street performances (LEFT) and high-flying amusement park rides

(RIGHT). Meanwhile, *Star Trek* fanatics have found plenty of *Enterprise*-ing ways to feed their obsession, from the fun and games at Sci Fi World on Inter-

national Drive (OPPOSITE RIGHT) to an inspired production at Manhattan South, an independent theater in Orlando (OPPOSITE LEFT).

WELCOME TO LASER LANE, *Business Week*'s nickname for Greater Orlando, recognizing its status as one of the nation's fastest-growing high-tech regions. Employment in the area's high-tech businesses has more than doubled in recent years.

Showbiz has made its mark on Orlando, where television and video production, recording, and filmmaking help boost the local economy. A number of children's programs are created at Nickelodeon Studios (ABOVE), one of the many attractions at Universal Studios Florida.

THE FUTURE OF ORLANDO STARTS with its children, and city schools offer a number of challenging and creative programs to nurture local youth. The area boasts one of the largest public school systems in the nation, with more than 130 schools serving some 130,000 students. In addition, prekindergarten and extended-day programs offer a variety of extra-curricular activities that push the limits of the creative spirit.

THE CITY BEAUTIFUL

FILLED WITH HOPE FOR THE future, early settlers embraced religion in the 1800s, starting traditions that still find many outlets in Orlando's houses of worship. The Cathedral Church of St. Luke has welcomed downtown worshipers for more than 60 years (TOP). Founded in 1885 by New England Congregationalists, historic Rollins College is now a non-denominational institution that offers Sunday services and other spiritual opportunities (BOTTOM).

THE CITY BEAUTIFUL

EAT MO' MULLET

WHETHER YOU'RE TRYING TO SELL your particular brand of cuisine or merely inspire a sunny disposition, an emphatic statement and good signage will get the point across.

THE CITY BEAUTIFUL

THANKS TO ITS ABUNDANT HONEY-bee population, Florida has for generations been a top honey producer. No matter their age, Central Floridians love the taste of sweet success.

ORLANDO

IT HAS BEEN SAID THAT ONE PER-
son's junk is another person's
treasure. Featuring everything
from common furnishings to
one-of-a-kind finds, the shops
of Antique Row near downtown
Lake Ivanhoe are a treasure
hunter's dream. Shopping at
garage, yard, and estate sales
is also a favorite pastime among
seasoned collectors.

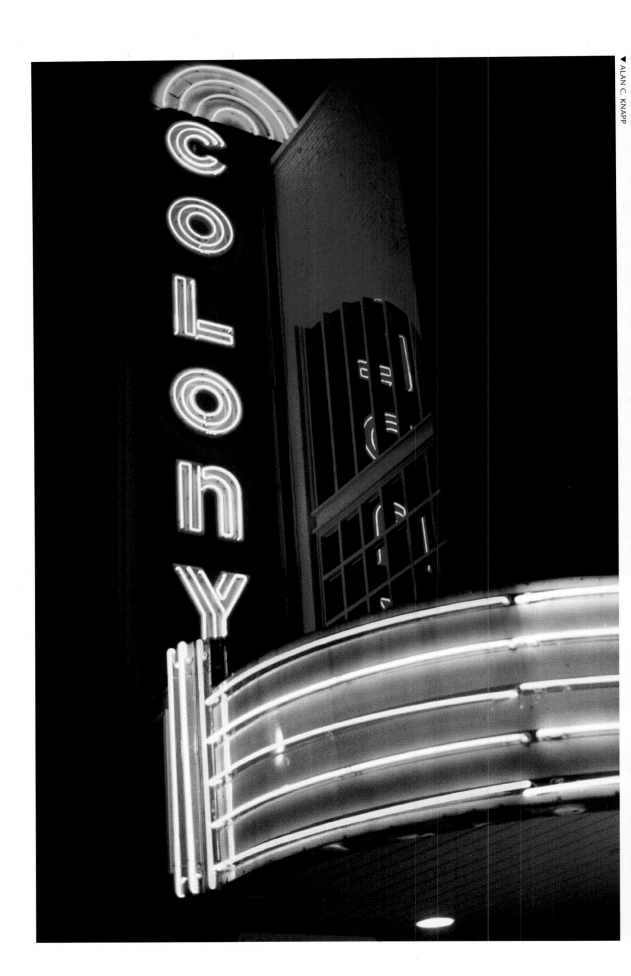

IGNS OF THE TIMES: These once-unwelcome neon giants shed new light on Orlando's business evolution.

O NE OF THE MOST POPULAR tourist destinations in the world, the Orlando area also attracts political figures, makeshift messengers, ardent nonvoters, and some of the most famous government leaders—past and present.

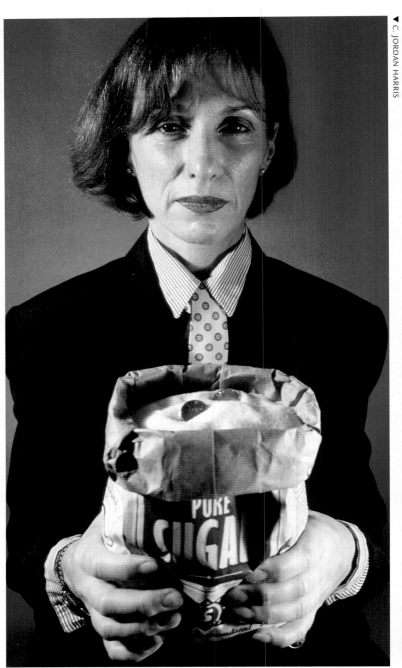

Whatever your political beliefs, rest assured someone in Orlando is fighting for the cause. Activists include (FROM OPPOSITE LEFT) state senator John Ostalkiewicz, well known for his continued probing of the local Department of Health and Rehabilitative Services; Orlando resident and environmentalist Mary Barley, who has helped clean up the Everglades by lobbying for a tax against big sugar companies; Lake Mary attorney Robert Petree, who advocated instituting night court in order to accommodate Orlando's working citizens; and William Boyer, who works on behalf of West Winter Park's African-American citizens.

THE FAMILIAR SHAPE OF FLORIDA conjures distinct images in the minds of almost every American. To outsiders, it most often symbolizes fun in the sun, but locals know it's also a terrific place to hang your hat.

ORLANDOANS MAY WORK HARD, but they also know how to relax. There's no greater way to spend a day away from the office than basking in the sun near one of the area's many lakes.

G RACEFUL SWANS AMID A COMMU-
nity on the move: Sometimes,
that's all the reminder you need
that Orlando is indeed the City
Beautiful.

PROFILES IN EXCELLENCE

A LOOK AT THE CORPORATIONS, BUSINESSES, PROFESSIONAL GROUPS, AND COMMUNITY SERVICE ORGANIZATIONS THAT HAVE MADE THIS BOOK POSSIBLE. THEIR STORIES—OFFERING AN INFORMAL CHRONICLE OF THE LOCAL BUSINESS COMMUNITY—ARE ARRANGED ACCORDING TO THE DATE THEY WERE ESTABLISHED IN THE ORLANDO AREA.

ABC FINE WINE & SPIRITS ✳ ALBERTSONS INC. ✳ AT&T ✳ BAKER & HOSTETLER LLP, COUNSELLORS AT LAW ✳ BARNETT BANK, N.A., CENTRAL FLORIDA ✳ BDO SEIDMAN, LLP ✳ BOYLE ENGINEERING CORPORATION ✳ BROAD AND CASSEL ✳ CAMPUS CRUSADE FOR CHRIST INTERNATIONAL ✳ CBIS ✳ CENTRAL FLORIDA INVESTMENTS, INC. ✳ CHRISTINI'S RISTORANTE ITALIANO ✳ CHURCH STREET STATION ✳ COOPERS & LYBRAND L.L.P. ✳ DARDEN RESTAURANTS INC. ✳ DEAN, MEAD, EGERTON, BLOODWORTH, CAPOUANO & BOZARTH, P.A. ✳ DELOITTE & TOUCHE LLP ✳ WAYNE DENSCH, INC. ✳ WALT DISNEY WORLD ✳ EMBASSY SUITES OF ORLANDO ✳ EPOCH PROPERTIES, INC. ✳ FIDELITY NATIONAL TITLE INSURANCE COMPANY ✳ FISERV CBS WORLDWIDE ✳ FISHER, RUSHMER, WERRENRATH, WACK & DICKSON, P.A. ✳ FLORIDA EXTRUDERS INTERNATIONAL, INC. ✳ FLORIDA HOSPITAL ✳ FLORIDA POWER CORPORATION ✳ FMC AIRPORT PRODUCTS AND SYSTEMS DIVISION ✳ FORUM ARCHITECTURE & INTERIOR DESIGN, INC. ✳ FRY HAMMOND BARR INC. ✳ GENCOR INDUSTRIES INC. ✳ GREAT WESTERN FINANCIAL CORPORATION/ GREAT WESTERN BANK ✳ GREATER ORLANDO AVIATION AUTHORITY ✳ GREATER ORLANDO CHAMBER OF COMMERCE ✳ HARCOURT BRACE & COMPANY ✳ HARD ROCK CAFE ✳ HBO & COMPANY ✳ HEALTH CENTRAL ✳ HUBBARD CONSTRUCTION COMPANY ✳ HUMANA ✳ HYATT HOTELS IN ORLANDO ✳ IBM CORPORATION ✳ LYNX/CENTRAL FLORIDA REGIONAL TRANSPORTATION AUTHORITY ✳ MATRIXX MARKETING INC., SOFTWARE SUPPORT DIVISION ✳ ORLANDO COLLEGE ✳ ORLANDO/ORANGE COUNTY CONVENTION & VISITORS BUREAU, INC. ✳ ORLANDO-ORANGE COUNTY EXPRESSWAY AUTHORITY ✳ ORLANDO ORTHOPEDIC CENTER ✳ ORLANDO REGIONAL HEALTHCARE SYSTEM ✳ ORLANDO SCIENCE CENTER ✳ ORLANDO SENTINEL COMMUNICATIONS ✳ ORLANDO UTILITIES COMMISSION ✳ ARNOLD PALMER'S BAY HILL CLUB & LODGE ✳ THE PEABODY ORLANDO ✳ PIZZUTI ✳ POST, BUCKLEY, SCHUH & JERNIGAN, INC. ✳ RECOTON CORPORATION ✳ SEA WORLD OF FLORIDA ✳ SIGNATURE FLIGHT SUPPORT ✳ SONNY'S REAL PIT BAR-B-Q ✳ SPLENDID CHINA ✳ SPRINT ✳ SUNTRUST BANK ✳ SUPERIOR PRINTERS, INC. ✳ TIME WARNER COMMUNICATIONS ✳ TUPPERWARE ✳ UNIVERSAL STUDIOS FLORIDA ✳ WESTINGHOUSE POWER GENERATION ✳ WLOQ ✳ YESAWICH, PEPPERDINE & BROWN

WHEN IT COMES TO MULTIMEDIA COMPANIES, ORLANDO SENTINEL Communications is committed to providing news and information to its customers any way they want it: in print, on-line, anytime. The multimedia company prints, publishes, and produces local news and information for more than 1 million Central Florida residents. Recently, Orlando Sentinel Communications launched a venture

with Time Warner Communications called Central Florida News 13 (CFN13). It is the region's first and only 24-hour local all-news cable channel, and reaches more than 400,000 homes in Central Florida.

The news channel is the latest addition to Orlando Sentinel Communications' multimedia business. Other operations include on-line services, specialty publications, direct marketing and printing services, and its core product—Central Florida's Pulitzer Prize-winning newspaper, *The Orlando Sentinel*.

"We are committed to being the most valued news and infor-

mation source in Central Florida—one of the fastest-growing regions of the world," says John P. Puerner, president and chief executive officer of Orlando Sentinel Communications. Close cooperation among the company's business units is important to this strategy.

"CFN13 is a critical step to developing Orlando Sentinel Communications into the community's around-the-clock news source," says *Sentinel* Editor John Haile. "To fill that time with quality news, we ask our *Sentinel* newspaper reporters to provide reports to the news channel also. Our reporting staff operates throughout

Central Florida in more than a dozen bureaus, giving CFN13 a range and depth that is unmatched in Florida."

SUCCESS IS A JOURNEY

A 24-hour news service is one of many pioneering moves making the *Sentinel* the region's most progressive daily newspaper. The *Sentinel* is published by Orlando Sentinel Communications and reaches more than half of metropolitan Orlando's 1 million adults on weekdays and 70 percent on Sundays.

The company also publishes many of Central Florida's leading magazines, including *Central Florida Family*, *Black Family Today*, *Magic Magazine*, and *Downtown Orlando Monthly*. For advertisers, it publishes a newcomers guide, *RELCON Renter's Book*, *New Homes*, and *Auto Finder* used-car guide.

The *Sentinel* is also a leader in providing on-line services to America Online (AOL) subscribers and Internet users. The company introduced Orlando Sentinel Online (http://www.orlandosentinel.com; AOL Keyword: OSO) in 1995, publishing one of the first and most successful major electronic newspapers on AOL. All of the *Sentinel*'s on-line services are now also available on the World Wide Web.

In 1996, the *Sentinel* increased its on-line presence with Digital City Orlando (http://orlando.digitalcity.com; AOL Keyword: Orlando). Digital City Orlando (DCO) is the region's major on-line city guide, linking 10 Central Florida counties. DCO expanded the *Sentinel*'s Central Florida on-line role from electronic newspaper publisher to on-line market maker.

IN PRINT, ON-LINE, ANYTIME, ORLANDO SENTINEL COMMUNICATIONS IS CENTRAL FLORIDA'S MOST VALUED INFORMATION SOURCE, OFFERING THE REGION'S LARGEST NEWSPAPER, ITS MOST POPULAR ON-LINE SITES, AND THE FIRST AND ONLY 24-HOUR CABLE NEWS CHANNEL.

"Digital City Orlando is like a town square," says Puerner, referring to the diverse number of information providers linked to the city guide. "Our electronic newspaper is an anchor tenant on the square. But there are many other neighbors, too."

Puerner continues, "We are building one place where on-line users can go for interactive classifieds, entertainment, news, weather, and sports coverage relevant to Central Florida."

Black Voices (http://www.blackvoices.com; AOL Keyword: BlackVoices) is another *Sentinel* on-line service that launched in 1996, featuring Afro-centric articles, photos, commentary, and message boards. The site quickly grew into the nation's premier African-American on-line service. Black Voices viewer hours on-line rocketed 1,760 percent in its first 15 months.

One-Stop Advertising

Advertisers use the *Sentinel* as their preferred way to reach Central Florida consumers. "There are so many ways for advertisers to tell their story through the *Sentinel*," says Bill Steiger, vice president and director of advertising. "We can take their message to every home and business in Central Florida." This message begins in *The Orlando Sentinel*, where advertisers can target specific zip codes or the entire market with their advertisements. *U.S. Express*, a *Sentinel* tabloid, is delivered to nonsubscribers, allowing total market coverage.

Niche services—such as Sentinel Tele-services (telemarketing), Sentinel Direct (direct mail), and on-line services—also offer new advertising opportunities. For example, powerful classified databases allow on-line viewers to narrow their search for goods and services by price, geography, and product specification. CFN13 adds a television component to Sentinel advertising services. Finally, Sentinel

in print   *on-line*   *anytime*

Signs produces advertising signage for customers.

A History of Integrity

On June 6, 1876, *The Orlando Sentinel* first published its newspaper under the name *Orange County Reporter*. Over the next century, the paper grew and merged with other local papers, taking *The Orlando Sentinel* name in 1982.

Tribune Co. of Chicago, the nation's 15th-largest media group in terms of revenue, reaches two of every three households in the nation with its newspapers, television, and radio stations.

Under Tribune Co. ownership, Orlando Sentinel Communications has invested in state-of-the-art printing presses and packaging facilities in its downtown production center. The company also built and operates a second production facility in Lake County.

As the newspaper has grown in size, so too has the scope of news coverage and investigative reporting. In 1988, the *Sentinel* earned its first Pulitzer Prize for an editorial series on mismanaged growth in Florida. Its second Pulitzer came in 1993 for an investigative news series about property seizures by a local law enforcement agency.

Orlando Sentinel Communications also helps the community it covers. Since 1995, the company's employees have volunteered more than 16,000 hours of their time in the community. The company and

its employees contribute about $2 million annually to community groups through the company's charity funds and corporate contributions.

"Central Florida is a vibrant market," says Puerner. "We are growing right along with our region. Every day, Sentinel businesses provide the most comprehensive array of news, advertising, and other information of local interest in our market."

ADVERTISERS USE ORLANDO SENTINEL COMMUNICATIONS' NEWSPAPER, ON-LINE SITES, SPECIALTY PUBLICATIONS, AND DIRECT MARKETING SERVICES AS THEIR PREFERRED WAY TO REACH CENTRAL FLORIDA CONSUMERS.

GEORGE WESTINGHOUSE HELPED LAUNCH THE AGE OF ELECTRICITY by building and equipping the first alternating current (AC) generating station, and supplying the first AC transmission and distribution system. He was granted a charter for the Westinghouse Electric Company in 1886, and for more than 110 years, his company has designed and manufactured systems for power plants that light America's cities and

power its factories. Today, Westinghouse Power Generation—an Orlando-based unit of the Westinghouse Electric Corporation—continues this tradition, working with utilities, independent power producers, government agencies, and industrial customers worldwide in nearly every aspect of producing electricity. From its local headquarters, Westinghouse Power Generation is a strong and vital part of the Westinghouse business family. The business unit's annual sales exceed $2 billion, 60 percent of which are international.

A STRONG GLOBAL ENTERPRISE

A successful global company is not simply an exporter of goods. Westinghouse Electric Corporation, through its Power Generation business unit, has established a business tradition as a partner in the economies of the nations where it does business, providing opportunities for mutual growth. Because of its unique approach to partnership and technology transfer, Westinghouse has set

the stage for a system of diversified growth welcomed around the world.

The business unit serves its global customers through an integrated manufacturing system in Asia, Europe, and North America, and in more than 200 sales and service locations in 60 countries. In addition to strategic alliances in Asia, Latin America, and Europe, the company's joint ventures in China and Europe enhance Westinghouse Power Generation's global scale and reach.

Today, with more than 300,000 megawatts of power generation equipment in operation throughout the world, Westinghouse has one of the largest installed bases of power-generating units in the industry. Westinghouse steam and combustion turbine generators deliver efficiency and performance excellence throughout the world.

THE POWERHOUSE BASED IN ORLANDO

Westinghouse Power Generation's services and capabilities range from

CLOCKWISE FROM TOP:
LOCATED ACROSS FROM THE UNIVERSITY OF CENTRAL FLORIDA, THE QUADRANGLE BUILDING IS ONE OF SIX WESTINGHOUSE POWER GENERATION SITES IN ORLANDO.

THE WESTINGHOUSE F CLASS GAS TURBINE IS AN INDUSTRY LEADER.

THE ORLANDO UTILITIES COMMISSION CURTIS H. STANTON ENERGY CENTER IS POWERED BY TWO WESTINGHOUSE STEAM TURBINE GENERATORS.

providing world-class power generation equipment to operating and maintaining its customers' power plants. The company provides power generation systems from 40 to 1,300 megawatts in simple and combined-cycle steam and combustion turbine-generator thermal islands. It also supplies complete turnkey services to power plants and can arrange permitting, provide all necessary equipment, and manage construction and start-up services.

With the world market for electricity growing substantially, Westinghouse is positioned to take a leading role in global power generation technology with its ongoing research and development of new and innovative energy-efficient systems.

"Westinghouse is committed to developing the technologies, products, and services that will enable its customers to better serve their stakeholders and achieve improved profitability in an increasingly competitive industry," says Randy H. Zwirn, president, Westinghouse Power Generation.

The company is working with the U.S. Department of Energy and university research centers to develop the next generation of fuel-efficient gas turbines. Westinghouse Power Generation also is participating in development of environmentally friendly biomass power plants that burn renewable crops like sugarcane or soybeans to produce electricity. A biomass demonstration plant is nearing operation in Hawaii. Other technologies under development include clean coal plants, solid oxide fuel cells, and compressed energy storage facilities—all of which are technologies for the 21st century.

Westinghouse is helping meet Central Florida's growing demand for electricity. Several electrical generating units from Florida Power & Light, Florida Power Corporation, and Orlando Utilities Commission are powered by Westinghouse equipment, including two units at the

Curtis H. Stanton Energy Center.

WESTINGHOUSE PEOPLE: MAKING A DIFFERENCE IN CENTRAL FLORIDA

Today, Westinghouse Power Generation employs more than 7,000 people worldwide, and has begun a new century of service. From its Orlando-based headquarters at The Quadrangle business complex near the University of Central Florida, and at factories and service centers around the globe, Power Generation continues to electrify the world by providing technologically superior power generating products.

Since coming to Central Florida in 1982, Westinghouse Power Generation has become an integral part of the community, providing career opportunities to local residents and college graduates worldwide.

More than 1,700 highly skilled engineers and strategic planning,

marketing, and support personnel call the Orlando area home. Power Generation's employees and families contribute to the community by volunteering in United Way, Junior Achievement, Special Olympics, Seminole and Orange county schools, and many other organizations. A longtime supporter of the Orlando Science Center, Westinghouse helped fund the Energize Electricity Exhibit, a featured exhibit at this state-of-the-art learning center.

GROWING WITH THE FUTURE

Today, Westinghouse Power Generation fulfills its founder's dream of leadership in the fields of power exploration and the production of electricity. Through growth, research, and technological expertise, Westinghouse Power Generation will continue to meet the needs of customers and the demands of growing economies worldwide.

STATE-OF-THE-ART SIMULATOR TRAINING ENABLES CUSTOMERS TO TRAIN PLANT OPERATORS BEFORE A UNIT GOES ON-LINE.

Florida Power Corporation

FOR NEARLY 100 YEARS, FLORIDA POWER CORPORATION HAS PROVIDED residents of Central Florida with efficient energy services. Since its inception as the St. Petersburg Electric Light and Power Corporation in 1899, the company has grown to serve more than 356 communities and 11 municipalities in 32 Florida counties. ✳ Today, Florida Power provides daily electricity service to more than 4.5 million people—about one-third of Florida's population. Producing a combined total of 7 million kilowatts, Florida Power Corporation is one of the largest electric utility companies in the state and one of the nation's leading energy companies. From new levels of performance to innovative customer relations programs, Florida Power Corporation has developed a patented system of service that goes beyond being visionary.

Central Florida is the fastest-growing region that Florida Power serves. Its wide range of commercial customers—from industrial giants to high-tech corporations to tourism properties—combined with its strong residential customer base make it an extremely important market for Florida Power. In order to show its appreciation, Florida Power has long been one of the area's most committed corporate neighbors. The company's commitment is evident in its active roles in economic development and corporate sponsorships. The company's extensive community involvement includes leadership roles in organizations such as the Economic Development Commission and the Greater Orlando Chamber of Commerce, and corporate sponsorship and participation in such important Central Florida organizations as the University of Central Florida, Rollins College, Orange County Public Schools, Junior Achievement, and Heart of Florida United Way. And, with nearly 1,300 employees, Florida Power is one of the area's largest employers.

High-Caliber Initiatives

Since its inception, the investor-owned Florida Power Corporation has been on the forefront of new and innovative hands-on service designed to meet the growing needs of Florida's ever increasing population. The company has been recognized for its ability to invent rather than reinvent solutions to ongoing energy issues, and to set higher industry standards as it strives to serve new and existing markets.

Florida Power Corporation is a subsidiary of the Florida Progress Corporation, a diversified electric utility holding company based in St. Petersburg. With assets of more than $5.8 billion, Florida Progress— a recognized utility leader—is built on a strong foundation made up of Florida Power Corporation and Electric Fuels Corporation, an energy and transportation company with operations in rail, marine services, and coal mining.

In 1996, Florida Power Corporation took an important step. In anticipation of changing markets, the utility reorganized into three strategic business units, allowing each to focus on its defined market segments. This new organization is vital in helping Florida Power grow in a deregulated business environment. The three business units operate as separate, relatively independent organizations within the corporation. Energy Supply is responsible for low-cost power generation. This unit oversees Florida Power's fossil fuel—coal, oil, and natural gas—operations in an effort to produce reliable power at the lowest possible cost.

To help meet the electricity needs of tomorrow's customers, the Energy Supply unit is building a new power plant complex. Florida Power was able to save on the costs of constructing this facility by purchasing plant components at favorable prices. This is expected to make the new plant among the most cost competitive and efficient in the Southeast.

The Energy Delivery unit focuses on maintaining reliable, cost-efficient transmission and distribution of electricity, while Energy Solutions is responsible for customer service, sales and marketing, and development of new products and services. Moving forward in a soon-to-be-deregulated environment, new products and services will be key to retaining and attracting new commercial and residential customers alike.

WITH STATE-OF-THE-ART EQUIPMENT AND ROUND-THE-CLOCK STAFFING, THE ENERGY CONTROL CENTER MONITORS AND CONTROLS THE GENERATION, TRANSMISSION, AND DISTRIBUTION OF ENERGY IN FLORIDA POWER'S 20,000-SQUARE-MILE SERVICE TERRITORY, WHICH SPANS 32 COUNTIES THROUGHOUT CENTRAL AND NORTH FLORIDA.

The company recently made national headlines with the creation of a new stand-alone company called Cadence, the industry's first-ever marketing alliance specifically targeted to serving large national accounts, such as retail stores, restaurants, convenience stores, grocery, and lodging. In a bold move, parent company Florida Progress Corporation joined forces with two of the nation's largest energy companies, Cinergy Corp. of Cincinnati and New Century Energies of Denver, to respond to the needs of national account customers. Cadence will provide single-source energy management services and products designed to lower energy costs for statewide and national companies.

Similarly, Energy Solutions is currently piloting a number of new products and services for its residential customer segment. The Surge Protection Service is a meter-based device that affords residential customers with a first line of defense against power surges, which can be frequent in the lightning capital of the United States.

Another new offering, Senior Privileges, features new products and services specifically designed for customers 55 years and older. These new organizations will allow each Florida Power business unit to better serve its customers while developing new business opportunities.

STRATEGICALLY POSITIONED FOR SUCCESS

Florida Power Corporation is strategically positioned in one of the fastest-growing areas of the country. The total population of its service area is expected to reach more than 5.1 million people near the turn of the century. The utility's service area covers approximately 20,000 square miles and includes the densely populated areas around Orlando, as well as the cities of St. Petersburg and Clearwater.

Advantages for Florida Power Corporation's long-standing service excellence and customer recognition include a management team that is committed to cost control, growth in its customer base, customer service, and delivery of reliable electricity. The utility's strengths also stem from its diverse, flexible energy mix of coal, nuclear energy, oil, and natural gas.

In 1995, Florida Power gained a winning edge by moving closer to some of its key customers. Following reorganization into strategic business units, Energy Delivery moved its headquarters to Orlando, while Energy Solutions has established central operations in Clearwater. These moves are in line with an overall philosophy to serve the diverse and immediate needs of customers.

While it is easy to perform well when conditions are at their best, it is a greater test of a company to rise above adversity. Over the years, the Florida Power service area was hit by several major storms, resulting in a temporary loss of electricity for thousands of Florida customers. Florida Power crews demonstrated their ability not only to quickly restore power to its customers, but also to provide time, skill, and energy in assisting other utilities that provide service to people in other damaged communities.

While demand for electricity increases daily as people and businesses move into the state, Florida Power Corporation has planned for the future with projected capital investments of almost $2 billion over the next five years. Innovative energy efficiency programs and a commitment to setting performance standards higher than ever signify Florida Power Corporation's ongoing efforts to raise its level of performance, stay ahead of the competition, and increase value to customers while lowering costs and improving service throughout Florida.

Florida Power Corporation is committed to finding innovative ways to do business. The levels of achievement reached today are only the forerunners of greater things to come.

FLORIDA POWER HAS MANY FACES AND WORKS WITH CUSTOMERS IN MANY WAYS. AN ADVANCED CUSTOMER SERVICE SYSTEM, INCLUDING THE ABILITY FOR CUSTOMERS TO USE AN AUTOMATED SYSTEM TO REPORT OUTAGES, HAS IMPROVED RESPONSE TIME AND CUSTOMER SERVICE. AND WHEN THE FLORIDA STORMS ROLL IN, SO DO THE FLORIDA POWER CREWS. IN CENTRAL FLORIDA ALONE, THERE ARE MORE THAN 9,000 MILES OF TRANSMISSION LINES— THE SAME DISTANCE AS TRAVELING TO CALIFORNIA AND BACK—AND THOUSANDS OF ELECTRICAL DEVICES.

CCORDING TO AT&T's COMMON BOND, A CREED FOR ITS EMPLOYEES, "We treat each other with respect and dignity, valuing individual and cultural differences. We communicate frequently and with candor, listening to each other regardless of level or position. Recognizing that exceptional quality begins with people, we give individuals the authority to use their capabilities to the fullest in order to satisfy their customers.

Our environment supports personal growth and continuous learning for all AT&T people. Our team spirit extends to being responsible and caring partners in the communities where we live and work." This statement represents the essential manner in which the company conducts business: valuing and respecting those who make the business work.

In Central Florida, this creed connects more than 3,500 AT&T employees who work in the Orlando area and in Tampa, as well as the more than 127,000 AT&T employees around the world.

One of the largest employers in Central Florida, AT&T focuses its business on global communications, including long-distance service, wireless communications, and Internet access. The company's

area business units that support these services include data processing, billing, customer management, network computing and installation, technology planning and engineering, consumer business and global communication services, and sales and marketing.

Representing its commitment to future generations and to education, AT&T also is the sponsor of the Spaceship Earth attraction at Walt Disney World's EPCOT Center, an attraction that is a journey through the history of human communication. Upon exiting the Spaceship Earth ride, guests are welcomed into the AT&T Global Neighborhood, an interactive exhibit area featuring Ride the Network and other attractions showcasing AT&T technology. Also at EPCOT, AT&T has a

hands-on exhibit area in the popular Innoventions attraction, featuring services such as the AT&T WorldNet℠, DIRECTV®, and AT&T Language Line®.

AT&T is also well represented at Universal Studios Florida with sponsorship of the E.T. Adventure® ride and AT&T at the Movies—an interactive exhibit showcasing new AT&T products, as well as the role AT&T has played in moviemaking history.

AT&T's diverse range of services makes communications easier, faster, and more convenient. As a leader in innovation, AT&T will build on its existing services to bring tomorrow's consumers even more creative and global communications solutions.

CELEBRATING DIVERSITY

AT&T takes great pride in the diversity of its employees. As a global company, AT&T celebrates the differences that make the world a fascinating place and supports the various cultural interests of its more than 20 employee organizations in Central Florida. These include organizations targeted to Hispanic, African-American, Asian-American, Native American, and female employees, as well as groups who support family care, educational, environmental, and many other local issues. Several of these AT&T Central Florida employee organizations have received national awards for their efforts.

GIVING BACK

Community involvement is an integral part of AT&T's Common Bond. Over the past several years, AT&T employees have generously

MORE THAN 120 AT&T ORLANDO EMPLOYEES PARTICIPATED IN THE KICKOFF OF AT&T CARES, A NATIONAL PROGRAM THAT GIVES EVERY AT&T EMPLOYEE A PAID DAY OFF TO VOLUNTEER IN THE COMMUNITY. IN ORLANDO, PARTICIPANTS DEDICATED THEMSELVES TO HELPING OUT AT THE SECOND HARVEST FOOD BANK, WHERE THEY SPENT THE DAY ORGANIZING FOOD TO BE DELIVERED TO NEEDY FAMILIES IN TIME FOR THANKSGIVING.

▶ J. SCOTT KELLY

contributed volunteer time and money to more than 150 organizations, including the Greater Orlando Area Chamber of Commerce's HobNob, United Way, and Junior Achievement. The majority of employee volunteer efforts are coordinated by the Central Florida chapter of the AT&T Telephone Pioneers, the largest volunteer network in the country.

In November 1996, the company launched its AT&T CARES program, the nation's largest corporate community service project, giving all employees one paid day off for volunteer work. More than 120 AT&T Orlando employees volunteered all day at Second Harvest Food Bank of Central Florida to prepare food supplies for those in need. Since then, hundreds of other employees have taken their days off to do volunteer work in the community.

AT&T has long been a champion of the power of effective education and has supported this belief by donating more than $500 million to innovative education programs since 1984. Most recently, AT&T announced its latest contribution to the education of America's children: the AT&T Learning Network℠, a $150 million commitment to help connect our country's schools with the wonders of computer technology. The program offers America's 110,000 public and private schools access to some of the newest infor-

mation and communications technologies, and the support to use them effectively.

SUCCESS BREEDS SUCCESS
Through the outstanding efforts and involvement of AT&T employees, the company has been recognized for many major achievements and endeavors. Some of these honors include the Corporate Volunteer of the Year award from the Central Florida Center for Community Involvement, selection as one of the top five corporations in the state in support of education by the Florida Department of Education, and the Friends of COMPACT Award for outstanding service to the youth of Seminole High School.

REACHING FOR THE FUTURE
As advances in technology and methods for learning continue

to evolve, AT&T will continue to develop and grow to keep pace with today's advances, and prepare for tomorrow's. For example, AT&T supports Florida's I-4 High Tech Corridor council. The Council was created in conjunction with the University of Central Florida, the University of South Florida, and a number of Central Florida companies to attract, retain, and grow high-tech industries in the state.

AT&T employees—in Central Florida and across the globe—are dedicated to keeping the world in touch. AT&T will continue to be the leader in providing communications solutions to people around the world—solutions people want and need—today, tomorrow, and always.

CLOCKWISE FROM TOP LEFT: THE NEW AT&T FACILITY IN LAKE MARY, WHICH OPENED ITS DOORS IN MAY 1996, HOUSES THE COMPANY'S INFORMATION TECHNOLOGIES SERVICES.

AT&T WIRELESS SERVICES, INC. IS THE NATION'S LARGEST PROVIDER OF CELLULAR SERVICE, OFFERING WIRELESS VOICE AND DATA COMMUNICATIONS. IN 1996, AT&T WIRELESS ANNOUNCED ITS NEW DIGITAL PCS, AN ALL-IN-ONE CELLULAR UNIT INCLUDING A TELEPHONE, FAX, AND PAGER.

EMPLOYEES AT AT&T ARE DEDICATED TO BEING THE VERY BEST IN THE BUSINESS. FROM CUSTOMER MANAGEMENT TO TECHNOLOGY PLANNING AND ENGINEERING, AT&T STRIVES TO PROVIDE SERVICES THAT MAKE COMMUNICATIONS FASTER, EASIER, AND MORE CONVENIENT.

FLORIDA HOSPITAL

THE CITY OF ORLANDO IS WIDELY REGARDED AS A LEADER IN health care, and Florida Hospital stands at the forefront of patient care, professional education, and medical research. The system is known internationally for its programs in cardiology, oncology, neurosurgery, orthopedic surgery, organ transplantation, and limb replacement. Other specialty areas include emergency medicine, obstetrics, outpatient services, pediatrics, psychiatry, general rehabilitation, diabetes, and women's medicine.

Florida Hospital is the largest private, not-for-profit hospital in the state. Founded in 1908, the 1,452-bed, acute health care system serves Central Florida and much of the Southeast, the Caribbean, and South America. It is the largest of the health care facilities that make up the Adventist Health System, Florida Hospital's parent company, which is operated by the Seventh-day Adventist Church.

The Florida Hospital system includes more than a dozen Centra Care walk-in medical centers, and several outpatient diagnostic centers and physician medical plazas. Each year, the system's nearly 10,000 employees, 1,640-plus physicians, and 850 volunteers serve more

than 57,000 inpatients, some 244,580 outpatients, and nearly 162,000 emergency cases. Its tradition of continued quality health care has earned Florida Hospital statewide, national, and international recognition, including the National Healthcare Forum Quality Award, the National Research Corporation Quality Leader Award, and the Governor's Sterling Award for Quality.

Over the years, Florida Hospital has remained true to its founding mission, which reflects its ongoing commitment to patients, staff, and community: "We endeavor to deliver high-quality service, showing concern for patients' emotional and spiritual needs as well as their physical condition," states the opening sentence of Florida Hospital's mission statement.

CARDIOLOGY SPECIALISTS

Cardiology has long been a Florida Hospital specialty. Since its beginning more than 25 years ago, the Florida Heart Institute at Florida Hospital has emerged as a leader in advanced cardiac care. It has been ranked as the largest cardiac center in the state and among the top five nationwide. Its staff includes

cardiovascular surgeons, cardiologists, and hundreds of highly skilled technicians and professionals.

To serve the needs of patients with peripheral vascular disease, Florida Hospital's renowned cardiology program offers the sophisticated tools for providing diagnostic invasive and surgical services for peripheral procedures: diagnostics, arterial, venous, simple, complex, atherectomy, therapeutics, and laser. More than 1,050 people are screened annually for peripheral artery disease at the Florida Hospital campuses located throughout Central Florida.

Since 1990, Florida Hospital has participated in numerous nationally and internationally recognized cardiac research studies and clinical testing for a variety of specialized drug treatments, medical devices, and procedural studies. In addition, the Florida Heart Institute at Florida Hospital offers patients the latest technological advances in cardiac services and programs such as rehabilitation, catheterization, angioplasty, open-heart and bypass surgeries, valve replacement, therapeutic cardiology, a chest pain center, pacemaker implantation, and monitoring.

A Leader in Cancer Treatment

The Walt Disney Memorial Cancer Institute (WDMCI) at Florida Hospital is one of the nation's leading cancer treatment centers and the

largest basic cancer research facility in Florida. It is staffed by a broad-based group of oncologists, surgeons, radiologists, hematologists, psychologists, nurses, therapists, technicians, and researchers covering a variety of cancer treatment. The integrated network of medical staff treats more than 3,000 people annually with programs that include comprehensive, state-of-the-art diagnostic treatment; research; education; and support services.

The Walt Disney Memorial Cancer Institute at Florida Hospital offers patients the latest in available cancer treatments: in- and outpatient surgery, biological therapy, surgery and radiation therapy combinations, chemotherapy, and innovative research programs. The institute also offers cancer-specific patient care through several award-winning programs: Gynecologic Oncology Center, providing specialized care for patients with precancers and cancers of the reproductive organs; Ovarian Cancer Screening Program, with state-of-the-art diagnostic services for women who are at high risk of ovarian cancer; and Hematology/Oncology Center for Children and Adolescents, offering the most advanced technology and expertise available for diagnosing and treating a variety of inherited and acquired blood disorders, including sickle cell disease, hemophilia, and leukemia.

Affiliations with leading cancer centers allow the Walt Disney

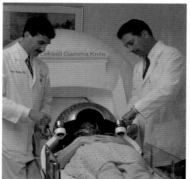

Memorial Cancer Institute at Florida Hospital to offer the most advanced treatment protocols to patients in Central Florida. Its collaboration with the Duke Comprehensive Cancer Center produced Central Florida's first Bone Marrow Transplant (BMT) Program, which includes the inpatient Bone Transplant Unit, the outpatient Bone Marrow Transplant Center, the Stem Cell Processing Laboratory, and a facility for stem cell biology research.

Florida Hospital's newest cancer treatment center, the Gamma Knife Center, is comprised of a multidisciplinary group of neurosurgeons, radiation oncologists, physicists, and nurses located on the first floor of the Medical Plaza at Florida Hospital Orlando. Powerful and precise, the gamma knife radiosurgery treatment uses a single dose of precisely directed radiation without an incision. This noninvasive outpatient procedure is offering new hope for patients with brain tumors, vascular malformations, and functional disorders.

CLOCKWISE FROM TOP LEFT:
THE CARDIOLOGY PROGRAM AT FLORIDA HOSPITAL IS RANKED AS THE LARGEST PROGRAM IN FLORIDA AND AMONG THE TOP FIVE NATIONWIDE.

THE WALT DISNEY MEMORIAL CANCER INSTITUTE AT FLORIDA HOSPITAL IS ONE OF THE NATION'S LEADING CANCER TREATMENT CENTERS AND THE LARGEST BASIC CANCER RESEARCH FACILITY IN THE STATE.

FLORIDA HOSPITAL LED THE WAY IN PROVIDING SOPHISTICATED CANCER CARE TO CENTRAL FLORIDA RESIDENTS BY DEVELOPING THE AREA'S FIRST BONE MARROW TRANSPLANTATION PROGRAM.

A SOPHISTICATED NEW TECHNOLOGY— GAMMA KNIFE RADIOSURGERY—ALLOWS PHYSICIANS TO PERFORM COMPLICATED BRAIN SURGERY USING A SINGLE DOSE OF PRECISELY DIRECTED RADIATION, RATHER THAN USING TRADITIONAL SURGICAL TECHNIQUES.

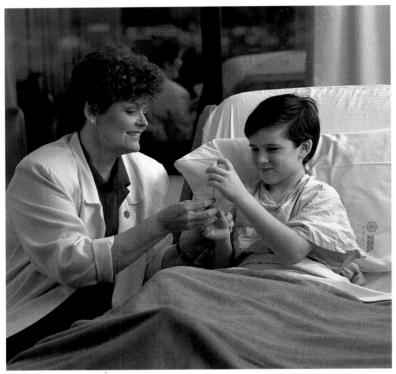

THE FLORIDA HOSPITAL DIABETES PROGRAM IS A RECOGNIZED LEADER IN EDUCATION, TRAINING, OUTREACH, AND CLINICAL CARE (LEFT).

FLORIDA HOSPITAL OFFERS A COMPREHENSIVE RANGE OF WOMEN'S SERVICES, INCLUDING OBSTETRICS, GYNECOLOGICAL CARE, MAMMOGRAPHY, AND MUCH MORE. THE PROGRAM HAS BEEN RECOGNIZED AS ONE OF THE TOP 10 WOMEN'S CENTERS NATIONALLY BY *Self* MAGAZINE (RIGHT).

In addition to its diagnostic and treatment capabilities, WDMCI operates Central Florida's largest basic cancer research program in some of the most advanced cancer research facilities in the state.

NEW ADVANCES IN DIABETES CARE

Since its inception, the Diabetes Center at Florida Hospital has been a leader in diabetes education, training, outreach, and clinical care for Central Florida. The self-management program is accredited by the American Diabetes Association and operates with national standards for diabetes education.

The Diabetes Center at Florida Hospital encompasses comprehensive education and care in the areas of prevention, intervention, and management. The center offers a health care team approach, emphasizing diabetes management and conducted by a full staff of registered nurses, registered dieticians, and behavioral counselors who are nationally certified diabetes educators. The center's ongoing support groups help to answer questions about diabetes in a monthly support group setting. These include

the Diabetes Support Group for adults with Type 1 or Type 2 diabetes; the Insulin Pump Group for patients who wear or are interested in insulin pumps; the Florida Hospital Kissimmee Diabetes Support Group; and the Parent Support Group for parents of children with diabetes.

Located across from Florida Hospital Orlando, the Diabetes Center serves more than 10,000 people each year. In addition to treatment and education programs, the center provides a specialized exercise program with personal training by exercise physiologists. The center also promotes early detection, treatment, and rigorous attention to self-care through the Diabetes Self-Management Program. This program is designed to provide diabetes patients with the skills necessary to care for themselves.

The Diabetes Center has established a foundation to support research into new therapies and treatment options, to reduce complications of the disease, and to discover new diabetes prevention methods. The goal of the center's research department is "to conduct research that will benefit the individual with

diabetes as it relates to therapy, prevention, and associated complications." The research department's experience includes ongoing research with the University of Florida and the National Institutes of Health.

WOMEN'S CENTER

Florida Hospital's Women's Center offers full-service obstetrical and gynecological care on both an inpatient and an outpatient basis to women of all ages. Florida Hospital is acclaimed nationally for women's medicine and is the only hospital in the state that has been recognized by *Self* magazine as one of America's top 10 hospitals for women.

The center's breast screening and education program provides breast diagnostic and screening procedures, breast assessment, and breast self-examination education. Services include low-dose film screen mammography, ultrasound, breast needle biopsies, and cyst aspirations. The osteoporosis screening and education program provides services for women with high-risk factors for osteoporosis.

Family-centered services offered by the Women's Center include parent education and a family-centered perinatal program. Florida Hospital is a leader in parent education, creating several courses that have served as models across the nation. In addition to Lamaze classes, this program supports the family-centered philosophy by offering childbirth preparation classes for the entire family—from siblings to grandparents. Additional services include the Our First maternity club for new parents; the Lactation Center, which provides breast feeding classes; the Fetal Diagnostic Center; birthing rooms; and birthing suites designed to fit the individualized needs of each new family.

Additionally, the Women's Center joins forces with the Walt Disney Memorial Cancer Institute at Florida Hospital to organize cancer screenings and educational programs for the entire community. Other women's health care services include cosmetic surgery, a menopause clinic, infertility services, continence treatment, adolescent services, heart checks, and a wide variety of support groups on subjects from breast cancer to endometriosis.

REHABILITATION AND SPORTS MEDICINE

Offered at nine Central Florida locations, Florida Hospital rehabilitation and sports medicine services encompass more than 25 comprehensive health care programs. Specialty areas include stroke rehabilitation, cancer rehabilitation, spinal cord and hand injury rehabilitation, a head injury program, treatment of neurological disorders, an amputee program, an orthopedic program, and audiology services. Rehabilitation and sports medicine programs also include biofeedback services as well as physical, speech, and occupational therapy.

Florida Hospital is the official hospital of the Orlando Magic National Basketball Association team and the Orlando Solar Bears professional hockey team. The hospital has also been named the official hospital of the University of

Central Florida Athletic Program and the official rehabilitation provider for the RDV Sportsplex. Florida Hospital is a partner with LGE Sport Science Inc. to provide patients with the latest in high-technology medical treatment for sports-related injuries and recovery needs.

CELEBRATION HEALTH

A continuously innovative, comprehensive health campus, Celebration Health is a 265,000-square-foot health care facility that includes physician offices, emergency services, fitness rehabilitation, and other health care programs for residents of Celebration, Florida, a new town located near Walt Disney World; residents of Central Florida; tourists; and international patients.

Plans and designs for Celebration Health are the result of a three-year, cooperative research and study effort between Florida Hospital and the Celebration Company, a subsidiary of the Walt Disney Company. Florida Hospital continues to collaborate with a team of health care leaders to further develop ongoing goals and objectives for Celebration Health. Among the team of visionaries is

FLORIDA HOSPITAL'S REHABILITATION AND SPORTS MEDICINE PROGRAM OFFERS A BROAD RANGE OF SERVICES FOR CENTRAL FLORIDA RESIDENTS. IT IS ALSO THE OFFICIAL HOSPITAL OF THE ORLANDO MAGIC AND THE ORLANDO SOLAR BEARS (TOP).

CELEBRATION HEALTH COMBINES THE BEST OF MEDICINE'S PAST AND FUTURE TO PROVIDE HEALTH CARE IN A UNIQUE MANNER TO THE RESIDENTS OF CELEBRATION AND OSCEOLA COUNTY, TOURISTS, AND INTERNATIONAL PATIENTS. THROUGH PARTNERSHIPS WITH NATIONALLY KNOWN COMPANIES LIKE JOHNSON & JOHNSON AND GENERAL ELECTRIC, CELEBRATION HEALTH PROVIDES PATIENTS WITH CONTINUOUSLY INNOVATIVE DIAGNOSTIC AND SURGICAL FACILITIES (BOTTOM).

former U.S. Surgeon General Dr. C. Everett Koop, Johnson & Johnson, Eli Lilly and Company, and General Electric Medical Systems.

Celebration Health includes a state-of-the-art surgery center, world-class diagnostic center, rehabilitation and sports medicine, health activities and fitness center, primary care services, specialty physicians, dental clinic, and pharmacy.

In addition, Florida Hospital's Celebration Health serves as a hub for community health activities. The new facility features a 60,000-square-foot fitness center along with a basketball and volleyball gym, swimming pool, therapy pool, cardiovascular fitness area, integrated rehabilitation center, spa services, weight and strength training, and health education services.

SPRINT

Throughout the Greater Orlando area, and indeed much of the state, Sprint is considered Florida's premier local telephone company. In fact, Sprint's colorful history dates back to the early days of telephony in Florida—back to the dawn of the 1900s, when Gilmer Heitman began providing phone service to 20 subscribers in southwest Florida, a grocer named Carl Hill Galloway offered phone service to his Maitland and Winter Park customers, and a Tallahassee physician, Dr. W.L. Moor, purchased a fledgling phone company to keep in touch with his patients. Eventually these humble start-ups led to the formation of two prominent Florida phone companies: United Telephone and Centel.

Today, both United Telephone and Centel are simply called Sprint—a name that assures more than 1.8 million customers throughout Florida that they'll receive quality service from a known and trusted global company with roots deep in their community.

Sprint supplies local service through more than 6.7 million customer lines in 19 states. The company's 48,000 employees provide 16 million business and residential customers with seamless integration of voice, data, and video communications. Sprint built and operates the country's only nationwide all-digital, fiber-optic network and is the leader in advanced data communications services, as well as the world's largest carrier of Internet traffic.

Sprint's Long Distance Division delivers services to more than 290 countries and locations, including connections to 100 percent of the world's direct-dial countries. Most recently, a commitment to straightforward pricing, easy-to-understand billing, and outstanding customer service earned Sprint the number one rank in customer satisfaction among residential long-distance customers by J.D. Power and Associates.

In Florida, the company's traditional service area stretches from the Panhandle to the Everglades, encompassing nearly 40 percent of the state's geography, in addition to providing advanced business services to areas throughout the entire state. The Telecommunications Reform Act, passed in 1996, will erase these traditional boundaries for local telephone companies. Sprint will provide a full package of products and services, including local and long-distance services, to customers throughout Florida, including all of Orlando.

Sprint is a leader in providing its customers with distance learning technologies and innovative applications such as Internet access and group videoconferencing. By paying special attention to customer service, Sprint consistently receives fewer customer complaints than any major local telephone company in the state.

From small businesses to Fortune 500 corporations, companies throughout Florida rely on Sprint's technical expertise and total business communications solutions.

Two key areas of growth for Sprint are the education and health care industries. Recently, Florida Hospital—the second-largest hospital in the state—chose Sprint as its single-source provider of telecommunications technology. Together, the two corporations are working to develop applications that will support telemedicine, teleradiology, and health information network services at the hospital's many sites throughout the metropolitan Orlando

SPRINT'S BEAUTIFULLY LANDSCAPED GENERAL OFFICE BUILDING, HEADQUARTERS FOR THE SOUTHERN REGION, IS LOCATED IN APOPKA, FLORIDA, JUST MINUTES FROM DOWNTOWN ORLANDO.

LEE LUCIA

area. In addition to providing telephone and teleconferencing equipment, Sprint will build and operate a self-healing synchronous optical network (SONET) using the latest transmission technology known as asynchronous transfer mode (ATM). Future plans will integrate Florida Hospital's Celebration Health, located in Disney's new town of Celebration.

In support of Florida's education system, Sprint was an active participant in NetDay '96—a national challenge by President Bill Clinton to "build a bridge to the 21st century" by bringing cyberspace into the classroom. Company volunteers wired schools throughout the state to gain access to the Internet. Sprint is also the total communications provider for Rollins College in Winter Park, connecting dorm rooms, administration, and classrooms with voice, video, and data services, as well as providing students with access to cable TV and computer networks.

Sprint's long-standing commitment to enhance the quality of life in the communities it serves is evident through the many community projects it supports each year. In 1995 and 1996, more than 800 employees participated in 231 projects involving education, crime prevention, and health care, totaling almost 22,000 hours. For this exceptional effort, Sprint was honored as the first utility to be named Central Florida's 1996 Outstanding Philanthropic Organization.

Sprint is moving into the forefront of technological development by designing and building a state-of-the-art, wireless personal communication services (PCS) network from scratch. To achieve its goal of becoming the national provider of choice for local, long-distance, wireless, Internet access, and data products and services, Sprint PCS—a partnership with three of the largest cable television operators in the United States—will provide more than 180 million Americans with a single, integrated package

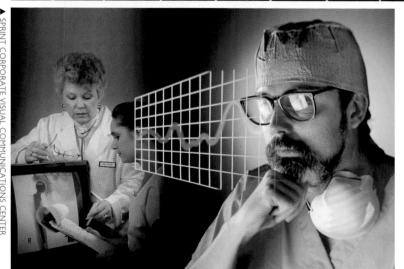

SPRINT IS A GLOBAL COMMUNICATIONS COMPANY—AT THE FOREFRONT IN INTEGRATING LONG-DISTANCE, LOCAL, AND WIRELESS COMMUNICATIONS SERVICES (TOP).

SPRINT HELPS HEALTH CARE PROVIDERS COMMUNICATE MORE QUICKLY AND EFFECTIVELY THAN EVER—BY VOICE, ON VIDEO, AND THROUGH IMMEDIATE ACCESS TO DATA (BOTTOM).

of communications services, all from one company.

Sprint has also formed Global One—a venture with Deutsche Telekom and France Telecom, the second- and fourth-largest telecommunications service providers in the world—to offer voice and data services to businesses, carriers, and consumers around

the globe through a single point of contact.

Locally, nationally, and internationally, Sprint's commitment to providing innovative services, cutting-edge products, and exceptional customer service will ensure it continues its mission of setting the standards others will follow.

AS THE REGION'S LARGEST PROBUSINESS ADVOCATE, THE GREATER Orlando Chamber of Commerce is committed to a solid business base built upon a sound community. Its vision for Greater Orlando and Central Florida is to be a family of communities functioning as a world-class hub of national and international commerce. The chamber's mission is to continue to build on the strengths of the

region, maintain a strong foundation, continually develop its identity, provide an innovative communications network, and maintain a solid community connection from which to build and grow.

"We are building a better community, creating a dynamic environment for emerging businesses within Central Florida, and establishing a central forum in which all of our 5,000 members—businesses, government, neighborhood associations, educational institutions, churches, and others—come together for a common good," says Chamber President Jacob V. Stuart. "I believe a community has the power to motivate its members to exceptional performance. It can set standards of expectation for the individual and provide the climate in which great things happen. That is what the Greater Orlando Chamber of Commerce is all about."

A MISSION TO SERVE

For more than eight decades, the Greater Orlando Chamber of Commerce has served the needs of Orlando-area businesses, recording the causes and effects that have changed this city's business climate from a quiet town into a shining international showcase.

In its early years, the Chamber was known as The Orlando Board of Trade. Led by J.N. Bradshaw, the organization targeted community campaigns to widen and improve roads, cope with federal taxation,

and protect the interests of area businesses. Today, the Chamber remains an essential partner to all areas of business and community development.

"Our goal is always to be a community melting pot with no agenda other than to further the betterment of the community," says 1997 Chamber Board Chairman Tico Perez. "We're on a mission to serve our members through a neutral system that brings everyone together without special interests."

STEPS TOWARD SOLUTIONS

From the creation of The Small Business Chamber in 1995—to meet the special needs of companies with fewer than 40 employees—to the development of the Chamber Trustees program involving the leadership of Central Florida's top 500 corporations, the Greater Orlando Chamber of Commerce is taking the roads less traveled and paving the way for others to follow.

"In the business world, everyone agrees that change and innovation are good only if someone else goes first," explains Tom Kornegay, head of Orlando's TeKontrol Inc. and 1997 Chairman of the Board of The Small Business Chamber. "The Chamber is comfortable in that leadership role. It invariably makes the first move and focuses on taking issues to the next level."

The Small Business Chamber was developed to provide growing companies with access to full-time business professionals, market research surveys, and other infor-

mation resources that most larger companies possess in-house. Dozens of programs, events, and guest speakers provide up-to-the-minute information on issues of importance to new and emerging businesses. Similarly, ChamberBenefits Inc., a wholly owned, for-profit corporation of the Greater Orlando Chamber, provides smaller companies sizable, cost-effective benefits based on bulk-buying and member-to-member discounts. These programs include a variety of employee health care services offered to growing businesses under the Chamber umbrella.

Launched in 1996, Chamber Trustees provides the framework for building community and preparing for the challenges of the next century. The goal is to bring together the senior executives of the area's largest employers for joint meetings with community, government, and industry leaders to provide a shared vision for the future and direct the quality of the region's growth.

The Chamber has developed three nationally recognized, award-winning community leadership programs: Leadership Orlando, Leadership Central Florida, and Youth Leadership. For more than 20 years, Leadership Orlando has introduced participants to the inner workings of the Orlando area and opened doors to valuable business contacts. More than 1,800 of today's Greater Orlando business leaders are Leadership Orlando graduates. Leadership Central Florida, the first program of its kind in the

BROWSERS ON THE WORLD WIDE WEB CAN ACCESS THE SERVICES OF THE GREATER ORLANDO CHAMBER OF COMMERCE THROUGH ITS EXTENSIVE SITE, WHICH NOT ONLY PROVIDES INFORMATION ABOUT THE CHAMBER AND ITS LEADERSHIP ORLANDO PROGRAM, BUT ALSO PROVIDES A LINK TO THE ORLANDO CHAMBER ELECTRONIC MALL (OPPOSITE PAGE).

nation, is designed for participants interested in issues of regional importance. The program builds partnerships to strengthen communities in nearby Brevard, Lake, Orange, Osceola, Polk, Seminole, and Volusia counties.

High school juniors from several area counties are selected each year to participate in the Youth Leadership program, a partnership of the Greater Orlando Chamber of Commerce and Junior Achievement of Central Florida, Inc. The students take part in a series of out-of-classroom experiences that teach them the inner workings of Central Florida tourism, law, government, and higher education systems.

Seeing the need to improve education programs for the future workforce of Central Florida, the Greater Orlando Chamber of Commerce has been a leading advocate of *WorldClass Schools, Inc.*, a statewide strategy designed to begin a new era of business-led school reform. Locally, the goals include raising standards and accountability for teachers and students, improving performance measures and technology, and developing curricula with real-world applications.

To keep Central Florida businesses thriving in the year 2000 and beyond, the Chamber has developed its most ambitious resource development campaign—Chamber 2000. Using a team approach, the campaign is designed to improve the community and maintain a consistently healthy business climate for the Chamber's 5,000-plus members, now and in the future.

"A healthy community should have a sense of where it should go and what it might become," says Stuart. "As a Chamber, we can't know all the forms the community will take, but we know the values and the kinds of supporting structures we want to preserve."

We want to give you the key *to our city.*

www.orlando.org

I N 1918, A GROUP OF ORLANDO RESIDENTS, PHYSICIANS, AND CONTRACTORS recognized the need to improve community health care services. Under the name of the Orange County Hospital Association, the group invested time and money, collected donations, purchased land, and hired a team to build the 50-bed Orange General Hospital, the city's first modern health care facility. ✳ But the association built more than a hospital. It established

a solid foundation for what would become the city's premier health care network—the Orlando Regional Healthcare System (ORHS). Today, the building that housed Orange General Hospital operates as one of six hospitals and numerous health care services united in the name ORHS, a comprehensive, not-for-profit, community-owned network of hospitals, special care centers, and health care professionals dedicated to improving the health and quality of life of more than 2 million Florida residents.

HEALTH CARE THROUGH TEAMWORK

ORHS has been voted one of the country's top 100 hospital systems and one of the area's top "family friendly" companies.

Reaching this level of community service takes more than one hospital, more than one doctor, and more than one staff. It takes teamwork.

The ORHS team, consisting of more than 8,000 employees throughout Central Florida, is

committed to excellence. A shareholder of the Voluntary Hospitals of America (VHA), ORHS is accredited by the Joint Commission on Accreditation of Healthcare Organizations.

Major ORHS hospital facilities include Orlando Regional Medical Center, a major hospital in downtown Orlando specializing in trauma, emergency care, cardiology, orthopedics, neuroscience, diabetes care, and critical care; Arnold Palmer

Hospital for Children & Women, one of only four such facilities in the nation dedicated exclusively to the care of children and women; Sand Lake Hospital, serving southwest Orange County residents and tourists staying nearby; M.D. Anderson Cancer Center Orlando, which provides state-of-the-art outpatient cancer care in a program jointly sponsored by ORHS and the M.D. Anderson Cancer Center in Houston; St. Cloud Hospital in Osceola County and South Seminole Hospital in Longwood; ORHS Health Sciences Center, a research and teaching facility for advanced science research, development, and training; Orlando Regional Healthcare Foundation, benefiting community health care programs; and Hubbard House, offering affordable and convenient living accommodations for family members of patients at ORHS facilities.

Additional ORHS services include the Visiting Nurse Association, Ambulatory Care Center, Orlando Regional Walk-In Medical Care, Outpatient Cardiovascular

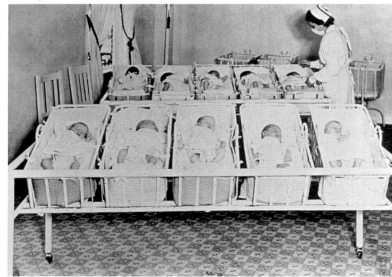

Center of Orlando, Orlando Regional Rehabilitation Services, and Orlando Regional Health Affiliates.

Together, these ORHS facilities and services offer a complete selection of specialized services from trauma to outpatient treatment, from pain management to wellness, and from adult services to child services. With the strength of all ORHS facilities working as a team and focusing on each patient and family member, ORHS is able to better meet growing health care needs in the community.

A MISSION TO SERVE

The Orlando Regional Healthcare System mission statement is to "improve the health and quality of life of the individuals and communities we serve." Since 1918, ORHS has earned a reputation as a community-owned health care system that looks beyond profits to embrace a mission of long-term service to all members of the community.

"Since 1918, Orlando Regional Healthcare System has grown hand in hand with Greater Orlando," says ORHS President and CEO John Hillenmeyer. "In the age of high-tech hospitals, our goal remains to provide residents with individual care and treatment. We plan to continue this tradition for generations to come."

As a private, community-owned organization, ORHS reinvests its services and funds back into Central Florida. Beyond personal health care services, ORHS improves the health of the community through education, offering such free public programs as 55PLUS®, which is tailored to the concerns of area seniors. Additionally, ORHS orchestrates numerous community initiatives, including programs designed to provide health care for the homeless, SAFE KIDS program to prevent childhood injuries, and resource services for the fight against Alzheimer's and other diseases.

To continue its mission in the future, ORHS is expanding and adding more services through new facilities and partnership programs.

While ORHS has enjoyed a history of growth and change, its mission remains constant—to provide Central Florida residents with quality, cost-effective health care as it has done for nearly 80 years.

CLOCKWISE FROM TOP:
WHEN PATIENTS NEED EMERGENCY AIR TRANSPORT TO AN ORHS FACILITY, THE HOSPITAL SYSTEM PROVIDES THE SERVICES OF ITS AIR CARE TEAM.

THE ORHS HEALTH SCIENCES CENTER SERVES AS A RESEARCH AND TEACHING FACILITY FOR ADVANCED SCIENCE RESEARCH, DEVELOPMENT, AND TRAINING.

THE ARNOLD PALMER HOSPITAL FOR CHILDREN & WOMEN IS ONE OF ONLY FOUR SUCH FACILITIES IN THE NATION DEDICATED EXCLUSIVELY TO THE CARE OF CHILDREN AND WOMEN.

THE NEONATAL INTENSIVE CARE UNIT AT THE ARNOLD PALMER HOSPITAL IS RENOWNED FOR ITS LIFESAVING SERVICES.

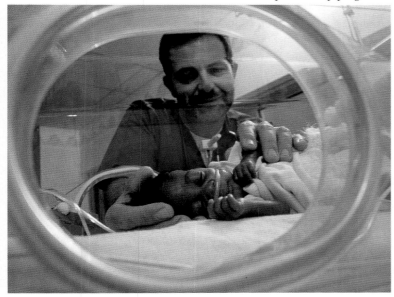

WHEN HUBBARD CONSTRUCTION COMPANY WAS FOUNDED IN 1920, its assets consisted of one mule, one wagon, and one shovel. Today, the company maintains more than 2,000 pieces of equipment valued at more than $100 million. From interstate highways to international airports, and from world attractions to new Florida communities, the men and women of Hubbard Construction

Company have paved the way for Orlando's growth, development, and economic expansion.

Headquartered in Orlando, Hubbard Construction Company is the leader in quality heavy construction throughout the state. The scope of the company's work covers a broad spectrum of both public and private construction projects. Its works include complex highway interchanges, roadbeds for rail transport, drainage systems, roads, bridges, underground utilities, golf courses, and real estate development. Its clients are served by hundreds of professionals at Hubbard and its affiliated divisions: Orlando Paving Company, Atlantic Coast Asphalt, and Mid-Florida Materials.

"Our company can only be best described as professional, dedicated, committed to excellence, and community spirited," says Jean-Marc Allard, chairman, president, and chief executive officer. "Our work is consistently producing cost-effective and professionally executed products. We rely on our professionals to continue our tradition of excellence. Our record is due primarily to the creativity, pride, and innovative spirit of the men and women who have been the heart of Hubbard for more than 75 years."

MARKS OF DISTINCTION

With close to $200 million in revenue for 1996, Hubbard Construction has been ranked by *Engineering News Record* as one of the top 50 highway and heavy construction contractors in the nation. Numerous landmarks reveal that Hubbard has shaped Florida's landscape from Orlando

to Jacksonville to Tampa and beyond.

Hubbard's quality design and construction can be seen in such projects as the Central Florida Greeneway, the Interstate 4 and Lake Mary interchange, the Osceola Parkway, State Road 436 in Orlando, and the All-Star Resort Boulevard and EPCOT Center Drive for Walt Disney World. Hubbard has also played a major role in the shaping of the Orlando International Airport, as well as the headquarters of the American Automobile Association in Lake Mary, the Marriott Orlando World Center, the Beeline Expressway, Florida's Turnpike, communities such as Lake Forest, the ongoing widening of Interstate 4 at Longwood, and the downtown Orlando "Lymmo" bus project.

Since its inception, Hubbard has often been the choice for road, highway, bridge, and interchange projects issued by the Florida Department of Transportation, as well as numerous city and county governments. Additionally, when Hurri-

cane Andrew hit South Florida in 1992, Hubbard Construction was the only contractor from Florida and one of six contractors in the nation selected by the U.S. Corps of Engineers to handle the unprecedented cleanup efforts.

BUILDING A SENSE OF COMMUNITY

Hubbard Construction is committed to making a difference in the communities where its employees live and work. "The people of Orlando are warmer and more genuinely interested in our community than any other part of the country," Allard explains. "We want to be involved in building a better community both on and off the work site.

"We at Hubbard Construction set out to achieve quality and excellence in every project we undertake," concludes Allard. "We are shaping the future every hour of our lives, whether building better business opportunities . . . or a better quality of life in Orlando and Central Florida."

HUBBARD IS BUILDING THE WORLD DRIVE EXTENSION, WHICH INCLUDES SEVERAL MAJOR INTERCHANGES AND BRIDGES FOR WALT DISNEY WORLD (LEFT).

HUBBARD CONSTRUCTION DID THE SITE PREPARATION, ACCESS STREETS, UNDERGROUND UTILITIES, AND PARKING LOTS FOR THE ORLANDO ARENA (RIGHT).

COOPERS & LYBRAND L.L.P.

BUSINESSES ACCOMPLISH FINANCIAL SUCCESS BY STRATEGICALLY formulating and achieving goals. Increasingly aware of the scope and depth of expertise required to plan sound strategies that lead to success, smart companies partner with seasoned professional services firms to address financial issues and establish a winning strategy. ✳ Helping companies reach their financial goals through a wide range of business and

financial services is what Coopers & Lybrand L.L.P. has successfully accomplished for nearly 100 years. The Orlando office, led by Market Managing Partner Pat Knipe, provides expertise through a variety of services including auditing, accounting, tax compliance and planning, management consulting, assistance with Securities and Exchange Commission matters, consulting on human resource issues such as benefit plans and compensation, technology services and statistical analysis, and information technology consulting.

Coopers & Lybrand has earned its reputation as one of the world's leading professional service firms by developing innovative services tailored to match the growing and evolving needs of each of its clients. In Central Florida, Coopers & Lybrand has earned the trust and business of clients that range from the largest public companies to emerging entrepreneurially

managed companies, as well as many of the area's largest city, county, and municipal governmental organizations. Expertise in all facets of business is what allows Coopers & Lybrand to successfully assist this wide range of clients— no matter how large or small—in achieving success in today's increasingly competitive global marketplace.

Coopers & Lybrand professionals in Orlando have assisted clients in their initial public offerings, mergers and acquisitions, and other major financial transactions that shape their businesses. The Orlando office's Entrepreneurial Advisory Services practice specializes in servicing the needs of growing closely held companies in the middle market. Whether a start-up or a growing organization in the middle market, this practice offers a team of professionals who are specifically trained in the accounting, tax, and computer tech-

nology needs of the closely held company.

The firm offers its clients the expertise of more than 16,000 professionals and staff in offices located in 100 U.S. cities and, through the member firms of Coopers & Lybrand International, more than 70,000 people in 140 countries worldwide, in a wide range of industries. In addition, the firm maintains a site on the World Wide Web (www.colybrand.com). Coopers & Lybrand has the resources, expertise, and reputation that ensure businesses that all their financial issues will be addressed through strategic planning and consulting.

"Our goals are clear and simple," explains Knipe: "Deliver the highest level of quality service our clients expect; develop individual initiative and help our people fulfill their potential; and foster a sense of teamwork among our people and with the communities in which we do business."

FROM ITS DOWNTOWN ORLANDO OFFICE LOCATION, COOPERS & LYBRAND L.L.P. DELIVERS HIGH-QUALITY SERVICE TO A WIDE VARIETY OF CLIENTS USING A TEAM-CENTERED APPROACH (LEFT).

THE COOPERS & LYBRAND SOLUTIONS THRU TECHNOLOGY OFFICE PROVIDES STATE-OF-THE-ART SOFTWARE PLATFORMS UTILIZED BY CLIENTS DURING INFORMATION SYSTEM SELECTION AND IMPLEMENTATION (RIGHT).

Orlando Utilities Commission

fOR MORE THAN 75 YEARS, CENTRAL FLORIDIANS HAVE COME TO RELY ON Orlando Utilities Commission (OUC) to keep the lights on, to keep the water flowing, and to lend a helping hand in the community. As Orlando has grown, so has OUC—keeping pace with the area's surging economic development by continuously improving its products and services and by staying ahead of the curve with leading-edge technology. All the while,

WEATHERING THE STORM TO KEEP CUSTOMERS IN SERVICE IS ALL IN A NIGHT'S WORK FOR OUC ELECTRIC DISTRIBUTION EMPLOYEES (TOP).

THE 468-MEGAWATT CURTIS H. STANTON ENERGY CENTER UNIT 2 BEGAN COMMERCIAL OPERATION JUNE 1, 1996, ON TIME AND UNDER BUDGET (BOTTOM).

OUC has earned both local respect and national acclaim for its customer service and impressive civic involvement.

Today, Orlando Utilities is also recognized for its consistent, reliable, and cost-efficient energy programs. Its environmental, conservation, and recycling systems have become vital resources to local industrial, residential, and commercial customers. OUC now serves more than 150,000 customers in a 400-square-mile service area.

THE POWER OF PARTNERSHIPS

The Orlando Utilities Commission is owned, controlled, and managed by a unique partnering among the citizens of Orlando. The Commission is comprised of five members, including the mayor of Orlando. Members—with the exception of the mayor, who is an ex officio member—serve without compensation and may serve

no more than two consecutive four-year terms.

Over the years, the Commission has strengthened its community partnership role. OUC returns to its stakeholders—the City of Orlando and its citizens—a significant portion of the general fund, helping to pay for police and fire services; sewer and sanitary facilities; street paving, cleaning, and lighting; parks and playgrounds; traffic engineering; airport operation; health department services; and other community operations.

AHEAD OF THE CURVE

Among the first in the nation to restructure its electric operations, OUC jumped ahead of the curve in preparing for industry deregulation and competition. To maintain its competitive edge, OUC cut costs and trimmed expenses to remain a low-cost provider of competitively priced and highly reliable power.

To meet the 21st-century needs of its customers, OUC embarked on several major endeavors in the 1990s. Its 468-megawatt Curtis H. Stanton Energy Center Unit 2 (SEC 2) began commercial operation in 1996—on time and under budget. The new power plant featured leading-edge technology to protect the environment and air quality. Designed to comply with the latest air quality regulations, SEC 2 was the first of its kind and size in the nation to use a selective catalytic reduction system to remove nitrogen oxides from the flue gas.

While always looking to the future, OUC has never lost sight of its commitment to reliability. In a 1996 study of 41 major electric utilities spanning the United States and England, OUC's distribution system ranked second in reliability. For years, OUC has also led other major Florida utilities in reliability.

BEYOND THE METER

Going beyond the meter, OUC is committed to maintaining its record of exceptional reliability by energy surveys, proactive inspections, and diagnostic checkups of customer equipment. An automatic outage reporting system has also been installed for sensitive and critical customers such as hospitals, airports, post offices, and other public facilities, as well as major commercial customers. Within 20 seconds, this monitoring system automatically reports outages, enabling OUC to respond immediately.

For residential customers, OUC conducts energy audits of homes, identifying improvements, such as insulation or heat pumps,

that could help lower customers' monthly utility bills; provides home fix-up programs that provide financial assistance to qualified residents to help weatherize homes; and rewards energy conservation with special rebate programs for customers who use efficient lighting systems.

On the Water Front

On the water front, OUC is leading edge, too. The utility launched Water Project 2000, which upgraded the entire water system to the ozone treatment process. The new water is called H2OUC—ozone-treated water that tastes as good or better than bottled water and costs substantially less.

The most comprehensive plan for expanding and modernizing the water system infrastructure in OUC's history, Water Project 2000 encompassed constructing new ozone treatment plants, converting existing plants to ozone, expanding and improving pipelines, and modernizing the computer control system so that the water plants can be operated by remote control.

Protecting the Environment

Environmental performance at OUC has continued to surpass all state and federal standards established by the 1990 Clear Air Act and the Safe Drinking Water Act. Preventing or reducing pollution at the source is at the core of OUC's environmental strategy. This includes eliminating hazardous materials, restricting their use, or substituting them with environmentally friendly products. In the area of environmental protection, OUC also provides storm water management, recycling programs, and programs to preserve endangered animals and wetlands. In addition, to improve reliability and for aesthetic reasons, more than 40 percent of OUC's electric system is underground.

A Commitment to Communities

OUC has always been committed to being a good neighbor, friend, and partner—not only to Orlando but also to other Central Florida communities it serves or affects. As a good corporate citizen, OUC is a major supporter of United Arts, United Way, Orlando Science Center, Public Television Channel 24, Minority/Women Business Enterprise Alliance, Metropolitan Urban League, and Habitat for Humanity, among others. OUC's PROUD Community Volunteer program has earned national recognition, and the utility has been named by *Central Florida Family* magazine as one of the Top 10 Companies for Working Families.

OUC combines community relations activities with highly proactive communications. Through its Neighborhood Outreach Program, Educational Outreach Program, and Speakers Bureau, OUC reaches out—in person—to thousands of people each year.

A Utility for the 21st Century

Responding to change and competition—while remaining steadfastly committed to reliability, protecting the environment, preserving resources, and serving the community—OUC has positioned itself as a utility for the next millennium. By building on its past and inventing its future, Orlando Utilities Commission has taken the steps necessary to safeguard the interests of its owners—the City of Orlando and its citizens.

As part of the most comprehensive plan for expanding and modernizing the water system in its history, OUC launched a fleet of new and refurbished water treatment plants that dispense H2OUC—ozone-treated water that tastes as good or better than bottled water and costs much less (left).

A good corporate citizen, OUC is actively involved in many community projects. The utility was a key contributor to the Power Station exhibit at the Orlando Science Center (right).

SunTrust Bank

WHEN LINTON E. ALLEN FOUNDED SUNTRUST BANK, HIS BUSINESS philosophy was "Build your community, and you build your bank." ✳ SunTrust has been building its community and growing with Central Florida since 1934. ✳ On February 14, 1934, in the midst of the Great Depression, SunTrust—then called First National Bank at Orlando—took to the road with unwavering growth and expansion. During the 1950s and 1960s, the bank boomed with the development of several affiliate banks. In 1973, First National, its affiliates, and its holding company were renamed SunBanks of Florida, Inc. SunBank continued to build on a foundation of strong performance and customer satisfaction. In 1985, SunBanks of Florida merged with the Trust Company of Georgia and later with Third National Bank Corporation of Tennessee, forming SunTrust Banks, Inc. But it was not until 1995 that all SunTrust subsidiaries, including Florida's SunBank locations, adopted the SunTrust name, establishing a connection between local banking institutions and their umbrella organization, SunTrust.

With more than $53 billion in assets, today SunTrust Banks, Inc. is one of the nation's 18 largest banking companies. Operating more than 680 banking locations in Florida, Georgia, Tennessee, and Alabama, SunTrust provides a wide range of personal, corporate, and institutional financial services. In Central Florida, SunTrust employs nearly 4,000 people at major entities, including SunTrust Banks of Florida, Inc., SunTrust Bank Central Florida, SunTrust BankCard, and STI Capital Management.

Locally, SunTrust continues to carry the banner of "Build your community, and you build your bank." George Koehn, SunTrust Bank Central Florida's chairman, president, and chief executive officer, sums it up best: "Our goal is to continue to build Central Florida by being the best bankers we can be and by applying our knowledge and skills to help our community grow."

GROWING ECONOMIC DEVELOPMENT

SunTrust's role in attracting, keeping, and growing businesses in Central Florida is legendary. As Orlando historian Ormund Powers notes in his book *Top Bank*, "There is scarcely any major business or civic endeavor in Orlando and Central Florida that has not come into being or been made better" without the help of SunTrust. As SunTrust has evolved, its strength has helped Orlando to earn its spot as a national and international destination for businesses and visitors alike. The bank helped the city earn its magic by financing the expansion of the Orlando International Airport and the Orange County Civic Center. Other civic endeavors in which SunTrust and its leaders have assisted include transforming the Tangerine Bowl into the Citrus Bowl; founding the University of Central Florida; attracting the first Minute Maid plant to Central Florida; persuading Martin Marietta Aerospace (now Lockheed Martin) to locate in Orlando; and securing the land tract now known as Walt Disney World Resort®.

Additionally, SunTrust was instrumental in the passage of an act by the Florida legislature to create a loan fund for African-American-owned businesses, and the company continues to participate in financial assistance activities, such as the minority- and women-owned business loan pro-

WITH MORE THAN $53 BILLION IN ASSETS, TODAY'S SUNTRUST BANKS, INC. IS ONE OF THE NATION'S 18 LARGEST BANKING COMPANIES.

gram for growing community businesses.

And because hospitals are a vital community component, SunTrust invests heavily in their future. In addition to serving the banking needs of area health care providers, SunTrust assists in capital fund-raising and special service projects.

INVESTING IN THE COMMUNITY

SunTrust's commitment to service extends beyond daily business calls. By working with leaders in government, health and human services, business, industry, education, and the arts, SunTrust actively searches for creative solutions to economic and social challenges. Philanthropy—through financial and in-kind donations, volunteering time and talent, and board involvement—is a significant part of SunTrust's past, present, and future contributions to Central Florida.

Annually, SunTrust staff members devote more than 150,000 hours to community service, building upon its mission that if the community succeeds, so too does SunTrust. These banking professionals serve on more than 200 community boards of directors, and the company serves as a patron of the arts, pledging more than $1 million to support

United Arts, a funding mechanism that supports such organizations as the Bach Festival Society, Orlando Museum of Art, Southern Ballet Theatre, Orlando Opera Company, Orlando Science Center, Orange County Historical Society, Crealde School of Art, Florida Film Festival, Brevard Art Center and Museum, Osceola Center for the Arts, and other area arts organizations.

Additionally, SunTrust is involved in educational support at every level, from elementary, middle, and high schools to community and four-year colleges and universities throughout its five-county service area.

In 1996, Central Florida charities received more than $1 million in SunTrust financial contribu-

tions. Local charities included the Orlando Science Center, Coalition for the Homeless, Adult Literacy League, Visiting Nurse Association, Central Florida Zoo, Salvation Army, Mothers Against Drunk Driving, Child Care Crisis Fund, and more than 100 additional museums, organizations, and community service programs. Interestingly, while SunTrust is Central Florida's 20th-largest employer, the company was the fifth-largest contributor to the United Way in 1996.

"We have seen firsthand that building the community can indeed build our bank," says Koehn. "It is a charge that we have taken to heart and will continue to embrace for many years to come."

As SunTrust has evolved, its strength has helped Orlando to earn its spot as a national and international destination for businesses and visitors alike. As such, the bank helped the city by financing the expansion of the Orlando International Airport (top left). Other projects include the Orlando Arena (top right).

SunTrust Bank serves as a patron of the arts, pledging more than $1 million to support a number of local organizations, including the Orlando Science Center (bottom).

WITH A CORPORATE NAME THAT IS KNOWN THROUGHOUT FLORIDA, ABC Fine Wine & Spirits is truly an Orlando success story. The story begins with the ambition of one man: Jack Holloway, a onetime Orlando cigar store clerk who laid the foundation of a company that has evolved into the largest family-owned alcohol beverage retail chain in the nation. ✳ Throughout the company's first years, Holloway pioneered new techniques, systems, and services to improve the efficiency of the business. This spirit of timeless determination has enabled the company to build on a well-known tradition of success and to maintain a solid business base which has spanned more than 63 years.

DISPROVING THE NONBELIEVERS

ABC grew to beat the odds in an industry that admittedly has its share of skeptics. Following the repeal of the 1934 Prohibition laws, Holloway suggested that his employer at the cigar store enter the liquor business. When his boss scoffed at the opportunity, Holloway searched for a partner to share in the development of a new local bar, but finding no takers, he ventured out on his own and, at the age of 24, opened one of Orlando's first post-Prohibition liquor stores.

Jack Holloway's Friendly Bar opened its doors in 1936 at the corner of Orange Avenue and Wall Street in the heart of downtown Orlando. Business was slow at first, and Holloway decided he needed to expand to gain a competitive edge. By World War II, Holloway had half a dozen stores and was on his way to building a business empire. In 1950, Holloway changed the name of his stores to ABC, a name commonly used by state-owned Alcoholic Beverage Commission stores. By 1960, ABC grew from a small corner bar to operating 20 ABC Liquor stores throughout Central Florida.

A SUCCESSFUL BLEND OF OLD AND NEW

It wasn't long before Holloway was ready to climb the next rung on the corporate ladder. Over years of growth and development, ABC branched out and applied its brand of success to a growing range of related products, expanding its stores and exploring growth in new markets.

MANY ABC LOCATIONS HAVE A WALK-IN, CLIMATE-CONTROLLED CIGAR HUMIDOR, AS WELL AS A CLIMATE-CONTROLLED WINE ROOM.

THROUGHOUT THE YEARS, ABC STORES HAVE EVOLVED INSIDE AND OUT. REMODELED STORES, WHICH ARE REFURBISHED AT A COST OF ABOUT $200,000 PER STORE, CARRY THE NAME ABC FINE WINE & SPIRITS AND ARE DESIGNED TO SHOWCASE PRODUCTS IN SPACIOUS ENVIRONMENTS RANGING IN SIZE FROM 8,000 TO 32,000 SQUARE FEET.

But it wasn't until the 1960s that significant growth came to the new chain. Acquisitions spawned new expansion and new service opportunities. Following the purchase of dozens of small and large competing chains and independent establishments, ABC Liquor grew in volume and size. By 1970, stores were expanded to include large retail outlets and adjacent full-service lounges.

As customer expectations climbed, ABC met them with new marketing and promotions programs, expanded product lines, and new locations for customer satisfaction and convenience. Stores were kept simple with well-stocked wine and spirits, and with friendly, professional service.

"YOU CAN'T STAND STILL"

While quality and service have remained a long-standing tradition at ABC, corporate leaders are committed to improving and expanding the company's core business. Today, ABC is still at the core of the downtown Orlando business district. But instead of one or two dozen stores, the chain is 173 stores strong and growing. ABC now operates under third-generation leadership, with Holloway's grandson Charles Bailes III serving as president and chief executive officer.

With estimated annual sales of more than $230 million, ABC continues its reign as the largest family-owned alcohol beverage retail chain in America. As the evolution of corporate leadership brought change to the company, consumers witnessed other new developments. ABC stores have evolved inside and out. The chain is phasing out the full-service lounges, and the stores are beginning to take on a new look and a new name. Remodeled stores, which are refurbished at a cost of about $200,000 per store, carry the name ABC Fine Wine & Spirits and are designed to showcase

products in spacious environments ranging in size from 8,000 to 32,000 square feet.

When *Beverage & Food Dynamics* named ABC its 1996 Retailer of the Year, Bailes told writer Howard Reill, "In business, you can't stand still. If you stand still, you're moving backwards. For us to present ourselves as a peddler of liquor is now becoming less acceptable if that's all we do."

ABC is catering to what Bailes calls "the entertainment lifestyle." By adding more than 1,000 new wines to an existing 2,000 varieties, ABC has spawned growing interest in its wine business and membership in its vintage wine club. New product lines include assorted party products, gourmet foods and cheese, customer gift baskets and gift wrapping, hand-rolled cigars, an extensive selection of import and microbrewery beers, direct mail baskets and gifts, customer wine storage, and statewide delivery service. New in-store merchandising techniques, such as walk-in humidors and climate-

controlled wine rooms, as well as state-of-the-art operation technology, are helping ABC in this transition.

While most companies may be content with their success, ABC Fine Wine & Spirits continues to take stock of itself and embrace the vision of Jack Holloway—seeking new opportunities and breaking new ground in an industry others might find too difficult to conquer.

NEW PRODUCT LINES AT ABC FINE WINE & SPIRITS INCLUDE ASSORTED PARTY PRODUCTS, GOURMET FOODS AND CHEESE, AND CUSTOMER GIFT BASKETS AND GIFT WRAPPING.

TUPPERWARE

WE HAVE THUMPED IT, SEALED IT, BURPED IT, AND STORED IT. IT CAN be found in homes, offices, boats, and briefcases around the world. For more than 50 years, Tupperware® brand products have been part of Americana. Today, Tupperware is one of the world's leading direct sellers with more than 1 million independent direct sellers demonstrating and selling Tupperware's premium food storage and serving containers, microwave cookware, and children's toys in more than 100 countries.

MAKING HISTORY

What began as an experiment in the 1930s has become a worldwide phenomenon. Self-styled Yankee trader and inventor Earl Tupper of Berlin, New Hampshire, invented a method of purifying a waste product of the oil refining process into a material that was durable, flexible, odorless, nontoxic, and lightweight. After manufacturing plastic gas mask parts during World War II, Tupper turned his attention to consumer products, and designed and manufactured a line of premium plastic food storage and serving containers. Tupper's products featured a unique, virtually airtight seal ideally suited to protect food from the drying air of electric and gas refrigerators.

Tupper introduced his new line in 1946, through department and hardware stores, but consumers were not used to high-quality plastic products and did not un-

derstand how to apply Tupperware's unique seal. Sales languished until the late 1940s when several direct sellers of Stanley Home Products discovered the unique benefits of Tupperware® containers and recognized the value of demonstrating them on the home party plan. Then sales took off.

One of those direct sellers was Brownie Wise, a single mother with a genius for people and a flair for marketing. Wise was so successful demonstrating and selling Tupper's plastics that he brought her into his company in 1951 to build the direct

selling system that has made the Tupperware party almost as famous as his products. The Tupperware demonstration has since become a global institution.

Wise designed the educational programs and built the fun and excitement into the Tupperware demonstration and the direct selling system that have made a career in Tupperware a growing opportunity for millions of women over a period of almost 50 years.

The Tupperware demonstration continues to evolve to provide an enjoyable, educational, and

CLOCKWISE FROM TOP:
THE TUPPERWARE WORLD HEADQUARTERS BUILDING IN ORLANDO WAS DESIGNED BY NOTED AMERICAN ARCHITECT EDWARD DURRELL STONE.

TUPPERWARE'S LUNCH BOX FOR JAPANESE SCHOOLCHILDREN WAS DESIGNED AT THE COMPANY'S DESIGN CENTER IN HONG KONG.

TUPPERWARE'S AWARD-WINNING TUPPERCARE® CHILDREN'S FEEDING LINE WAS DESIGNED IN EUROPE AND IS SOLD IN MANY AREAS OF THE WORLD.

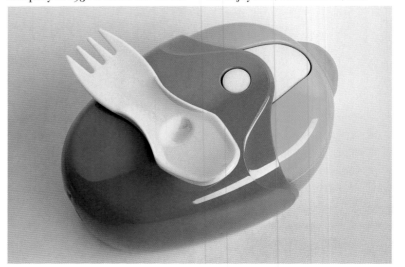

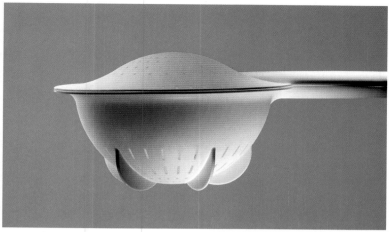

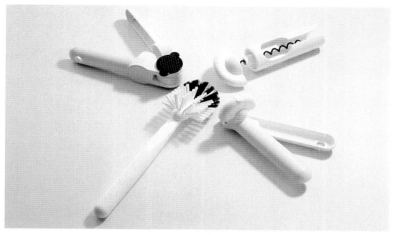

personalized shopping experience that is relevant to the wants and needs of today's consumers in culturally diverse markets.

Tupperware's direct selling system offers a flexible earnings opportunity, putting part-time to six-figure incomes within reach, plus added incentives, prizes, bonuses, travel, and abundant occasions for peer recognition and personal encouragement.

The Tupperware® brand has achieved unparalleled market penetration, with Tupperware® products found in more than 90 percent of American households. The Tupperware® brand has been ranked among the top 20 brands in price/value criteria, and each product is designed and manufactured to be perfect for its purpose and perform for a lifetime.

Tupperware continues to symbolize eminently practical and useful design. The graceful form of Tupperware® products and their quality and functionality over the years have also been recognized and honored in permanent collections of a number of the world's fine arts museums and industrial design centers, and have won design awards in the United States, Europe, and Japan. Tupperware has earned the accolade "extraordinary design for everyday living."

Since 1990, Tupperware has expanded into eastern Europe, including Poland, Hungary, and the Baltic states, and has established a presence in the Balkans as well

as the Federated Republics of Russia. From its operations in the Pacific Rim, Tupperware has entered India, Indonesia, and the People's Republic of China. Together, these nations contain nearly half the world's population. And Tupperware is leveraging its operations in Latin America to expand into new markets there. More than 85 percent of Tupperware's $1 billion-plus in worldwide sales is generated outside the United States.

Tupperware's charitable focus is also worldwide. Helping others has been the hallmark of a career in Tupperware for almost 50 years: offering the tools of opportunity especially to women, assisting customers with products and information to care for their families, and supporting charities with fundraising events and direct donations. Reflecting the company's urgent sense of compassion and feeling of shared responsibility for children, Tupperware has established the Give a Child a Chance Program. Through it, Tupperware supports with direct grants or in partnership with the sales force a variety of programs and services for children around the world.

And for the first time since Tupper sold the company in 1958, Tupperware has become an independent enterprise once again. On November 1, 1995, the board of directors of Premark International, Tupperware's parent company, authorized management to establish Tupperware as an independent

company, which was completed May 31, 1996. Tupperware stock is traded on the New York Stock Exchange under the symbol TUP.

Each year, thousands of international visitors, representing valued members of the Tupperware sales force as well as consumers, travel to Tupperware Corporation's world headquarters in Orlando to enjoy the symbols of recognition and tributes to success that honor the achievements of its independent direct sellers around the world. Thousands of residents come to the Tupperware Convention Center to enjoy theater, ballet, and symphony, as well as rock concerts, other live performances, and community events.

Today, the sun never sets on Tupperware, with a demonstration beginning somewhere every two seconds, on average, and more than 100 million people attending Tupperware demonstrations each year.

CLOCKWISE FROM TOP LEFT: TUPPERWARE'S AWARD-WINNING DOUBLE COLANDER WAS DESIGNED IN THE UNITED STATES AND IS SOLD IN MANY COUNTRIES AROUND THE WORLD.

TUPPERWARE'S LINE OF INGENIOUSLY DESIGNED KITCHEN PRODUCTS OFFERS CONSUMERS SOLUTIONS FOR FOOD PREPARATION, CLEANUP, AND SERVING. CREATED WITH EXTRAORDINARY DESIGN FOR EVERYDAY LIVING, PRODUCTS SHOWN HERE INCLUDE (FROM TOP LEFT) A GARLIC PRESS, THE UPLIFTER™ CORKSCREW, THE TOPLIFTER CAN OPENER, AND THE COMFORTCLEAN™ DISH BRUSH.

THE BEAUTIFUL FORM AND COLOR, CONVENIENCE, AND EASY MAINTENANCE OF THE MICROWAVE COOKWARE SET EARNED JAPAN'S PRESTIGIOUS G-MARK AWARD FOR DESIGN.

I N 1952, ONE OF THE FIRST INDEPENDENT COMMUNITY HOSPITALS IN CENTRAL Florida—West Orange Memorial—opened to serve the needs of a small rural community. Over the years, the promise of new growth turned many such communities into budding new sources for development, and the need for a central health care institution grew with the population. ✳ In 1993, West Orange Memorial met the challenge. Hospital officials relocated the West

THE HEALTH CENTRAL MISSION IS TO IMPROVE THE HEALTH OF ITS COMMUNITY BY PROVIDING LEADERSHIP TO INTEGRATE QUALITY HEALTH CARE SERVICES FOR EVERYONE (TOP).

HEALTH CENTRAL OFFERS A FULL RANGE OF CARE, FROM OBSTETRICS TO CARE FOR THE ELDERLY (BOTTOM).

Orange Memorial team to a new facility with a new name—Health Central. Uniquely independent from a hospital chain, Health Central prides itself on being an integrated health care facility. The 141-bed, acute care hospital is connected to physicians' offices, health services, and related retail shops. The medical mall includes a rehabilitation center, a prosthetics and brace company, a home health care company, and a complete vision center.

IMAGEWORKS PHOTOGRAPHY

SETTING THE PACE

One of the most unique aspects of Health Central is its award-winning design. Located on 64 acres of meticulously landscaped grounds, the building is the product of extensive research and planning, integrating the best elements of dozens of health care settings into one facility.

Inside the hospital, every detail is designed with patients and visitors in mind. The five-story, glass-enclosed atrium—which has towering, 20-foot palm trees; a dancing fountain; and a grand piano that continuously plays soothing music—provides a comforting atmosphere, as opposed to the institutional look of most hospitals. Recessed lighting is utilized throughout the public areas of the building, eliminating the glare produced by fluorescent lights, and the colorful, oversized hospital rooms are equipped with sofas and daybeds for overnight visitors.

Designed as a one-stop shop for all medical needs, Health Central's physician offices are integrated with the inpatient and outpatient units of the hospital, with doctors' offices located on one side of the hallway and hospital departments on the other. This arrangement benefits both physicians and patients, and is one of the many unique aspects that set Health Central apart from its competitors.

HEALTH CARE IN ACTION

The Health Central mission is to improve the health of its community by providing leadership to integrate quality health care

services for everyone. This plan has been put into action with a blend of health care services to meet many different needs. For example, Health Central's School Nurse Program has placed registered nurses in public schools within Health Central's district. For the first time in more than 10 years, nurses are in the schools every day for six hours to provide immediate, chronic, and preventive care, as well as education. Health Central is the only facility in the area with such a program.

Other community services offered by Health Central include educational classes; Senior Central, the facility's program for those 55 years and older; a mall-walking program; free health screenings and immunizations; support groups; and health fairs.

Health Central offers a full range of care, from obstetrics to care for the elderly. Some of the many services include birthing rooms; case management; cosmetic surgical procedures; emergency room services; general surgical services; intensive and progressive care units; state-of-the-art MRI, spiral CT scanner, mammography, and digital radiology; respiratory therapy; sleep center; smoking cessation; and the Health Central Women's Center.

As the Orlando-Central Florida area approaches a new era of development, Health Central is proud to be involved in the continued growth of the community. With plans for expansion under way, the forward-looking health care provider will continue to serve the population of west Orange County for many decades to come.

fOR MORE THAN 100 YEARS, THE NAME DELOITTE & TOUCHE LLP HAS BEEN synonymous with leadership in providing services that guide businesses to success. As a community leader in Orlando, Deloitte & Touche understands the pulse of Central Florida. This insight, combined with the resources of one of the largest and most highly regarded professional services organizations in the world, enables the company to consistently

exceed its clients' expectations. The key to the firm's success is its ability to focus effectively on understanding clients' needs. Deloitte & Touche is a firm of business advisers whose ultimate goal is helping local businesses become more efficient, more effective, more competitive, and more profitable than ever before. The firm works to meet these goals with the assistance of 20,000 employees in more than 100 offices across the United States.

"BRINGING YOU THE WORLD"

As a leading provider of accounting services to one of Florida's fastest-growing business markets, the Orlando team of professionals serves clients in many different industries, ranging from manufacturing to hospitality. In addition to accounting and auditing, tax, and management consulting services, the firm offers a wide range of customized services. These include information systems consulting, business systems consulting, corporate finance consulting, cosourcing, litigation support, reorganization advisory services, and valuation consulting and appraisal services.

As the business world awakens each day, Orlando's team of professionals share the latest information through the firm's high-tech office systems. "We have harnessed today's PC and network technology to enable the profession's best and brightest practitioners to deliver the most efficient and cost-effective professional services," says Partner Mike Harding. The strength and size of the firm's professional network are complemented by the power and growth of its worldwide

organization, Deloitte Touche Tohmatsu International. With more than 63,000 people in 125 countries, Deloitte Touche Tohmatsu International meets the global needs of clients operating worlds apart.

"We are a world leader in mergers and acquisitions, joint ventures, and capital-market services," says Partner-in-Charge Mike Zychinski. "As a global firm, we assemble service teams that match our clients' cultures, business environments, structures, and geographies. Our portfolio includes one-fifth of the world's largest corporations, testimony to the high quality of our services throughout the world."

BUILDING A BETTER COMMUNITY

The Orlando team of professionals finds solutions to complex business problems for area businesses ranging from midsize companies to the largest and most prominent business leaders. But the firm has another focus as well.

"Our Orlando practice is defined by a culture of excellence in client and community service," says Zychinski. "We are privileged

to work with a dynamic group of growth-oriented, entrepreneurial clients, which is reflective of the Central Florida marketplace. We also believe in investing in our community through our efforts with local civic and not-for-profit groups."

Harding agrees: "Our Orlando team works hard to develop a healthy economic and civic environment, and to contribute energy and resources to charities that are building a better future for Central Floridians. We know that quality of life is at the heart of a successful community."

AT DELOITTE & TOUCHE, UNDERSTANDING THE BUSINESSES OF ITS CLIENTS IS THE FOUNDATION OF THE FIRM'S APPROACH. BEFORE STARTING A PROJECT, DELOITTE & TOUCHE'S ENGAGEMENT TEAM IS GIVEN A TOUR OF THE CLIENT'S OPERATIONS (TOP).

MIXING A LITTLE BUSINESS WITH PLEASURE, THE DELOITTE & TOUCHE TEAM ENJOYS A ROUND OF GOLF WITH ONE OF THE FIRM'S CLIENTS (BOTTOM).

I N TODAY'S FAST-PACED SOCIETY, THE MEASURES OF SUCCESS AND EXCELLENCE are integrity, community service, and longevity. For more than four decades, Orlando College has met the measures of excellence in education in the Greater Orlando metropolitan area. Established in Orlando in 1953 as Jones College, today's Orlando College has changed with the times. Mrs. Jones School for Secretaries was the founding institution in Jacksonville and dates back to 1918 as the parent school. In 1947, the college was chartered by the State of Florida as a non-profit, degree-granting institution, and in 1982, changed its name from Jones College to Orlando College.

Orlando College was accredited in 1975 as a senior college by the Accrediting Council of Independent Colleges and Schools (ACICS), and offers master, bachelor, and associate degrees. ACICS is a national organization that accredits more than 600 schools nationwide, making it one of the largest accrediting bodies in the country. The organization has established high standards of academic and administrative requirements for participating schools. These criteria assure the student that the curriculum is valid and worthwhile.

Today, Orlando College is a member of Florida Metropolitan University (FMU), a subsidiary of Corinthian Colleges Incorporated with headquarters in Santa Ana, California, and offers a collection of educational programs that are in tune with their respective industries. FMU has eight schools in its statewide structure. With colleges in Tampa, Clearwater, Brandon, Lakeland, Melbourne, and Orlando, FMU offers an institution that meets the flexible needs of today's students. In addition, students can select from day, evening, and Saturday classes to meet their individual needs. Each program within the university maintains a level of academic excellence that successful graduates and industry professionals will confirm as being clear, concise, and up to date.

Two modern campuses are available for students in the Orlando area. North Campus is located at 5421 Diplomat Circle, near Lee Road, and is I-4 accessible, making it convenient to students in the downtown Orlando area, as well as those in the northern suburbs. South Campus is located at 2411 Sand Lake Road, making access convenient to students from the south side of Orlando.

CLOCKWISE FROM TOP:
NORTH CAMPUS IS LOCATED AT 5421 DIPLOMAT CIRCLE, NEAR LEE ROAD, AND IS I-4 ACCESSIBLE, MAKING IT CONVENIENT TO STUDENTS IN THE DOWNTOWN ORLANDO AREA, AS WELL AS THOSE IN THE NORTHERN SUBURBS.

ORLANDO COLLEGE WAS ACCREDITED IN 1975 AS A SENIOR COLLEGE BY THE ACCREDITING COUNCIL OF INDEPENDENT COLLEGES AND SCHOOLS (ACICS), AND OFFERS MASTER, BACHELOR, AND ASSOCIATE DEGREES.

EDUCATION WILL ALWAYS BE A TIME OF SEARCHING AND DISCOVERY FOR ANY STUDENT. AT ORLANDO COLLEGE, IT IS ALSO A TIME OF EXCITEMENT AND REWARD.

With more than 16 academic programs available—two master degrees, four bachelor degrees, and 10 associate degrees—the Orlando College student can select a career path in court reporting, paralegal, business administration, commercial art, computer science, management/marketing, film and video, or medical assisting. Course work in all of the programs is designed to provide the knowledge and skills graduates need in order to become more competitive in the workforce.

As students approach graduation, the Career Planning and Placement Office helps with résumé preparation, interview coaching, and appointment setting and follow-up, making the first job search a less daunting task.

The Orlando College student can count on instruction from a professional and enthusiastic faculty that makes the learning experience exciting and rewarding. With an average class size of about 15, the student will not be lost in a sea of nameless faces. Instead, the students find themselves in an environment of hands-on teaching, modern equipment, new technology, and the latest information. Many programs provide for externships at related businesses, where the student can apply the skills he or she has attained. Independent Study and Directed Study programs provide the student with alternatives

to the traditional classroom lecture environment. Credit for the adult student's life experiences can help to accelerate completion of his or her program of study.

Education is always a time of searching and discovery for any student. At Orlando College, it is

also a time of excitement and reward. With a proud history of successful graduates and dedication to future graduates, Orlando College is pledged to the same commitment to quality in teaching and excellence in education that has been its trademark since 1953.

CLOCKWISE FROM TOP: ORLANDO COLLEGE STUDENTS CAN CHOOSE FROM A VARIETY OF PROGRAMS, INCLUDING COMPUTER SCIENCE.

SOUTH CAMPUS IS LOCATED AT 2411 SAND LAKE ROAD, MAKING ACCESS CONVENIENT TO STUDENTS FROM THE SOUTH SIDE OF ORLANDO.

ORLANDO COLLEGE'S SOUTH CAMPUS OFFERS A MEDICAL ASSISTANT TRAINING PROGRAM.

FRY HAMMOND BARR INC.

FOUNDED IN 1957 BY THREE ENTERPRISING ADMEN DRIVEN BY THE principles of reputation, capability, chemistry, and hard work, Fry Hammond Barr Inc. is one of Orlando's most influential advertising agencies. One of the longest-established advertising agencies under original management in Florida, Fry Hammond Barr takes pride in the long-term business relationships it has forged over the years. As agency President

and Chief Executive Officer Peter C. Barr says, "Our business is all about people and it's our people who make us unique."

Fry Hammond Barr was established when the Orlando-based Charles Fry Agency merged with the Robert Hammond Advertising Company. Barr, then a recent graduate of the University of Florida, joined the team during the corporate union. As the company flourished, so did its staff and client base. Today, the full-service marketing communications firm boasts 40 award-winning employees who create and produce advertising and other communications material for American, Canadian, and overseas markets.

KEYS TO SUCCESS
From its original offices along Lake Eola Park, Fry Hammond Barr has witnessed the great changes Orlando has undergone in the past 40 years. Even so, Barr is the first to note that success comes not from looking

to the past, but from anticipating the future: "Like a race, if you look back you won't keep the pace. Our past, in terms of our reputation in the business, makes us competitive, but we have always remained focused on tomorrow. That is what has made us successful."

The firm's corporate philosophy, Integrated Marketing Communications, has also contributed to its success. Fry Hammond Barr stresses the importance of combining the strengths of each department to reach a client's goals and objectives.

"Advertising and public relations should follow the same path," Barr explains. "All forces should be heading in the same direction to promote, advertise, and sell. We use research to prepare for a project. We use our departments to look at a business plan and to prepare a communications program. There is a lot more to our business than creativity. Without the background and support of all possible resources,

the end result will be a campaign that may earn the firm an award, but won't sell the client's product or service. Unless we look at the whole picture, our client's needs will not be met."

In 1984, this detail-driven approach earned Fry Hammond Barr the prestigious Florida Department of Citrus fresh fruit account, a victory over more than 100 agencies competing from around the nation. More than 10 years later, the Department of Citrus still relies on the branding capabilities of Fry Hammond Barr. Other longtime clients include Dixon Ticonderoga, The Pencil People, Panama Jack sun care products, the *Orlando Sentinel*, and Stein Mart Inc., a national department store chain, among others.

COMMUNITY LEADER
The staff at Fry Hammond Barr insists that leadership is not limited to the workplace and should extend to the Orlando community. Many employees serve on local committees or work with student interns. Barr has served on dozens of community boards and is the past president of the Greater Orlando Chamber of Commerce and past chairman of the Downtown Development Board. He established student scholarships at the University of Central Florida and the University of Florida, and is a member of several area economic development, education, and industry organizations.

With a reputation for quality performance and community giving, Fry Hammond Barr intends to witness Orlando's next 40 years, serving the area with experience and dedication.

CLOCKWISE FROM TOP:
PETER C. BARR, PRESIDENT AND CHIEF EXECUTIVE OFFICER OF FRY HAMMOND BARR INC.

THE STAFF AT FRY HAMMOND BARR INCLUDES (FROM LEFT) ASSOCIATE CREATIVE DIRECTOR JOHN CASON, ACCOUNT SUPERVISOR NANCY ALLEN, ASSOCIATE CREATIVE DIRECTOR TOM KANE, AND EXECUTIVE PLANNING DIRECTOR GUY STEPHENS.

FRY HAMMOND BARR'S LEADERSHIP INCLUDES (SEATED FROM LEFT) VICE PRESIDENT/CONTROLLER, CFO, AND COO MARY ALICE KOLESAR; EXECUTIVE VICE PRESIDENT PETER C. BARR JR.; (STANDING FROM LEFT) EXECUTIVE CREATIVE DIRECTOR TIM FISHER; EXECUTIVE MEDIA DIRECTOR MARJORIE DOBBIN; AND EXECUTIVE ACCOUNTS DIRECTOR JEFF STERNBERG.

IBM Corporation

IBM OPENED ITS ORLANDO OFFICE IN 1957 TO SERVE THE CENTRAL Florida marketplace. Since then, IBM has provided business, industry, government, and educational institutions with information system solutions comprised of computer hardware, software, and all types of related services. Yet IBM's most valuable contribution has been its more than 150 Orlando customer advocates. ✳ "Our employees are the customer advocates," says Bud Echols, business unit executive for the Orlando field office. "Our employees are out there to listen and understand the requirements of our customers, and then provide the help they need in utilizing information technology to more effectively manage their organizations."

CUSTOMER SERVICE IS GOAL NUMBER ONE

"We want to be more responsive to our customers' needs than ever before," adds Echols. To achieve that goal, the IBM Corporation worldwide has developed an ongoing system for restructuring its marketing and service organizations. The focus is on lowering costs, improving quality, and shortening response time to customers. Employees involved in solutions, hardware, software, services, education, financing, and maintenance functions are now highly specialized and work together in flexible teams established by the corporation's newly created Worldwide Marketing Processes.

Customers at every level are benefiting from IBM's ongoing changes and improvements. The need by IBM customers for a broader range of information technology expertise is the motivation behind IBM's drive to reposition itself as a value-added, technology-based services organization and the premier provider of products and services in the information technology industry.

IBM helped pioneer the information processing industry, offering state-of-the-art products as the industry has evolved. From the electromechanical punch card machines and vacuum tube calculators of the 1940s to today's powerful computers, IBM technology has continued to lower the cost of computing, provide more functions, and extend the range of information handling systems.

COMMUNITY COMMITMENT

IBM is focused on enhancing the communities in which its teams live and work. Over the last 10 years, IBM has been the largest contributor of money, equipment, people, and technological resources in the United States—more than $12 million to nonprofit organizations and educational institutions across the United States and around the world in more than 153 countries.

In Orlando, IBM is committed to education, health and human services, arts, environment, and sports. In Orlando-area education, IBM supports Junior Achievement with volunteers in the classroom, Foundation for Orange County Public Schools, and World Class Schools. The corporation also supports such health and human service organizations as the five branches of United Way in Central Florida and Meals on Wheels.

In the area of the arts, IBM is an advocate of the United Arts Council, with involvement in the University of Central Florida's Shakespeare Festival, as well as the Orlando Science Center. The firm also has volunteers who have teamed with Seniors First to help clean area streets as part of the Adopt-a-Highway Program.

In sports, IBM was a corporate sponsor and provided many employee volunteers for Orlando Olympic Soccer.

"We are here to serve more than businesses," Echols says. "We are here to serve the community—mind and soul."

IBM CORPORATION HAS REPOSITIONED ITSELF AS THE PREMIER PROVIDER OF INFORMATION SYSTEMS SOLUTIONS.

▶ TERRY D. CUFFEL

1958 - 1977

1960   Wayne Densch, Inc.

1960   Orlando Science Center

1961   Humana

1962   Boyle Engineering Corporation

1963   Orlando-Orange County Expressway Authority

1966   Barnett Bank, N.A., Central Florida

1968   Darden Restaurants Inc.

1968   Gencor Industries Inc.

1968   Sonny's Real Pit Bar-B-Q

1970   BDO Seidman, LLP

1970   Central Florida Investments, Inc.

1970   Epoch Properties, Inc.

1970   Arnold Palmer's Bay Hill Club & Lodge

1970   Superior Printers, Inc.

1971   Walt Disney World

1971   Time Warner Communications

1972   Hyatt Hotels in Orlando

1972   LYNX/Central Florida Regional Transportation Authority

1972   Orlando Orthopedic Center

1973   Sea World of Florida

1974   Church Street Station

1974   HBO & Company

1974   Post, Buckley, Schuh & Jernigan, Inc.

1975   Albertsons Inc.

1975   Greater Orlando Aviation Authority

1976   Pizzuti

1977   WLOQ

WAYNE DENSCH, INC.

fOR NEARLY FOUR DECADES, WAYNE DENSCH, INC. HAS BEEN AN integral part of Central Florida. After seven years as a successful Budweiser beer distributor in Waukegan, Illinois, Wayne Densch was awarded the Anheuser-Busch distributorship for Central Florida in 1960. One year after opening delivery routes for the four-county Central Florida market, consisting of Orange, Lake, Seminole, and Osceola counties, sales increased 98

percent from 261,540 to 517,053 cases.

Densch's booming business soon outgrew its facility on West Kaley Street, as well as its second location on 27th Street, and finally settled on three acres along West Holden Avenue, a site still within reach of downtown Orlando. Since then, the site has expanded four times, and new land parcels have been purchased to accommodate the company's rapid growth. In February 1994, a branch facility

was constructed in Seminole County on 1st Street in Sanford.

Until his death in May 1994, Densch continued to lead the company into nonstop growth. A caring man with an exceptional personal character, he also set into motion charitable programs and community service projects supporting education and the arts.

RISK TAKER, SUCCESS MAKER

Known for his innovative, dynamic, entrepreneurial, and aggressive spirit, Densch shared the visions of Eberhard Anheuser and Adolphus Busch of a national beer market and of transforming a budding company into an industry powerhouse.

Prior to 1960, the state of Florida had only three Anheuser-Busch distributors. Budweiser's competitors, such as Schlitz and Canadian Ale, were successful in the Orlando market; but in 1961, Wayne Densch, Inc.'s market share rose to 25 percent. The company grew from six original employees

to nine employees, and sales grew to more than 1.4 million cases by 1965.

Tremendous growth in case volume sales continued over the next several years, with more than 3.5 million cases in 1975, more than 5.6 million in 1985, and more than 10 million cases sold in 1996.

A significant contribution to the success of the company was Densch's commitment to customer service. "Wayne always maintained the highest level of service standards. Wayne created a family environment through his true devotion to his employees, customers, and to his product," says Leonard E. Williams, president and chief executive officer. "You have to be a committed team to be successful, and Wayne saw to it that his team—his family—had opportunities to break new ground."

Under Densch's guidance, the company became quite a force in the beer distribution industry. "The company earned a good relationship with its customers. Clients grew to respect this reliable firm that offered a quality, fresh product every time and on time," says John Tipple, executive assistant.

Tom McCarty, vice president of operations, agrees: "Wayne set the stage for how we operate today, with a dedication to service, a superior product, and a respect for our customers. It is truly the key to our success."

As Budweiser and the Anheuser-Busch family of products grew to become the nation's best-selling beers, Wayne Densch, Inc. settled into its role as the king of the market, adding Heineken USA products to its expansive list of brands and packages. The com-

pany's staff has grown to approximately 300 employees, and its client list has expanded to include such newcomers to Orlando as Martin Marietta, Walt Disney World, Sea World of Orlando, and Universal Studios.

A Part of Life in Orlando

Wayne Densch was proud to be a part of the fabric of life in Orlando and donated millions of dollars to the community. In 1986, Densch contributed $1 million to the athletic program at the University of Central Florida (UCF) for scholarships. In gratitude, the university named its athletic building the Wayne Densch Sports Center, as well as retiring the UCF Knights' number 1 football jersey in Densch's honor.

In 1992, the Wayne Densch Charities were created, and the organization continues to provide assistance "to the poor, elderly, homeless, and distressed in Central Florida." In 1993, the company was presented the Anheuser-Busch Dimensions of Excellence Bronze Award in recognition of community involvement and sales excellence.

The company's civic contributions include its participation in various customer training programs focused on alcohol awareness and its involvement in Anheuser-Busch's Know When to Say When national awareness program.

Wayne Densch, Inc. is proud of its corporate citizenship. As a company with annual gross sales of more than $130 million, it contributes more than $15 million each year in state taxes.

Embracing the Future

While business methods, the marketplace, and client expectations have changed since 1960, Wayne Densch, Inc. remains a corporate and civic leader. In 1995, one year after the death of Wayne Densch, the company underwent a reorganization, initiating new delivery methods and embracing new technology to serve customers better.

The firm's new electronic invoicing system, route books, radio frequency product scanning, and electronic data and fund transfer systems offer better, faster, and more accurate information to customers. Today, the firm's 300 employees use the new technology to serve more than 3,500 customers in a market share that has grown to nearly 60 percent. From new technology to community citizenship, Wayne Densch, Inc. continues to emphasize the bedrock of its rise to the top: quality equals success.

ORLANDO SCIENCE CENTER

THE CENTRAL FLORIDA MUSEUM AND PLANETARIUM OPENED IN 1960 with the belief that science should be experienced rather than observed. The Science Center, adjacent to the historical museum in Orlando's Loch Haven Park, became the catalyst for new adventures in hands-on science experiences for children and their parents. In order to keep up with changing technologies, and to improve science and math education opportunities for Central Florida school-children, the Planetarium expanded its focus and in 1984 became the Orlando Science Center.

The Orlando Science Center outgrew its 26-year-old facility, and moved into its new, state-of-the-art home—the largest science showcase in the Southeast—in 1997. The new facility was built at a cost of more than $45 million, and features everything from an indoor cypress swamp to a voyage through the human body.

TOUCHING THE IMAGINATION

The Orlando Science Center touches the imaginations of the young and the young at heart. In KidsTown, children can learn how a city functions in a town built to kid-size scale. Children can explore the growth of a tree from the inside out as they climb around, into, and under the Science Story Tree.

In Science City, guests can lift a car using a series of levers and ropes, while others enjoy exhibits and activities related to mathematics, physics, mechanics, structures, electricity, and magnetism. In Cosmic Tourist, children of all ages can study different aspects of space exploration through hands-on displays.

BEYOND THE IMAGINATION

The Orlando Science Center takes people of all ages beyond their imaginations in the Science Center's 310-seat Dr. Phillips CineDome, which offers filmgoers a chance to view large-format films on an 8,000-square-foot screen.

Central Florida's high-tech companies hold center stage in Light Power, Imaginary Landscapes, and ShowBiz Science. Visitors can learn how filmmakers alter perceptions, how simulations allow scientists and engineers to test ideas, and how light and lasers behave. BodyZone sets the stage for discovering how the human body works. In the Science Center's Darden Adventure Theater, people experience science-related performances courtesy of an in-house performance troupe called the Einstein Players. The Science Center is also developing educational programs that can be sent via satellite to more than 30,000 classrooms nationwide.

Four Discovery Labs equipped with state-of-the-art equipment provide an arena for training teachers in science at the Teacher Leadership Center. The Center provides educators with hands-on experiences in teaching biology, physics, chemistry, computers, mathematics, and other topics. Programs are also available for preteachers, and the nearby Early Childhood Lab assists preschool students and their teachers.

The crowning touch to the Orlando Science Center is its 800-square-foot Crosby Observatory. The silver dome houses Florida's largest publicly accessible refractor telescope, through which visitors can observe wonders of the night sky during weekend observatory viewings.

The Center continues to remain abreast of changing technologies and scientific discoveries, and admirably fulfills its role of furthering scientific education. There is truly something for everyone at the Orlando Science Center.

ORLANDO SCIENCE CENTER

THE CROSBY OBSERVATORY ATOP THE ORLANDO SCIENCE CENTER HOUSES FLORIDA'S LARGEST PUBLICLY ACCESSIBLE REFRACTOR TELESCOPE, THROUGH WHICH VISITORS CAN OBSERVE WONDERS OF THE NIGHT SKY DURING WEEKEND VIEWINGS (TOP).

THE ORLANDO SCIENCE CENTER HAS BECOME THE CATALYST FOR NEW ADVENTURES IN HANDS-ON SCIENCE EXPERIENCES FOR PEOPLE OF ALL AGES (BOTTOM).

ORLANDO SCIENCE CENTER

I N TODAY'S HIGH-TECH WORLD, THE ORLANDO-ORANGE COUNTY EXPRESSWAY Authority is taking on a new role. Its motto, We Build More Than Just Highways, is a testimony to the agency's new mission: to meet the transportation needs of Orange County while working to improve the community's quality of life. From a business development program designed to encourage equal employment opportunities for minority and women's business enterprises to

enlisting the support of community partners to implement future transportation solutions for Central Florida, the Orlando-Orange County Expressway Authority is embarking upon a new course toward community problem solving.

INTELLIGENT TRANSPORTATION

Moving area citizens toward "intelligent" transportation, the Orlando-Orange County Expressway Authority's leading program is a cashless toll collection system called E-PASS. Introduced in 1994, the system consists of an electronic device installed under the front bumper of cars that automatically deducts toll transactions from a prepaid account. As the number of E-PASS customers increased, the Authority opened dedicated E-PASS Only lanes at area toll plazas, allowing E-PASS users to bypass traffic lines and pass through toll plazas more quickly. Today, E-PASS is operational at 10 mainline and 36 ramp toll plazas.

By the middle of 1997, more than 105,000 electronic devices, or transponders, were issued for about 65,000 accounts, and nearly 40 percent of peak-hour toll transactions were generated by E-PASS participants. The E-PASS Service Center quickly became a key point of contact and communication with expressway customers, giving the Authority a new opportunity to deliver improved customer service.

Other high-tech highway solutions include a similar E-PASS program in neighboring Osceola County and the development of programs featuring fiber-optic technology. The Orlando-Orange County Expressway Authority is rapidly

becoming one of the leading innovators in transportation and communication solutions.

ALL ROADS LEAD TO COMMUNITY

The Orlando-Orange County Expressway Authority was created in 1963 by the Florida legislature. In 1996, the Authority generated more than $83 million in revenue. By the year 2020, estimated annual earnings will top more than $200 million. Revenue collections are used to pay debt service on outstanding bonds, as well as to fund operations, maintenance, planning, engineering, and construction costs.

In order to further stimulate the local economy, the Orlando-Orange County Expressway Authority assists qualified minority- and women-owned businesses with several employment opportunity programs. The programs help these businesses as they seek to bid on Authority projects. In 1995, the Authority awarded $3 million in contracts to minority- and women-owned businesses in Central Florida. To that end, the agency's Business Development Office is maintaining a community outreach program that provides businesses with technical assistance, counseling, bid process

training, and networking assistance.

As Central Florida grows, so do the responsibilities of the Orlando-Orange County Expressway Authority. "Our privatized toll collection is unique, and we have quickly become an internationally recognized authority for transportation innovation," says Orlando-Orange County Expressway Authority Chairman A. Wayne Rich. "Our system is among the best in the country in bringing electronic toll services to a community on a mass scale. We are committed to providing number one service to Central Florida drivers."

THE ORLANDO-ORANGE COUNTY EXPRESSWAY AUTHORITY'S MOTTO, WE BUILD MORE THAN JUST HIGHWAYS, IS A TESTIMONY TO THE AGENCY'S NEW MISSION: TO MEET THE TRANSPORTATION NEEDS OF ORANGE COUNTY WHILE WORKING TO IMPROVE THE COMMUNITY'S QUALITY OF LIFE.

ONE OF THE LARGEST MANAGED CARE COMPANIES IN THE NATION, Humana Inc. has been a leading member of the Central Florida health care community since its inception in 1961. Today, Humana serves the health care needs of more than 56,000 residents of Central Florida and operates the largest health management organization (HMO) in the state. With its strong commitment to customer service and

affordable, quality health care, Humana provides a leading-edge commitment to the expansion of managed care in the private and public sector. A specialist in affordable health plans and services to employee groups and Medicare beneficiaries, Humana's services include preventive care, patient follow-up programs, and a network of more than 30,000 hospitals and physicians, and 23,000 pharmacies nationwide.

HUMANA IS COMMITTED TO PROVIDING UP-TO-DATE INFORMATION AND EDUCATION ON HEALTH CARE TO THE RESIDENTS OF CENTRAL FLORIDA (LEFT).

THE NEW LOOK FOR HUMANA EXEMPLIFIES THE COMPANY'S COMMITMENT TO THE "SPIRIT OF SERVICE (RIGHT)."

HEALTH CARE BY DESIGN

Humana operates a, proactive customer-first approach based on an integrated services system that enables health care providers and customers to work together to improve health options and performance. "Achieving the best quality, service, and financial outcomes requires high performing, informed consumers, physicians, and a health plan that supports them with meaningful, timely information. That's why our partnerships with physicians and customers are ideal for communicating information about outcomes, prevention, and wellness. As leaders in our industry, Humana is always looking for ways to increase benefits and services, and to provide affordable, quality health care," says Nancy Smith, executive director of Humana-Central Florida.

Humana's Central Florida service area, which includes Orange, Seminole, and Osceola counties, consists of more than 800 physicians and specialists in a network of 14 area hospitals. Humana's 200-plus associates work directly with customers to tailor

services to specific customer care programs, quality improvement, sales, case management, delivery system development, and data support.

With a hand on the pulse of the market, Humana designed an HMO to serve both Medicare patients and others through employer-sponsored programs. Additional services include a preferred provider organization (PPO), a point-of-service plan, administrative, Civilian Health and Medical Program of the Uniformed Services (CHAMPUS), and a select number of indemnity plans and Medicare-related health insurance benefits for seniors.

Humana's designs for new and expanded health care programs include involvement in the National Committee for Quality Assurance accreditation for federally qualified health plans. This organization recently gave Humana-Central Florida a three-year full accreditation. Only 20 percent of HMOs in the nation have earned full accreditation as of April 30, 1997. Future health options stem from Humana's leading-edge technology, which includes a highly sophisticated claims operation dedicated solely to the administration of managed care plans. The Claims Adjudication System (CAS) allows instant access to all data necessary to settle a claim. Through the use of electronic claims submission and automated claims adjudication, the process lowers premiums and promotes faster turnaround on claims.

VALUING SERVICE AND SOLUTIONS

In an effort to better meet patients' needs, Humana developed patient surveys for ongoing satisfaction

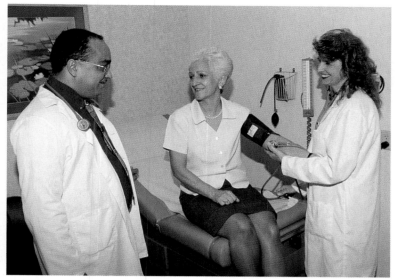

studies, which assist the company in the design and development of new or expanded services. Surveys from 92 percent of Medicare beneficiaries have consistently ranked Humana as a leader in quality health care. Surveys have also noted a high rate of patient satisfaction regarding the hospitals available and the ease of making appointments, as well as greater patient understanding of insurance coverage and the claims process.

Valuing the physicians' stake in health care quality, Humana works closely with its participating physicians in order to optimally manage complex health care needs and discover better ways to improve the delivery of health care services. Additionally, all Humana physicians are required to participate in a system of checks and balances for proven quality assurance, thus improving the overall health of Humana members.

For employers, Humana provides the Employer Report Summary, a consumer report for health care that shows employers how their benefits compare to other corporate benefits, monitors the types and number of employee inquiries, and pinpoints areas of employee concern that could also be costing the firm health care dollars.

In addition to providing quality health coverage through the managed care sector, Humana also offers personal physician care in one of four wholly owned offices located strategically throughout the Central Florida area. Specializing in quality preventive care, the offices offer board certified/eligible physicians in family practice and internal medicine. Humana's wholly owned offices—Personal Care Physicians of Orlando, Personal Care Physicians of Casselberry, Personal Care Physicians of Lake Mary, and Personal Care Physicians of Apopka—accept Medicare assignment, CHAMPUS/Tricare, workers' compensation, Humana-HMO, PPO, Gold Plus Plans, and private indemnity insurance.

TRUE TO THE MISSION

Throughout the years, the mission of Humana has remained the same: to achieve an unequaled level of measurable quality and productivity in the delivery of health care services that are responsive to the needs of patients, physicians, employers, and consumers. To reach its mission, Humana has established seven key values that provide the framework for the company to deliver on its promises: customer health and happiness, mutual respect, trust and integrity, teamwork, continuous improvement, a sense of urgency, and commitment. These values have become more than daily practice at Humana; they are posted in every

office area as a tribute to Humana's drive toward service excellence and quality solutions.

As Humana continues to study new methods to deliver the highest quality of care at affordable prices, the company's product diversity and financial management strategies continue to provide the company with stability during times of industry flux and reform, which, in turn, ensures customers of quality products and service. "We have remained true to our commitment to provide excellent quality, services, and financial outcomes," says Smith. "Our associates work as a team of experts, ready to meet today's challenges while blazing a trail for the future of Central Florida's health care system."

CLOCKWISE FROM TOP LEFT: HUMANA'S SERVICE EXTENDS BEYOND PROVIDING QUALITY HEALTH COVERAGE BY ALSO OFFERING PERSONAL PHYSICIAN CARE IN ONE OF FOUR WHOLLY OWNED OFFICES THROUGHOUT CENTRAL FLORIDA.

THE FOUNDATION OF HUMANA'S SUCCESS IS A SENIOR MANAGEMENT TEAM COMMITTED TO SEEING THAT CENTRAL FLORIDA IS PROVIDED WITH THE HIGHEST QUALITY HEALTH CARE.

NANCY SMITH, EXECUTIVE DIRECTOR OF HUMANA-CENTRAL FLORIDA, TAKES THE LEAD IN ORGANIZING THE BEST PROGRAMS AND SERVICES TO MEET THE NEEDS OF HUMANA MEMBERS ACROSS THE AREA.

Boyle Engineering Corporation

BACK IN 1962, J.R. "LESTER" BOYLE FOUNDED A SMALL ENGINEERING company based on two values—integrity and trust. Today, as one of the nation's top 100 engineering and design firms, Boyle Engineering Corporation remains committed to those same values. ✴ With an Orlando-based regional headquarters, the firm prides itself on providing professional engineering services to create and improve infrastructure for

public and private clients in the United States and around the world. From new techniques for water treatment to state-of-the-art weight-in-motion stations for the nation's interstate highways, Boyle applies the latest in engineering systems to solve some of the world's toughest design and construction problems.

BOYLE SERVED ON THE TEAM THAT DEVELOPED THE CASTLE OF MIRACLES IN KISSIMMEE, WHERE TERMINALLY ILL CHILDREN AND THEIR FAMILIES GATHER TO ENJOY THE CENTRAL FLORIDA AREA.

Advanced Technologies

To meet client needs, Boyle assembles teams of specialists from around the world with expertise in diverse engineering fields, including water resources, treatment, and distribution; wastewater collection, treatment, and reuse; streets, highways, and bridges; light and heavy rail; and drainage and flood control. Boyle's team also includes computer and CAD experts; instrumentation and control specialists; architects and landscape architects; electrical, mechanical, and structural engineers; planners; surveyors; and many other professionals.

These teams of specialists apply their skills to the most compli-

BOYLE DESIGNED AND CONSTRUCTED 15 DIFFERENT AT&T CALLING CENTERS THROUGHOUT THE ATLANTA AREA THAT WERE USED BY THE ATHLETES AND THEIR FAMILIES, CORPORATE SPONSORS, AND THE MORE THAN 2 MILLION VISITORS WHO ATTENDED THE 1996 SUMMER OLYMPICS.

cated projects in the industry. For example, the logistics and details involved in taking a prison from the conceptual stage to final completion are staggering, but Boyle had a successful formula for the California Department of Corrections. The firm applied its state-of-the-art computer technologies to its civil engineering services for the construction of the world's largest women's prison, and an adjacent prison with similar form and function. Boyle was instrumental in the preparation of a master site plan, improvement of off-site roads, and design of all on-site utilities and supporting infrastructure, such as water treatment, telephone and communications systems, fencing, roads, and parking areas.

Through Boyle's new supervisory control and data acquisition (SCADA) system, an automated system is giving employees at Maryland's Anne Arundel County Department of Public Works the ability to perform functions that once required service calls. The SCADA system provides telemetry and

computer technology that allow centralized monitoring and control of facilities spread out over a large geographic area. The new system allows a small group of operators and dispatchers to focus on one computer screen to see and control all of the county's water facilities and wastewater operations, while additional manpower and resources are allocated to other areas.

Boyle chemists use computational chemistry through new computer systems designed to help scientists and engineers find new ways to meet stricter water treatment requirements. The process has taken a test that once lasted months and has condensed it to a matter of microseconds.

Boyle's computer technology systems have added new degrees of efficiency and analytical capability to engineering design. The new tools continue to help public and private clients understand and manage facility operations, and give engineers the ability to map and model every level of customer service and project development.

Award-Winning Performance

For more than 50 years, Boyle has maintained a reputation for providing excellent service to its clients. Boyle's work has been honored locally and nationally by numerous organizations, including the Florida Institute of Consulting Engineers (FICE). Most recently, FICE presented Boyle with a 1997 Honorable Mention for the AT&T Calling and Business Centers at the 1996 Summer Olympics in Atlanta. Boyle designed and constructed 15 different centers throughout the Atlanta area that were used by the athletes and their families, corporate sponsors, and the more than 2 million visitors who attended the Olympic Games. In 1995, FICE awarded Boyle an honorable mention for its work with the nonprofit organization Give Kids the World, Inc. Boyle served on the team that developed the Castle of Miracles in Kissimmee, where terminally ill children and their families gather to enjoy the Central Florida area. Additionally, Boyle's involvement in the creation of the Hubbard House for the Orlando Regional Medical Center earned the firm the Golden Brick award from the Downtown Orlando Partnership.

The firm has completed numerous award-winning projects in Florida, including honorable

mentions for the Water Independence for Cape Coral project and the Eddie D. Edwards Water Treatment Plant in Fort Myers, which provided one of the first large-scale applications of membrane-softening treatment for a U.S. municipal water supply. Boyle was also part of the team for the 1996 FICE Grand Award-winning T. Mabry Carlton Jr. Water Treatment Plant in Sarasota County. This 12.0-mgd facility is the largest electrodialysis reversal water treatment plant in the world and will eventually serve 250,000 people.

The firm also won the engineering industry's most prestigious award, the Grand Conceptor, for the Water Conserv II project. The American Consulting Engineers Council recognized this project for

its innovative advanced treatment and distribution system, which utilizes reclaimed water to irrigate more than 12 square miles of citrus groves throughout Central Florida.

The firm continues its award-winning tradition with national and international recognition for design and service across the country. The Jamboree Road Extension in Irvine, California, received the 1993 Project of the Year award presented by the American Society of Civil Engineers; the Cuchillo Dam project in Truth or Consequences, New Mexico, earned the 1994 Civil Works Merit Award presented by the Chief of Engineers' Design and Environmental Awards program; and the Arnold Ground Storage Tank project in Washington, D.C., which provides critically needed storage to meet peak demand for water in suburban Washington, was recognized for "distinguished architectural treatment."

With more than 20 national and international offices, the company continues to provide professional engineering and related services coast to coast. From major U.S. airport designs, trolley systems, and environmental integration programs to ongoing charitable contributions in nearly every community in which the firm's employees live and work, Boyle is working to meet the needs of a growing world.

THIS AWARD-WINNING PROJECT, KNOWN AS WATER CONSERV II, IS BELIEVED TO BE THE WORLD'S LARGEST OF ITS KIND. WATER CONSERV II USES ADVANCED TREATMENT TECHNOLOGY TO CONVERT MUNICIPAL SEWAGE INTO SAFE, CLEAN WATER TO IRRIGATE CITRUS GROVES IN CENTRAL FLORIDA.

A RECOGNIZED LEADER IN ADVANCED WATER TREATMENT TECHNOLOGY, BOYLE DESIGNED A 2.0-MGD EXPANSION TO THE MARCO ISLAND REVERSE OSMOSIS WATER TREATMENT PLANT.

I N 1877, 52-YEAR-OLD WILLIAM BOYD BARNETT ARRIVED IN JACKsonville, Florida, with his wife and son. A banker by trade in his home state of Kansas, Barnett soon opened the First National Bank of Jacksonville. In the years that followed, this family-owned company would change the course of Florida banking. ✳ Today, Barnett Bank, N.A., Central Florida—which was established in Orlando in 1966—has 61 branch offices in Orange, Seminole, Osceola, and Brevard counties. With $40 billion in assets, Barnett Banks, Inc. is the leading financial institution in Florida, and ranked among the top 25 banks in the United States.

A NEW ERA BEGINS

From the beginning, Barnett was committed to creating a new era in banking. His key to success was said to have been his personal golden rule: "It always pays in the long run to treat a customer as you would be treated. Always be fair and square in your dealings."

Following Barnett's death in 1903, son Bion Hall Barnett carried on that tradition, even during the Great Depression. While other banks fell, the Barnetts held on. In a unique move to shore up Florida banking, the Barnetts formed Barnett National Securities Corporation, which acquired failed banks and reopened them to meet customer needs.

The Barnetts' banking business continued to grow. During the years of World War II, the bank met the needs of a bustling military town. After the war, the bank expanded its services to fill the growing consumer demand, and by the 1950s, it began selling limited stock to the public. The 1960s transformed Barnett National Securities Corporation into a parent company, enabling it to acquire other banks throughout the state. By 1969, it was clear that a new strategy was working to change the company into a single, statewide identity.

A VISION FULFILLED

Barnett's modern vision is to "improve the lives of our customers and the well-being of our communities." Community involvement, quality of work life, and diversity through innovation and training remain at the forefront of all Barnett banking systems.

Through the convenience of multiple banking locations, Barnett works to improve banking for customers. This has become a key factor in the company's research and development of new banking programs, featuring newcomers' guides with banking and relocation information; supermarket banking services and airport locations; and a sophisticated, award-winning Web site, all designed to increase Barnett accessibility. Increasing the bank's access to customers also means expanding services, as well as providing new technologies and innovative training programs for local banking teams.

Through its involvement in programs such as Habitat for Humanity, Junior Achievement, and United Way, Barnett works to improve the well-being of the communities it serves. In 1995, Barnett and Publix became founding sponsors of the Take Stock in Children Foundation, a public, nonprofit organization designed to assist Florida's at-risk children by improving education and helping to reduce youth crime.

The firm has also received national and local recognition for its support of its employees. Named one of the top 10 companies for working families by *Central Florida Family* magazine, Barnett's Quality of Work/Life Program dates back to its early roots with its mission to "champion a work environment that fosters self-worth, values diversity, and empowers individuals."

TODAY, BARNETT BANK, N.A., CENTRAL FLORIDA—WHICH WAS ESTABLISHED IN ORLANDO IN 1966—HAS 61 BRANCH OFFICES IN ORANGE, SEMINOLE, OSCEOLA, AND BREVARD COUNTIES.

Gencor Industries Inc.

THE 1960S USHERED IN AN ECONOMIC BOOM THAT NEARLY SPANNED the entire decade. Early in that decade, businessman E.J. Elliott seized the economic moment in Alliance, Ohio. Bringing together the talents of local workers, he incorporated a company that manufactured key products for the construction industry. Today, Gencor Industries Inc. is a worldwide capital machinery manufacturer with facilities in seven states and eight countries. Employing cutting-edge technology, the company enjoys leading market share in such diverse areas as the highway construction industry, machinery for the production of sugar, and equipment for processing such oil seeds as corn, peanuts, sunflower, and soybeans. Gencor also produces pelleting machinery for processing grains into scientifically compound animal feeds, as well as machinery for producing food starches and mining precious metals. In addition, Gencor manufactures machinery for remediation of contaminated soils, industrial combustion systems, and electronic process controls.

Gencor Industries Inc. has been a low-profile corporate citizen of Orlando since 1968. After transforming a World War II bomb factory into a state-of-the-art industrial complex, E.J. Elliott, president and chairman of the board, created programs that trained thousands of area workers in welding, fabricating, and assembly of heavy machinery. Through retraining funded by Gencor, jobs were created for a large number of Central Florida residents. Today, Gencor Industries Inc. is the largest heavy equipment manufacturer in Central Florida.

A Leader in Its Fields

As one of Central Florida's top employers and a global industry leader, Gencor is continually advancing construction and process machinery technology, and "staying two generations ahead of all competition," according to Marc Elliott, vice president of marketing. "Gencor was built on a reputation of identifying mature leading companies that complement existing product lines with comparable synergies to bring together under the Gencor name," says Elliott.

In the 1980s, the company made numerous successful acquisitions of national and international corporations. In 1985, the company acquired Beverley Group of Billingshurst, England, a leading European manufacturer of industrial thermal fluid heat systems and industrial waste incinerators. Acquisitions from 1986 through 1996 ranged from Midwest manufacturers of heat-transfer systems and asphalt-mixing plants to the world's leading manufacturer of industrial process machinery.

"Gencor has broadened into all types of process machinery manufacturing and design with manufacturing facilities and offices in more than nine countries around the globe," E.J. Elliott says. "Our key mission is to be the technological and market leader in industries and markets driven by the essential needs of growing world populations."

Gencor has become synonymous with integrity, quality, and technological innovation. Virtually every innovation in energy release, heat transfer and recovery, alternative fuels, asphalt production, and the environmental sciences during the last 15 years has been spawned by one of Gencor's enterprises.

A Good Neighbor

Gencor believes that to be a good neighbor, a company should conduct itself with class and dignity, keep its facilities and headquarters in order, and help its neighbors to the best of its ability, all while keeping a modest profile. As a result, hundreds of families in the Orlando area and thousands around the world benefit from Gencor's generosity. Gencor's corporate contributions—as well as those of its management and employees—to the local economy, social activities, and nonprofit causes are significant. E.J. Elliott notes, "Huge machinery built at Gencor factories in Orlando with the hands of Orlando residents finds its way to the far corners of the world. But in Orlando, you hardly notice us. We think that's a good way to be."

CLOCKWISE FROM BOTTOM LEFT: GENCOR WORLD HEADQUARTERS

SUGAR BATCH CENTRIFUGE

ASPHALT MIXING PLANT

W HEN BILL DARDEN AND HIS TEAM OPENED A SEAFOOD RESTAURANT in Lakeland more than 29 years ago, few could have predicted the enormous impact it would have on the nation's dining habits. His restaurant, Red Lobster, was an immediate success, and it marked one of the early entries into the "casual dining" industry that has been growing ever since. Darden also saw a lot of growth poten-tial in Orlando, where he located the headquarters for his fledgling company.

Red Lobster succeeded for reasons that went far beyond seafood. Darden developed a system that fed the public's hunger for no-frills dining in a moderately priced, full-service restaurant. Inspired by the popularity of quality seafood items at two of his earlier restaurants—Jacksonville's Thunderbird Inn and Orlando landmark Gary's Duck Inn—Darden handpicked his concept team in 1968 and charged them with designing a new seafaring dining experience. The question was: Could such a concept succeed in a mass market? The answer can be found in today's sales and market reports, which rank Orlando-based Darden Restaurants Inc. as the nation's second-largest restaurant company.

RECORD GROWTH

Darden Restaurants Inc. is known today as the "new restaurant company with a 29-year history." What began as Bill Darden's innovative approach to developing a niche between fine dining and quick-service restaurants soon became a new venture for national food giant General Mills Inc. In 1970, just two years after opening the first Red Lobster, Darden sold his concept and his chain of three restaurants (and two more under construction) to Minneapolis-based General Mills. With General Mills' financial support, Red Lobster would no longer remain a secret of the South.

The 1970s brought growth and change to General Mills. In 1971, an in-house department was established for worldwide seafood purchasing, and just three years later, General Mills opened its 100th Red Lobster restaurant in Omaha. By the late 1970s, as the slogan proclaimed, Red Lobster had become "Where America goes for seafood."

In 1981—when the 300th Red Lobster opened in Dallas and chainwide sales exceeded $500 million—the company was ready to use lessons learned at Red Lobster to research another casual dining concept. Using the general recipe for Red Lobster's success, an internal team developed a concept for an Italian restaurant. Through focus groups and surveys, the company made the new restaurant chain customer-driven, taking into consideration customer recommendations for restaurant designs, menu items, and decor. The result, The Olive Garden, debuted in Orlando in 1982. Today it is the largest Italian restaurant chain in the nation.

ON THEIR OWN

In a tax-free spin-off to shareholders, General Mills Restaurants

THE OLIVE GARDEN DEBUTED IN ORLANDO IN 1982, AND IS NOW THE NATION'S LARGEST ITALIAN RESTAURANT CHAIN (LEFT).

RED LOBSTER HAS GROWN TO BECOME THE NATION'S LARGEST FULL-SERVICE RESTAURANT CHAIN (RIGHT).

separated from its parent company, General Mills Inc., in 1995. The new restaurant company returned to its roots, forming Darden Restaurants Inc. In the process, Darden became the largest publicly traded casual dining restaurant operator in the nation, and became Florida's newest corporate headquarters.

No Time Like the Present

Darden was off and running with more than 700 Red Lobsters in North America with total sales of more than $2 billion, and more than 470 Olive Garden restaurants with total sales of more than $1.2 billion.

The company remains committed to the future through growth of its core concepts, potential acquisitions, and internally developed concepts like Bahama Breeze, already an Orlando favorite.

"Unlike many competitors that are separated from their parent corporations, we have a strong balance sheet, and we have tremendous resources to meet our mission and to do the things needed for growth, whether it's research-ing, testing, or developing," said Darden Chairman and CEO Joe Lee. "We have proven concepts, an experienced management team, motivated employees, an unrivaled purchasing network, national marketing power, and an unflagging spirit of innovation."

Lee continues, "As a stand-alone company, we are able to react and execute more quickly, and to focus on our customers more than ever. A diverse workforce and the diversity of our guests require our very best effort."

The philosophy that the employees are at the core of Darden Restaurants' success story can be witnessed on office plaques bearing founder Bill Darden's sentiment: "I am convinced that the only edge we have on our competition is the quality of our employees, as reflected each day by the job they do."

Committed to Community

Richard Walsh, senior vice president corporate relations, says the Darden spirit reflects the company's devotion to people. "It's very important to give back to the community. Many of us have been in this community for 25 years or more. It's where we live and raise our families. We have grown along with the city, and we care where it is going and how it gets there," Walsh explains.

Over the years, in communities across the nation, Darden Restaurants has given more than $10 million in community grants, and employees have donated hundreds of thousands of volunteer hours to programs, including the Orlando Science Center; United Arts; Special Olympics; and Darden's own community fund-raisers, the Olive Garden's Pasta for Pennies and Red Lobster's Partners in Preservation.

From a single seafood restaurant to the nation's largest independent casual dining company, Darden Restaurants remains one of Orlando's true success stories. In the years to come, the company is committed to providing its restaurant customers with the best quality, value, and service, and to continuing as one of Orlando's premier employers.

SONNY'S REAL PIT BAR-B-Q

SONNY TILLMAN—FOUNDER OF SONNY'S REAL PIT BAR-B-Q—KNEW THAT IN the South, barbecue is not just a meal; it is an experience. In 1968, he came up with an idea to turn this experience into a sweet and savory new business. He wanted to offer customers good food at low prices, and he wanted it cooked slow but served fast and in a friendly way. Today, Sonny's Real Pit Bar-B-Q in Orlando is the nation's fastest-growing barbecue chain.

Sonny's is also one of the largest privately held companies in Florida. There are nearly 100 Sonny's Real Pit Bar-B-Q restaurants throughout six southeastern states: Florida, Georgia, Kentucky, Louisiana, Mississippi, and North Carolina. Annual sales for the company are estimated at more than $130 million.

BELIEF IN THE BEST

The first Sonny's restaurant—which opened in Gainesville, Florida—expanded and enhanced the role of barbecue for generations to come. Barbecue went from being exclusively the fare of backyard picnics to becoming a featured favorite on the dining-out menu. Floyd Earl "Sonny" Tillman has said he believes that by doing the

best job possible, he has kept his dream alive, even when "people had just about convinced me that I was out of my mind."

Through his venture, Tillman built a dining tradition that was almost instantly successful. With less than $2,000, Tillman expanded by opening more restaurants and becoming more well known throughout Florida. His innovative spirit still at work, Tillman began franchising Sonny's Real Pit Bar-B-Q restaurants in 1977. The first Orlando franchise opened in 1978 on Oak Ridge Road and the chain continued its successful climb to the top.

Robert and Jeff Yarmuth, who owned and operated several successful Sonny's franchise restaurants in the Orlando area, took over the

franchise company in 1991. The Yarmuths moved Sonny's corporate headquarters from Gainesville to Orlando in 1991 and guided the company's marketing and franchising programs to its current expansion rate.

"With a well-proven concept developed by Sonny Tillman and the restructuring of the company over the last few years, I believe the Sonny's system is now uniquely positioned to become a greater force in this industry and to continue to be one of the premier restaurant chains in the country," says Robert Yarmuth, president and chief executive officer of Sonny's Franchise Company. "Our growth over the last three to four years illustrates our potential, and our loyal and growing customer

SONNY'S REAL PIT BAR-B-Q RESTAURANTS ARE FAMILIAR SIGHTS THROUGHOUT THE SOUTHEAST (RIGHT).

"THIS COMPANY CAN ONLY GO AS FAR AS OUR VISION AND THE QUALITY OF OUR PEOPLE," SAYS ROBERT YARMUTH, PRESIDENT AND CEO OF SONNY'S FRANCHISE COMPANY (BELOW).

base illustrates our well-earned reputation for a quality product."

MEETING CUSTOMER NEEDS

With the average meal costing between $5 and $6, Sonny's offers a healthful alternative to fast-food dining—a mixture of tangy and sweet sauces, and lean cuts of meat. In addition, new customer desires have emerged over the years, and Sonny's has worked to meet them. The original product line now includes smoked turkey, a 40-plus-item salad bar, and Brunswick stew.

"We have built a bond with our customers—a relationship of fairness and trust," Robert Yarmuth says. "You have to know your customer. Sonny was a 'people genius.' He was street smart. He worked in the pit right alongside his employees, talking with customers as they walked in and out. He developed relationships with people at every level."

On that solid foundation, the Yarmuths' plan is to develop Sonny's in a steady and responsible manner. They are looking to intro-

duce Sonny's into new market areas such as the Midwest and Northeast. By the end of the decade, the Yarmuths expect to have more than 140 restaurants recording sales in excess of $200 million. The chain has been recognized for its marketing innovations and its use of global information systems (GIS) to combine maps and demographic data for business development. While Robert Yarmuth agrees that GIS and other technology can prove to be important tools of the trade, he notes that human contact is key. Technology, he says, cannot replace walking up and down streets, going into local barbershops and fire stations, and talking to people. "After all, computers don't eat barbecue. People do," Robert Yarmuth says.

This recognition that people make a difference has resulted in a solid employee base, a loyal customer following that stretches across many states, and programs designed to give back to each of the communities served by Sonny's. From continuing education programs for staff to the support of

such area charities as Give Kids the World and March of Dimes, Sonny's is committed to a goal of total customer satisfaction. "You can advertise all you want, but eventually you have to prove who you are," Yarmuth says. "We have proven that we are a 'people' company inside and out."

The Yarmuths' goal is to maintain quality growth at a sustainable rate, adding stores that strengthen the chain's dominance in the Southeast, increasing chain purchasing and marketing power, and building sales volumes to reach a solid per store average. When all is said and done, Yarmuth says true growth and success will come from what many call Sonny's "magic."

"Our challenge is to keep that original spirit. Magic is magic. How can you explain magic?" Yarmuth concludes. "The key words are fun, trust, value, respect, and friendly and attentive service. The restaurant business is about feeding and satisfying people. This company can only go as far as our vision and the quality of our people."

BDO Seidman, LLP

A S PART OF THE WORLD'S SEVENTH-LARGEST ACCOUNTING AND CONSULTING organization, BDO Seidman, LLP is a powerhouse firm with extensive resources and a global reach. Yet the firm is also renowned for its community ties and close relationships with clients, which is more reflective of smaller, local accounting practices. It is this characteristic that sets BDO Seidman apart. ✳ In Orlando, BDO Seidman is known for its commitment to the people and organizations that improve the city's quality of life. Professionals in the office participate in numerous civic and charitable groups, providing expertise and support to an array of causes.

A key element in the firm's community outreach program is its support of Central Florida's education systems. In particular, the University of Central Florida (UCF) is a focal point for BDO Seidman's support. More than one-half of the professionals in the Orlando office are graduates of UCF, Orlando's hometown university, and the majority of the office's professional staff are recruited there.

To support UCF and its efforts to produce the community's future workforce, BDO Seidman representatives are involved as supporters, fund-raisers, and board members with the UCF Foundation, UCF Alumni Association, UCF Knight Boosters, and the School of Accounting Advisory Board. In addition, they are supporters of UCF's Alumni Trust, a major fund-raising initiative that has endowed scholarship money for National Merit Scholars.

The firm's enthusiastic commitment and support of UCF is complemented by involvement in many other community organizations. Among them are the Economic Development Commission of Mid-Florida, Inc.; Greater Orlando Chamber of Commerce; Orlando/Orange County Convention & Visitors Bureau, Inc.; Central Florida Hotel & Motel Association; Downtown Orlando YMCA; Florida Citrus Sports Association; Greater Seminole County Chamber of Commerce; Downtown Orlando Partnership; SHARE of Central Florida; Women's Resource Center; Heart of Florida United Way; and Junior Achievement of Central Florida, Inc. Given the office's staff of 30 people, this translates into an active group of professionals who are supported by the firm to invest in their community with contributions of human capital as well as financial support.

RICH IN TRADITION

BDO Seidman, LLP was founded in New York City in 1910 and quickly gained a reputation for successfully handling complex tax matters. By the 1940s, the firm was operating coast to coast, providing a variety of public accounting services to individuals and businesses. Then, as now, the practice was oriented toward the emerging midtier sector of the economy, ranging from small, family enterprises to sizable, publicly held corporations.

Under the leadership of J.S. Seidman, the firm continued to grow in reputation as a leader in accounting and auditing. In 1968, BDO Seidman reorganized as a general partnership under managing partner L. William Seidman, who later became chairman of the Economic Policy Board in former President Gerald Ford's administration. BDO Seidman boasts more than 1,700 partners and staff throughout the United States. Each BDO office offers highly individualized services and partner involvement. The firm has expertise serving clients in real estate, hospitality, vacation ownership, manufacturing, high-tech products and services, government contracting, warehouse and distribution, financial institutions, a broad range of service businesses, and more. BDO's capabilities in financing and capital are also extensive, and include private placements, initial public offerings, and other Securities and Exchange Commission (SEC) matters.

BDO Seidman's rich history of service quality and innovation continues today. Individuals, corporations, and governments continue to rely on BDO Seidman not only to provide superior accounting and auditing services, but also for its tax expertise. The firm's current market base consists of midtier companies—with annual sales of $5 million to $100 million—which are primarily closely held businesses or management-controlled public companies. The firm's experience in working with growth companies and publicly held businesses has been recognized with a number of service excellence awards and other honors from industry groups worldwide.

MORE THAN ONE-HALF OF THE PROFESSIONALS IN BDO SEIDMAN, LLP'S ORLANDO OFFICE, INCLUDING THE ACCOUNTANTS PICTURED HERE, ARE GRADUATES OF THE UNIVERSITY OF CENTRAL FLORIDA. THE FIRM ACTIVELY SUPPORTS THE UNIVERSITY AND MANY OTHER CIVIC AND CHARITABLE ORGANIZATIONS IN THE COMMUNITY.

I

N 1965, GOLF LEGEND ARNOLD PALMER PLAYED IN AN EXHIBITION MATCH AT A young golf course called Bay Hill on the outskirts of Orlando. He shot a 66 that day and began a love affair with the course. In 1970, he consummated the relationship by purchasing the course, club, and adjoining lodge. ✳ Since that time, Arnold and his wife, Winnie, have called Bay Hill their winter home. Lodge guests and club members often get more than a glimpse of the King at his

home club. He eats in the dining room, and practices and tees off along with everyone else, just like a member of the club.

"Our members have gotten kind of used to it over the years, but guests sometimes get downright giddy when they see him," says Pamela Rush, Bay Hill's general manager. "They're surprised that he's so visible."

The course was originally designed in 1961 by Dick Wilson. Palmer and Ed Seay modernized and upgraded Bay Hill in 1979, and again in 1989. The course is a fair test of golf and truly reflects Arnold Palmer's aggressive, go-for-it spirit.

Today, Bay Hill is a private club with a cap of 400 golfing members. A short waiting list holds the names of anxious prospective members. For those who reside outside of the Orlando area, nonresident memberships are still available.

Orlando's best-kept secret may be the lodge at Bay Hill. The lodge harkens back to a time when private clubs offered comfortable, on-site accommodations to visiting guests. This is still very much the tradition at Bay Hill, where lodge guests are treated as club members during their stay. "We're the antithesis of the large golf resort," Rush explains. "Our service is very personal. Everyone on our staff strives to treat our guests like members of the family."

Arnold and Winnie Palmer are, surprisingly, very hands-on in the running of Bay Hill. They are involved in all of the decision making and are at the heart of the pampering that members and guests receive.

The lodge at Bay Hill is quaint, with only 58 rooms. Guests receive such membership privileges as use of the dining rooms and lounges. Additional amenities include a swimming pool, tennis courts, and a private marina. In 1997, construction was begun on a fitness center with an equipment room, sauna, whirlpool spa, massage therapy facilities, and personal salon. The lodge and club also offer meeting rooms for business conferences and seminars for up to 500 people.

While golf packages are available at the lodge year-round, summer offers the best value. Overnight accommodations, breakfast, greens fee, cart fee, and more are all inclusive. Summer seasonal rates are effective from first day of May through September 30. Bay Hill is also home to the

Arnold Palmer Golf Academy, where instructors work with players individually to improve specific areas of their game.

Bay Hill also has been home to the Bay Hill Invitational since 1979. One of the more popular stops on the PGA TOUR, it boasts one of the most outstanding fields year after year. In fact, the tournament was ranked the fifth-favorite TOUR stop by the pros themselves in a poll taken in 1996.

Located in a secluded setting outside Orlando, just minutes from all of the area's famed theme parks, Arnold Palmer's Bay Hill Club & Lodge is a golfer's dream come true. It is indeed the only opportunity anywhere to play on a PGA TOUR event course that is also owned by and played regularly by the King of golf: Arnold Palmer.

THE GOLF AT BAY HILL IS A CHALLENGING BUT FAIR TEST OF A PLAYER'S SKILLS. ARNOLD PALMER LIVES, AND PLAYS, AT BAY HILL DURING THE WINTER MONTHS EACH YEAR (LEFT).

ARNOLD AND WINNIE PALMER ARE VERY INVOLVED IN THE EVERYDAY OPERATIONS AT BAY HILL (RIGHT).

WHEN DAVID AND BETTIE SIEGEL COFOUNDED CENTRAL FLORIDA Investments, Inc. (CFI) in 1970 to promote local real estate development, the company was a home-based business with a good idea. Nearly 30 years later, Orlando-based CFI is one of the fastest-growing companies in the world. A multimillion-dollar firm with more than 4,000 employees, CFI has a diverse business portfolio, including Westgate Resorts, a family of five timeshare resorts; telecommunications, hotel, and resort management; magazine publishing; retail stores; real estate development; family attractions; hospitality guest services; restaurants; travel agencies; and more.

LEADING WITH ENTREPRENEURIAL SPIRIT

The rapid growth of CFI is attributed to the innovative vision of its president, David A. Siegel. As *USA Today*'s 1996 Real Estate/ Construction Entrepreneur of the Year for the State of Florida, Siegel emphasizes the true meaning of entrepreneurial spirit: vision, risk taking, perseverance, ingenuity, and innovation.

"I started my first business, a paper route, at the age of four. Throughout the years, beginning when I was a youngster, I have learned what it takes to succeed in business—hands-on involvement and education. I learn every nuance of an industry before I become involved with it," says Siegel. "But, most importantly, I know my customers' needs."

CFI began as a real estate development company with little money and an office located in the family garage. Siegel has since built an empire that spans dozens of international markets, including Europe and every major Latin American country. In 1976, CFI ventured into the family attraction industry when it opened Mystery Fun House, located in Orlando across from Universal Studios.

CLOCKWISE FROM LEFT:
DAVID SIEGEL, PRESIDENT, CFI

WESTGATE LAKES OFFERS OWNERS AND THEIR GUESTS AN OPPORTUNITY TO ENJOY A FIVE-STAR VACATION EXPERIENCE WITHOUT EVER HAVING TO LEAVE THE RESORT.

WESTGATE VACATION VILLAS IS THE LARGEST SINGLE-SITE TIMESHARE RESORT IN THE WORLD.

The attraction has been an Orlando icon for more than 20 years, offering year-round fun house classics such as a mirror maze, spinning tunnel, giant video arcade, trolley rides, minigolf, children's parties, and laser tag in Starbase Omega.

Even with family entertainment, residential properties, hospitality guest services, and retail sales under its belt, CFI is always looking for a new challenge. For instance, in 1991, Siegel introduced the company to the wireless communications industry with the opening of CFI Cellular Telephone Company. Currently, the company is the second-largest cellular products dealer in Central Florida. Likewise, Everything But Water opened its first store in 1984. Today, this retailer of fine swimwear for women boasts 34 locations across the country.

CFI's diverse business lineup also includes the Florida Vacation Stores—full-service travel agencies that sell Florida vacation packages in a mall-like setting; Fairgrounds Mall in Tampa; and Hotel Royal Plaza, an official hotel of Walt Disney World.

FOUNDING FATHER OF TIMESHARE

David Siegel credits much of CFI's success to the timeshare phenomenon. The company entered the timeshare industry when other business experts found the industry an unpopular choice due to its market complexity. In 1980, Westgate Resorts, Ltd., a subsidiary of CFI, began the development of Westgate Vacation Villas. Today, Westgate Resorts is a family of five timeshare resorts: Westgate Vacation Villas, Westgate Lakes,

Westgate Towers, Westgate Miami Beach, and Westgate Daytona Beach. In addition, Siegel owns two other timeshare properties: The Seasons and Club Orlando.

Marketed as a vacation sanctuary, Westgate Vacation Villas opened in 1982 with 16 villas. The villas promoted a cost savings over long hotel stays, as well as the ability to make consumers feel at home on the road with one- to three-bedroom villas, fully equipped kitchens, screened patios, master bath whirlpool tubs, and other luxurious amenities. Today, Westgate Vacation Villas is the largest single-site timeshare resort in the world with more than 1,100 villas and expansion plans for 2,000 new villas over the next few years.

"What we've been pitching for years, people now believe. Timesharing has come into its

TODAY, WESTGATE RESORTS IS A FAMILY OF FIVE TIMESHARE RESORTS, INCLUDING WESTGATE DAYTONA BEACH (TOP LEFT).

OTHER CFI ENTERPRISES INCLUDE FISHERMAN'S COVE RESTAURANT (BOTTOM LEFT) AND MYSTERY FUN HOUSE FAMILY AMUSEMENT CENTER (RIGHT).

own, and we are the pioneers," says Siegel, who has been dubbed the "king of timeshare" by local news media. "We now operate close to 50 percent of the timeshare resort sales business in Orlando, we're expanding our international markets, and we're planning to go public in the near future."

Westgate Resorts, Ltd. expanded its timeshare resort business in 1996 when it opened Westgate Lakes, a 97-acre resort with approximately one mile of secluded lakefront property. Westgate Lakes offers owners and their guests an opportunity to enjoy a five-star vacation experience without ever having to leave the resort. The property offers more than 600 luxury one-, two-, and three-bedroom villas, as well as fine dining and entertainment. It is the home of Westgate Watersports: Home of Peterson's World Championship Ski School, which is operated by Bill and Kyle Peterson, both of whom are international waterski title winners. Plus, the resort also features a kids club program that offers daily supervised activities for children ages four to 12.

In support of the timeshare properties, CFI now operates six

DAVID SIEGEL EXAMINES BLUEPRINTS FOR THE RENOVATION OF THE HOTEL ROYAL PLAZA.

international timeshare customer service offices located in Argentina, Brazil, Chile, Guatemala, Mexico, and Venezuela. CFI also has more than 500 brokers in 39 countries. "We have a very strong relationship with the South American populations," says Siegel. "They particularly like our Westgate Lakes and Westgate Miami Beach property."

Within the industry, customer service is a priority. From the first day a consumer tours a property, to each day an owner stays on property, Westgate Resorts maintains a total involvement strategy. Not only is each guest assigned a personal vacation concierge, but top executives are seen daily on property speaking with owners and guests. "We are able to continue to lead the industry because of our unique involvement with our guests," says Siegel. "It is important to understand clients' needs, and by interacting with them, we discover valuable insights."

CFI's approach seems to be working. Owner participation has doubled. In fact, Interval International, one of the world's largest timeshare exchange companies, named Westgate Vacation Villas the number one sales-producing timeshare resort in the world, with Westgate Lakes as number two and Westgate Miami Beach as number four. With a timeshare owner base of more than 100,000 and sales reaching $211 million in 1996, Westgate Resorts, Ltd. is breaking new records as the industry's timeshare resort leader.

SIEGEL PLAYED THE PART OF SANTA CLAUS DURING THE ORANGE COUNTY SHERIFF'S OFFICE'S ANNUAL SHOP WITH A COP PROGRAM FOR DISADVANTAGED CHILDREN.

BELIEVING IN COMMUNITY

Siegel does not enter a room unnoticed. Whether evoking smiles and greetings from staff, handshakes from business associates, embraces from customers, or words of thanks and praise from local charity staff, Siegel's reputation for corporate and civic citizenship is well recognized.

With a firm belief in family and community, Siegel and Central Florida Investments, Inc. have been widely recognized for community service contributions. Siegel has received such distinctions as the 1995 Honorary Doctorate of Human Letters from Florida A & M University for community service. In 1996, Siegel was honored with the chairmanship of the Heart of Florida United Way's Alexis de Tocqueville Society. Siegel has also been recognized for his work with the Salvation Army and as a Boy Scout leader for disabled children. As an active sponsor and member of numerous other local and national charities, Siegel continues to be a community leader.

Both Siegel and CFI employees donate thousands of service

hours and financial contributions to local charities, including Boggy Creek Gang, Children's Wish Foundation, Edgewood Children's Ranch, and Tangelo Park Foundation. "We believe in giving back to our community," says Siegel. "Our community is only able to grow collectively if everyone is able to participate in a positive manner, be it physically or financially."

In 1995, CFI set a record for the largest Heart of Florida United Way corporate contributions drive during its first year of participation. In 1996, CFI increased the dollar amount of contributions by nearly twice as much with the 100 percent participation of its employees. Another favorite charity of CFI employees is Toys for Tots. In both the 1995 and 1996 campaigns, the company was the largest single contributor.

"CFI is a company made up of dedicated employees. I'm not the company. It's the 4,000 plus employees who work with me that make this company a business and community leader," Siegel says. "We have always gone the extra mile, whether it be in the quality of products used in our villas, the amenities we provide, the treatment of our customers, or our involvement in the community. In a way, our high standards force the competition to upgrade their products and services; our standards are what have always set us apart. We will continue to do what's right for the people and the places where we live and grow. It's the only way we know how to do business."

INTERVAL INTERNATIONAL, ONE OF THE WORLD'S LARGEST TIMESHARE EXCHANGE COMPANIES, NAMED WESTGATE MIAMI BEACH AS ONE OF THE TOP SALES-PRODUCING TIMESHARE RESORTS IN THE WORLD.

▶ AERIAL INNOVATIONS, INC.

WESTGATE RESORTS, LTD. EXPANDED ITS TIMESHARE RESORT BUSINESS IN 1996 WHEN IT OPENED WESTGATE LAKES, A 97-ACRE RESORT WITH APPROXIMATELY ONE MILE OF SECLUDED LAKEFRONT PROPERTY.

EPOCH PROPERTIES, INC.

WELL KNOWN THROUGHOUT THE REAL ESTATE INDUSTRY FOR ITS creative architecture and landscape design, Epoch Properties, Inc. has become an industry trendsetter, with its focus on luxury apartment communities planned to ensure their value for years to come. One of the nation's premier specialists of multifamily housing development, the company has built more than 26,000 multifamily

rental apartment communities in more than 56 cities throughout the United States since 1970.

Producing more apartment communities than any other development company in the state, the Winter Park-based company develops multifamily properties and provides property management services through a second company—Epoch Management, Inc., which is led by its own president, John Ariko. A certified property manager and an accredited management organization with more than 200 employees, Epoch Management has managed more than 57,000 apartments in 13 states throughout its corporate history.

Yet despite this history, President James H. Pugh Jr. insists, "We are an understated company, and we let our reputation speak for itself. But more important, we

are substantive. We want to be the one company on which our investor partners can rely."

BUILDERS OF SUCCESS

The founder and first chairman of the board of Epoch Properties, Inc. was Earl Downs, one of the pioneers in the nation's multifamily apartment industry and a leader in the creation of Epoch's successful corporate culture.

For the last 27 years, Jim Pugh has served as president of the firm. A Florida native, Pugh contributes his unique understanding of both Florida's business climate and the state's commitment to community pride. A graduate of the University of Florida, Pugh has maintained his focus on the pulse of future industry. His experience as an Airborne Ranger Infantry Company commander in the U.S. Army has been a strong influence on how Pugh does business.

"The military teaches you about discipline," says Pugh. "At Epoch, we stay within our ability to manage. Through the good times—when there is a lot of equity capital and lots of interested investors—we could easily do 10 deals per year, but we limit ourselves to five. We don't try to do more than we are capable of doing. We have a disciplined approach to development by staying in the multifamily niche market. Some of our competitors try to do more than they are capable of doing. We do what we know, and we do it well."

Also leading the charge at Epoch is Greg Jacoby, chief financial officer and a graduate of the University of Central Florida; Kyle D. Riva, vice president of finance and a graduate of Florida State Uni-

versity and Rollins College in Winter Park; and Julie M. Arnold, a graduate of the University of Central Florida and comptroller of Epoch Properties. Epoch's construction project managers include Manning E. Willson and Robert S. Novell.

AWARD-WINNING SERVICE

Each of Epoch Properties' apartment communities is carefully designed to best utilize its location and environment through careful attention to the balance between the development of a community and the ecosystems that surround it. This concept has brought the company many national awards, as well as national publicity in such publications as *Housing*, *Professional Builder*, and *Florida Trend*. The company earned the Feature Performance Award from *Professional Builder* magazine and is recognized annually as one of the giants

of housing in an industry listing of the nation's top 100 builders.

Because of its instrumental role in the development of The Springs, Central Florida's premier housing community, Epoch Properties received an award at the White House recognizing the project as the Outstanding Planned Unit Development in America. Epoch communities have broken records by continuously winning the industry's top honors, such as the Aurora Award for architectural excellence.

The company's strategy includes joint venture partnerships with leading institutional investors and lenders with the ability to finance large-scale, multifamily communities. Such partners include Aetna, Bear Stearns, Citibank, Disney, Manufacturers Hanover, New York Life, Prudential, Lincoln National Life Insurance Company, Pacific Mutual

Life Insurance Company, Florida Capital Assets Corporation, and many others.

"Our joint ventures have contributed greatly to our success," Pugh says. "The reason we've been here 27 years is because we put a lot of equity into our deals. By working in joint ventures, we have created a culture in which our investors succeed and continue to invest.

"People believe in our integrity," Pugh continues. "The bottom line is that we do what we say we're going to do. If we set up a joint venture and predict the final cost to be $20 million, then the final cost is $20 million. We live up to our word. Epoch Properties, Inc.'s excellent reputation is based on this reliability."

CLOCKWISE FROM TOP LEFT:
PLANTATION PARK AT LITTLE
LAKE BRYAN
ORLANDO, FLORIDA
320 UNITS

THE HEADQUARTERS FOR EPOCH
PROPERTIES, INC.
WINTER PARK, FLORIDA

THE SUMMIT AT METROWEST
ORLANDO, FLORIDA
280 UNITS

Superior Printers, Inc.

CHUCK AND CHARLOTTE SENGEL HAD AN IDEA. OPEN A QUICK PRINT shop in the heart of Central Florida, provide the highest level of personal service and attention to clients, and maintain a consistent and superior level of quality. The idea was both exciting and challenging. The business would offer an opportunity to be involved in a growing industry, and it would create a legacy on which the Sengel family would build their dreams.

In 1970, Superior Printers opened its doors for business under the name Superior Minute Print Co. The company soon found it was doing much more than "minute" printing and changed the name in 1976 to Superior Printers, Inc. The company has evolved into one of Orlando's most respected commercial printers. Today, Superior employs 34 people and has two satellite locations in addition to its main offices and plant on Fairbanks Avenue in Winter Park.

THE OWNERS OF SUPERIOR PRINTERS, INC. ARE (FROM LEFT) CHARLOTTE SENGEL, TERRI SENGEL, AND ED SENGEL.

HOMESPUN SUCCESS

Superior Printers began as a traditional mom-and-pop shop with a committed work ethic and deep family values. While it has grown in staff, size, and capability during its nearly 30 years in business, the company prides itself on old-fashioned honesty in business.

The energy level at the offices of Superior Printers reflects the fast-paced work flow required for today's competitive printing environment. Staff members move in and out of the well-equipped departments, processing each job through its various stages with efficient know-how and professional confidence. A fast-paced business—still owned and operated by the Sengel family—Superior Printers, Inc. is committed to quality and excellence for its clients. This has held true since 1970, when the firm was founded, and it is a spirit shared by all those who are a part of the organization today. "Every now and then, I stop and think about what my parents started back then. They built this business on the very things we take for granted today. While determined to succeed, they never sacrificed their values of honesty and integrity, quality and personal service," says Ed Sengel, president of Superior Printers. "We don't want our clients to settle for second best—that's not why they choose to do business with Superior. They expect the best quality and service and that is what we commit our organization to providing. It is the same commitment my parents made to their first clients in 1970, and it provides the foundation upon which Superior Printers' reputation has been built. We're proud to say that tradition continues today."

That tradition also includes service to Central Florida's nonprofit organizations. Sengel says the family business has always advocated giving something back to the communities it serves. In addition to its numerous business and civic organization memberships, Superior Printers is a corporate sponsor of Orlando public television station WMFE

COMMUNICATION IS ESSENTIAL THROUGH EVERY STEP OF THE PRODUCTION PROCESS.

Channel 24. The company also sponsors the Children's Miracle Network, Habitat for Humanity, and Orlando Science Center, and is also a partner with Junior Achievement of Central Florida and Children's Make-a-Wish Foundation.

On the Cutting Edge

In recent years, businesses across Central Florida have been faced with rising costs and tougher service deadlines. Responding to that growing trend, Superior Printers has created high-tech production systems that are now key elements in the company's plans for the future. The company provides sheet-fed commercial printing of one to six colors.

Unique among print service companies, Superior probably offers a broader range of capabilities than any other commercial printer in Central Florida. At any given time, visitors will find in-house print projects ranging from short-run stationery packages, fliers, and forms to color brochures, newspaper inserts, booklets, and annual reports.

To achieve all of this, Superior has added a state-of-the-art electronic prepress department. The company's full-service prepress work flow allows it to scan images, output a digital proof, and output high-resolution

film—all in-house. Utilizing the latest technology in high-end color scanning and high-resolution image setting, Superior Printers can achieve the quality its customers demand and the turnaround they require.

"We will continue to stay abreast of the current technology—and invest in that technology—when there is a real and immediate benefit to our clients in terms of service and quality," says Sengel. "We are in an industry of custom manufacturing, and we face the constant challenge of finding ways to profitably produce printing jobs on ever tightening schedules and budgets. Printers unable or unwilling to invest in these technologies to meet their customers' demands

will find themselves in similar situations that typesetters were faced with in the 1980s. Superior Printers intends to stay in the forefront of Central Florida's commercial printers and will continue to build on those relationships that have been established over the last quarter century."

I N 1964, WALT DISNEY GAVE EVANGELIST BILLY GRAHAM A TOUR OF Disneyland in Anaheim, California. Graham is reported to have told Disney, "What a wonderful world of fantasy you created, Walt," to which Disney replied, "Look around. You see people and families of all ethnic backgrounds smiling together. This is the reality. Out there is the fantasy." This true account is just one of many that exemplify the spirit behind Disney, the man, and

the magic of his legendary theme park attractions. Richard A. Nunis, chairman of Walt Disney Attractions and a veteran of the Walt Disney Company, explains, "People always wonder why Walt Disney World is so successful. It's our people. Walt always believed in the magic of people."

ORLANDO'S MYSTERY INDUSTRY

With a string of successful business ventures that climaxed in 1955 with the landmark opening of Disneyland, Walter E. Disney chose Orlando

for his largest and most secretive business mission ever. In the early 1960s, Disney and his "imagineers" at the newly formed WED Enterprises envisioned a total vacation resort destination that would feature an Experimental Prototype Community of Tomorrow (Epcot). As with any new project of this magnitude, early details were kept secret from the public and the press.

Central Florida was quietly chosen as the location for the new Disney project because of the area's year-round good weather, high level of tourism, and availability of land

at a reasonable price. In an effort to avoid the congestion problems that plagued Disneyland, the Walt Disney Company bought up more than 27,000 acres of pristine Florida land from 100 Orlando-area property owners. The property was purchased by dummy companies for the "mystery industry," fueling press speculations about the identity of the land buyer.

On November 15, 1965, a public announcement revealed the mystery to be a project that would turn Central Florida into a unique entertainment and vacation center. Disney estimated the cost at $100 million, a fraction of the final investment, and he worked on concepts for the Florida project until his death in December 1966.

"WHEN YOU WISH UPON A STAR . . ."

Brother and business partner Roy O. Disney, along with the creative team at WED Enterprises, worked to turn the Walt Disney World Resort dream into a reality. Just two months before his own death, on October 1, 1971, Roy O. Disney wit-

THE WALT DISNEY COMPANY

THE WALT DISNEY COMPANY

nessed the nationally televised opening of the Walt Disney World Resort in Orlando. Today, his son Roy E. Disney, vice chairman of the Walt Disney Company, continues to be involved with the company as it reaches new heights.

Since opening, the Walt Disney World Resort has hosted more than 500 million guests at its three major theme parks: the Magic Kingdom®, Epcot®, and Disney-MGM Studios.

Epcot opened in 1982. Its Future World continues to be a place of discovery, while its World Showcase demonstrates the cultural achievements of 11 nations in a global display of entertainment, food, art, and architecture.

Disney-MGM Studios, which opened in 1989, continues to provide guests with a behind-the-scenes look at the world of moviemaking and Disney animation. The park features more than 50 major shows, shops, restaurants, ride-through adventures, and a backstage movie tour.

"Today, we are proud that the Walt Disney World Resort has developed far beyond Walt's original vision," says Judson Green, president of Walt Disney Attractions. "The diversity of our product and entertainment continues to attract millions of people every year." In addition to the three theme parks, its vast offerings include three water parks; two theater and nightclub centers; six golf courses; 80 swimming pools, lakes, and recreation areas; and more than 15 resort hotels. Among the recent additions are Disney's Blizzard Beach (1995), Disney's Wedding Pavilion (1995), Disney's BoardWalk (1996), Disney Institute (1996), Disney's Wide World of Sports (1997), Downtown Disney (1997), and Disney's Animal Kingdom (scheduled to open in 1998).

"... YOUR DREAMS COME TRUE"

Walt Disney once said, "The greatest moments in life are not concerned with selfish achievements,

but rather with the things we do for people we love and esteem." As the largest employer in Central Florida and a significant member of the community, Walt Disney World is committed to embracing and supporting the needs of the diverse community with an emphasis on children and families, education, and the environment.

Programs that demonstrate this commitment include the Disney VoluntEars Program, through which Disney cast members can volunteer their time. Community service projects are created to address the needs of nonprofit organizations, and VoluntEars are often seen participating in a variety of events benefiting the community overall.

As part of Walt Disney World's commitment to education, programs such as Disney's Teacherrific Awards and Disney Dreamers and Doers were created. The Teacherrific program honors local teachers who have demonstrated innovative and effective teaching practices, and it distributes more than $200,000 annually in cash awards to winning teachers and the schools they represent. The Disney Dreamers and Doers program honors students from across the state of Florida who have overcome great personal challenges and displayed the qualities of courage, confidence, curiosity, and constancy—Walt Disney's four secrets to making dreams come true.

Additionally, through the Disney Scholars program, full, four-year

college scholarships are awarded annually to 16 deserving Central Florida senior high school students. Furthermore, sharing an educational message through entertainment is the Disney Crew traveling puppet show, which has communicated its antidrug message to more than 1.7 million elementary-school-age children.

Environmentally speaking, Walt Disney World's contributions include donating excess building materials to nonprofit organizations; donating prepared meals and unserved food to nonprofit organizations through the Disney Harvest program; and creating the Disney Wilderness Preserve, a joint partnership between government, private industry, and the not-for-profit community. The preserve was implemented to protect 8,500 acres of environmentally significant land. Disney purchased the land, and in turn donated it to the Nature Conservancy so it can be managed and restored in perpetuity.

From its environmental initiatives to its communications and transportation networks, the Walt Disney World Resort has influenced the way many companies do business. "It will always be our vision to inspire and entertain our guests, and leave them with wonderful memories that last a lifetime," says Green. "And, we will always remain committed to supporting the caring community in which we live."

CLOCKWISE FROM TOP LEFT: The *Partners* STATUE, WHICH DEPICTS THE PARTNERSHIP BETWEEN WALT DISNEY AND MICKEY MOUSE, IS ON PERMANENT DISPLAY IN THE HUB OF THE MAGIC KINGDOM.

DISNEY-MGM STUDIOS, WHICH OPENED IN 1989, CONTINUES TO PROVIDE GUESTS WITH A BEHIND-THE-SCENES LOOK AT THE WORLD OF MOVIEMAKING AND DISNEY ANIMATION.

THE WALT DISNEY WORLD RESORT PROVIDES FAMILY-ORIENTED ENTERTAINMENT TO MILLIONS OF PEOPLE EACH YEAR.

Time Warner Communications has a presence in more than 560,000 homes in a nine-county area of Central Florida. While the name has changed over the course of this 30-year relationship, the mission of providing customers with the best possible service and the benefits of the latest state-of-the-art technology to meet their communications needs has continued unabated. ✳ Time Warner Communications, whose parent is

Time Warner Inc., is the world's leading media and entertainment company. Time Warner Inc. includes operations in magazine and book publishing, film and home video, television programming, and recorded music.

Time Warner Communications is the country's second-largest cable company, serving more than 12 million homes stretching across 37 states, and has its roots deeply embedded in Central Florida. The more than 1,200 employees of the Central Florida Division of Time Warner not only work in the area, but live there, too.

TIME WARNER'S FIBER-OPTIC NETWORK OPERATIONS CENTER ALLOWS CUSTOMERS TO ACCESS A VARIETY OF DIGITAL SERVICES (LEFT).

THIS OPTICAL FIBER FUSION SPLICING UNIT PERFORMS VITAL FUNCTIONS (RIGHT).

LEADING THE WAY IN FIBER OPTICS

In 1988, Orlando was selected as one of the first Time Warner locations in the country to begin the conversion to fiber optics. Fiber provides greater bandwidth and allows Time Warner to add a variety of new program choices and services, including telecommunications and transmission of voice, data, and video. Time Warner Communications is expanding its offerings to include these types of services, as well as business telephone service and cable modems.

A significant part of providing quality service is delivering a quality product. By the year 2000, all Time Warner cable customers in Central Florida will receive their favorite programs through a sophisticated, state-of-the-art network of fiber-optic lines.

The installation of fiber is at the forefront of current trends in building broadband networks through which digital services can be delivered into homes all across America. Time Warner is an industry leader in the development of fiber

optics, winning an Emmy award in 1994 for its accomplishments.

Fiber optics has revolutionized the delivery of television signals and other services. Fiber optics provides greater reliability and ensures that customers receive the highest picture quality available, more channels from which to choose, and the ability to carry additional types of services.

In Time Warner systems, for example, the addition of fiber has resulted in a greater number of available channels. And as technology moves closer to the delivery of digital services, fiber has the potential to add more than 200 new digital channels. It allows Time Warner to continue providing additional value for its customers.

FULL RANGE OF SERVICE

In 1993, Time Warner tested future technology in Central Florida by choosing Orlando to launch the Full Service Network (FSN), a research and development project that provided interactive television services to a select group of customers. The Full Service Network

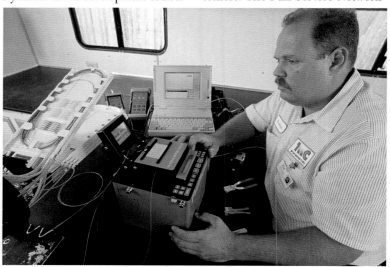

was the first in the world to integrate technology from the cable, computer, and telephone technologies to provide a wide range of new services.

Another new area of business for Time Warner is telephone service. Time Warner Connect is providing local and long-distance telephone and cable services to multiple family complexes. In addition, Time Warner provides business telephone accounts with local access to long-distance carriers.

Time Warner is also introducing Road Runner, a service that provides cable modems for high-speed computer access to on-line services. Road Runner takes advantage of fiber optics to allow PC users access to on-line services at speeds hundreds of times faster than other conventional telephone lines.

In 1997, Time Warner Communications partnered with Orlando Sentinel Communications to provide the first 24-hour local news channel: Central Florida News 13 (CFN 13). This unique Time Warner service focuses on local news and information around the clock.

CLOSE TIES TO THE COMMUNITY

Time Warner has maintained its close ties to the communities of

Central Florida. Employee community volunteers participate in local community events. The result is a Time Warner presence in a wide range of holiday parades, ethnic festivals, charity walk-a-thons, and sponsorships. Time Warner also is active in a variety of non-profit organizations around Central Florida.

Time Warner is committed to supporting education, providing free cable connections to schools in its service areas, and conducting free training workshops with hundreds of Central Florida teachers to demonstrate how they can incorporate educational cable programming into their classrooms.

In addition, Time Warner participates in several education foundations that sponsor activities such as Teacher of the Year awards and recognition programs.

Equally as important as Time Warner Communications' participation in the community is the company's focus on providing high-quality customer service. Giving customers added value is the goal at Time Warner Communications. By staying on top of the latest technological developments and by maintaining a commitment to providing quality customer service, Time Warner continues to enjoy its strong relationship with Central Florida.

THE HYATT NAME IS ONE OF THE OLDEST AND MOST RESPECTED IN THE hospitality industry. The relationship between Orlando and Hyatt Corporation has been a long one indeed. In 1972, the Hyatt Orlando opened near Walt Disney World, carrying with it a national tradition of service excellence. Hyatt Regency Grand Cypress Resort opened 12 years later, followed in 1992 by Hyatt Regency Orlando International Airport, one of the city's newest and most modern hotels.

The Hyatt Hotels in Orlando are among the more than 176 Hyatt hotels and resorts worldwide. The Hyatt Hotels Corporation operates more than 105 hotels and resorts in the United States, Canada, and the Caribbean. Hyatt International, through its subsidiaries, operates nearly 71 hotels and resorts in more than 34 countries.

A FULL-SERVICE RESORT

Hyatt Orlando continues its more than 20-year tradition of Hyatt hospitality from the heart of the Sunshine State. Located near EPCOT Center, MGM Studios, Universal Studios, and Sea World, Hyatt Orlando is a primary host for vacationers and convention meetings. In addition, the nearby location of Florida's main thoroughfares affords guests quick access to such attractions as Busch Gardens and the Kennedy Space Center.

Hyatt Orlando is known for its unique brand of hospitality, offering more than 900 oversized guest rooms, which are arranged in four courtyards. Each courtyard has its own swimming pool and spa, and all guests may enjoy the hotel's three lighted tennis courts, 1.3-mile fitness trail, and two playgrounds. For golfing aficionados, two of Central Florida's finest resort golf courses—Falcon's Fire Golf Club and the new Disney sensation, Celebration Golf Club—are located within two miles of the hotel.

The hotel offers a variety of dining experiences, ranging from quick deli meals and picnic foods at the Market Place to haute cuisine at the Summerhouse and Fio-Fio. All restaurants at the Hyatt Orlando offer special menu items for children.

For those traveling for business as well as pleasure, the Hyatt Orlando offers an elegant Caribbean-style

CLOCKWISE FROM TOP LEFT:
A GUEST ROOM AT THE HYATT ORLANDO

THE HYATT REGENCY ORLANDO INTERNATIONAL AIRPORT'S SIX-STORY ATRIUM

A MEETING ROOM AT THE HYATT REGENCY ORLANDO INTERNATIONAL AIRPORT

THE HYATT ORLANDO'S ENTRANCE

design with more than 45,000 square feet of meeting space, including a 20,000-square-foot exhibition hall. The resort also offers a 24-hour business center to meet any business service need.

NATURE'S PARADISE

Hyatt Hotels opened its second area hotel in grand style. The 750-room Hyatt Regency Grand Cypress Resort—a destination in itself—opened in 1984 near the Walt Disney World Village. The resort hotel features cascading fountains, priceless artwork, tropical birds, and award-winning restaurants. For relaxation, the resort offers 1,500 acres of rolling lawns and tropical gardens. A half-acre free-form pool flows through grottoes and caves, under bridges, and down a 115-foot water slide, and springs from 12 waterfalls.

For the active traveler, the Hyatt Regency Grand Cypress features a 45-hole, Jack Nicklaus-designed golf course. The 7,054-yard par 72 course is ranked among the world's most innovative and challenging tournament courses. In addition, guests have access to a nine-hole pitch-and-putt course. The resort also features 12 all-weather tennis courts, as well as horseback riding at a full-service equestrian center. Guests eager to take advantage of warm-weather water activities can rent canoes and paddle or sail boats on the 21-acre Lake Windsong. Additionally, a variety of innovative exercise and relaxation programs are offered at the resort's state-of-the-art health and fitness club.

Other advantages for Grand Cypress guests include five award-winning restaurants; a professionally staffed child care center; the exclusive Regency Club for business and leisure travelers; 24-hour room service; 65,000 square feet of meeting space; a 17,000-square-foot exhibition hall; and one of Florida's largest ballrooms, which is designed to hold up to 2,700 people.

Behind the scenes, a staff of more than 1,000 employees ensure that each guest's needs are met. Employees of the Hyatt Regency Grand Cypress are recognized for outstanding service and dedication through the Circle of Excellence program and the Employee of the Month awards, which honor the most inspiring and helpful service representatives.

GATEWAY TO THE WORLD

In 1992, the City of Orlando welcomed its first and only airport hotel—the Hyatt Regency Orlando International Airport. Located inside the main terminal of Orlando's gateway to the world, the hotel boasts a 42,000-square-foot atrium and 446 soundproof rooms. Within walking distance from any in-flight gate, the Hyatt Regency Orlando International Airport is elegant and comfortable, with an open-park-like atrium.

Billed as the city's premier business hotel, as well as the "hotel of tomorrow," the Hyatt Regency Orlando International Airport boasts state-of-the-art comfort and design. Business travelers will find the hotel especially equipped to meet all their business needs. It features more than 48,000 square feet of meeting space, including a 150-seat amphitheater complete with simultaneous language translation capabilities and three revolving stages. The hotel also offers a 13,000-square-foot exhibition hall, fiber-optic teleconferencing systems, and two conference suites that can be divided into six rooms. In addition, there are five boardrooms, four of which are equipped to host private functions.

The airport Hyatt provides business travelers with a fully staffed, state-of-the-art business center with private offices and telecommunications services. In addition, each guest room is designed with personal work space areas and desk phones with computer dataport systems. For pre-

sentations, the hotel offers Total Audio Visual Services (TAVS), which provides equipment and setup services for video, data display, communications systems, lighting and special effects, projectors and lenses, multi-image accessories, sound systems, recorders, and other program needs.

In addition to its special business features, the Hyatt Regency Orlando International Airport houses two award-winning restaurants, as well as a swimming pool, a spa, and a fully equipped health and fitness club. The Business Plan and Hyatt Gold Passport floors offer exclusive services and travel benefits.

From families and guests on a search for fun in the sun to the business traveler on the run, the Hyatt Hotels in Orlando offer the latest guest services available while continuing the long-standing tradition of elegance and luxury that has become Hyatt's trademark.

CLOCKWISE FROM TOP LEFT: THE HYATT REGENCY GRAND CYPRESS OFFERS FIVE AWARD-WINNING RESTAURANTS.

THE HYATT REGENCY GRAND CYPRESS FEATURES AN ARRAY OF RECREATIONAL ACTIVITIES.

THE HALF-ACRE SWIMMING POOL AT THE HYATT REGENCY GRAND CYPRESS FEATURES 12 FREE-FORM WATERFALLS, A SWINGING BRIDGE, TWO WATER SLIDES, AND LUSH VEGETATION.

MOVING TO BE AMERICA'S BEST SEEMED LIKE JUST ANOTHER internal motivational slogan when it was adopted by the public transportation agency operated by Orange, Seminole, and Osceola counties back in 1992. The agency—then called Tri County Transit—was virtually unknown in its own market. In fact, those who *did* know of Tri County—mostly passengers—were not happy with it. With such dilemmas, how could the agency hope to become America's Best?

Tri County changed its management, name, fleet colors, and operating philosophy. As LYNX, it developed programs that appealed to both riding and nonriding customers, and demonstrated the growing agency's determination to be a player in the market. Five years later, LYNX was recognized as Public Transportation Company of the Year, ridership had doubled, public awareness had tripled to more than 90 percent, and satisfaction had reached 95 percent, all of which indicated success in its goal of being America's Best.

THE RETAILING OF PUBLIC TRANSPORTATION

"We are customer driven," says Deborah Cooper, director of marketing and public affairs, "and that's very different from most government agencies." Cooper explains that more established transit authorities tend to treat riders as a captive audience. "In Central Florida, we made many changes based on the idea that everyone is either a riding or nonriding customer. We want all our customers to be happy with public transportation."

The way Cooper describes the LYNX public is typical of the LYNX difference. "They are not 'riders' or 'passengers,' but 'customers,'" she says. "By changing the way we talk about them, we changed the way we think about them." Paul P. Skoutelas, executive director of LYNX from 1991 to 1997, is credited with bringing about this change in mind-set. "Paul's approach to language reinvented the way our agency treats the people who depend on us. You don't take customers for granted," Cooper says.

Although Skoutelas spearheaded the changes, it was Chairman of the Board Jacob V. Stuart who launched the retail marketing of public transportation in Central Florida prior to Skoutelas' arrival. In 1991, Tri County Transit went from obscurity to objet d'art when Stuart ordered the main bus station to be painted bright pink.

In 1992, with Skoutelas aboard, a contest asking the public to suggest a new name was held. Of the nearly 10,000 entries received, the name LYNX was chosen because good public transportation "lynx" people together. A new logo was created, the routes were renamed "links," each stop was identified with a brightly painted pink paw print, and the entire bus fleet was repainted. Soon, a dazzling array of jewel-toned coaches with the

MORE THAN 5,000 PAWS IDENTIFY THE BUS CONNECTIONS—OR LINKS—SERVED BY LYNX/CENTRAL FLORIDA REGIONAL TRANSPORTATION AUTHORITY.

LYNX name and logo were prowling the streets. Drivers' uniforms were changed from "Ralph Kramden" dark blue to customer-friendly golf shirts and khaki slacks. Current bus drivers were schooled in how to deal with passengers as customers, and new drivers were carefully screened for customer-service skills.

By almost any measure, the campaign was a success. Ridership began to increase, and even non-riding customers called the agency to thank them for the new stops and to comment on the sudden increase in fleet size. However, few of the stops or buses were actually new; many people simply had never noticed them before. To many transit professionals, this was a coup. To marketers, it was classic retailing: an improved product should get improved packaging.

CHANGES MORE THAN SKIN DEEP

The LYNX product was improving. Under the leadership of Director of Planning and Development Rob Gregg, links were added or improved as quickly as funding allowed. Recalls Gregg, "We wanted to make our system more convenient—going more places more often—if we wanted to truly serve the public." But how? The LYNX fleet had only one-fifth as many buses used by comparable markets, and some were nearly 20 years old.

More efficient routing was implemented, and preventive maintenance was emphasized. The Inspection Purrfection program reduced breakdowns, allowing the few LYNX buses to provide more service hours. Skoutelas, a seasoned public spokesperson, used his lobbying skills to help secure funding for new buses. By 1997, the fleet had grown to nearly 250, and there was talk of a 500-bus fleet by the year 2000. Ridership had doubled and planning for a rail system was under way.

A REPUTATION FOR INNOVATION

The magnitude of change engineered by LYNX was not inexpensive, and yet, it was implemented on a bare minimum of cash outlay, thanks to the authority's willingness to do things in new ways, such as the LYNX advertising sales program. Essentially, LYNX leases the space on both sides of its buses at rates competitive with local billboards. Cooper, who organized the program, took advantage of the unique Central Florida advertising market to arrive at the rates. "We have two surfaces as big as billboards on every bus that can go anywhere an advertiser needs, and can even be in areas where billboards are restricted," she says. Today, advertising sales generate approximately $3 million in annual cash and trade revenues that go back into the funds used to operate the system. As Cooper points out, "That's $3 million the public does not have to provide."

The LYNX reputation for innovation—based on everything from its rainbow fleet and advertising profits to the LYNX Jazz Festival and litter of feline mascots—has earned the authority numerous awards in the industry and a better than 95 percent favorability rating among area residents.

LYNX employees are proud of their accomplishments, and Executive Director Leo Auger says he expects the awards to continue: "We don't plan to rest on our laurels. We're going to stay innovative, keep setting records, and help make life in Central Florida the best it can be with convenient, affordable, reliable public transportation."

CLOCKWISE FROM TOP LEFT: LYNX IS A COLORFUL PART OF CENTRAL FLORIDA.

THIS EXCITING AFRICAN ARTiculated BUS IS ONE OF LYNX'S MOST POPULAR DESIGNS.

THIS WALGREEN'S BUS IS JUST ONE EXAMPLE OF LYNX'S NATIONALLY RECOGNIZED ADVERTISING BUSES.

WITH A SHARED VISION OF UNCOMPROMISING EXCELLENCE IN orthopaedic care, Drs. J. Darrell Shea and Robert C. Mumby established the Orlando Orthopaedic Center (OOC) in 1972 to better serve the community. Today, OOC has grown to include more than 12 orthopaedic physicians in four Central Florida locations, which continue the founders' tradition of medical excellence in serving

hundreds of patients in the tri-county area. In 1997, OOC celebrated its 25th anniversary of excellent service in the Orlando area.

Dedicated to meeting the complex medical needs of a fast-growing community, the center remains committed to earning the trust and respect of patients, other professionals, and the community. Its goal is to exceed expectations; ensure a creative, challenging, and compassionate professional environment; and strive for continuous improvement at all levels.

PUTTING EXPERIENCE TO WORK

Experienced, personalized care for all patients—from children to seniors and from amateur sports enthusiasts to professional athletes—has always been the goal of the Orlando Orthopaedic Center. OOC provides a solid range of orthopaedic medical services, with a team of specialists that include spine, total joint replacement, oncology, hand, sports medicine, foot and ankle, pediatrics, podiatry, and other dedicated professionals.

OOC physicians go beyond standard practices to ensure patient care. Among them, cofounder Shea, whose experience includes serving as head of Orlando's Lucerne Spinal Center and president of the Orange County Medical Society, adheres to the philosophy that conservative treatment and patient education ensure quality relationships with patients and referring physicians.

Dr. G. Grady McBride, president of OOC, is Central Florida's leading instructor of arthroscopic spinal surgery, a procedure that provides a quick recovery time, thereby allowing the patient to get back to a regular schedule. McBride's lectures and teaching procedures have been televised, allowing physicians and patients nationwide to benefit from his expertise.

Fellow OOC physician Jeffrey P. Rosen, M.D., is one of the area's leading experts on sports medicine and total joint replacement. Rosen's brand of community education has established one of the strongest doctor-patient relationship programs in Central Florida.

As Central Florida's only leading orthopaedic oncologist, Dr. Craig P. Jones has developed a program designed to help patients through the physical treatment and emotional challenges of cancer. Through unique one-on-one education, Jones treats the hearts and minds of patients throughout Central Florida.

Modern technology can take a physical toll on many people—from homemakers and students to data processors and other professionals. Lawrence S. Halperin, M.D., works to educate patients on the most appropriate treatment for hand and wrist injuries. Halperin works closely with employers and employees alike to get employees back to work quickly and safely.

Neck and back pain is one of the most critical areas in orthopaedics, and spine specialist Dr. Stephen R. Goll is one of the most proactive surgeons in Central Florida. With a focus on prevention, he often tours area work sites to assist in educating employers as to how to teach proper lifting techniques. Goll was recently named Department Chair of Orthopaedics at Florida Hospital and has been invited to speak to surgeons across the nation about the spine.

Professional sports are on the move in Central Florida. Dr. Samuel Blick is an orthopaedic sports medicine physician—fellowship trained in the area of sports medicine, with an emphasis in knee ligament injuries. Blick was recently named one of the team physicians for the Orlando Sun Dogs, and he also volunteers at local sports events and at the Florida Hospital Family Practice residency program.

Orlando Orthopaedic Center also boasts such leading physicians as Dr. David D. Dore, who works to educate women on the prevention and treatment of osteoporosis, also known as the "silent disease." Dore is fellowship trained in total joint replacement and is chief of

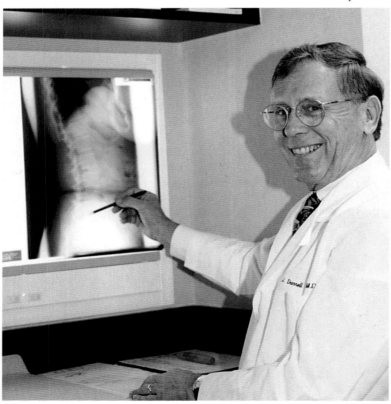

J. DARRELL SHEA, M.D., COFOUNDER OF ORLANDO ORTHOPAEDIC CENTER

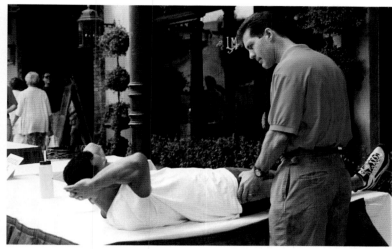

orthopaedics for Columbia Park Medical Center.

OOC physicians believe that the physical demands of intense training need specific attention in order to avoid serious injuries. For Olympic hopefuls and performing artists, Dr. Robert C. Palumbo has fellowship training in sports medicine of the knee and shoulder, and also adult foot and ankle injuries. As well as volunteering his medical expertise to budding gymnasts, professional dancers, and other athletes, Palumbo is the medical director of the Orlando Regional HealthCare System Performing Arts Rehabilitation Center and a reviewer for the *American Journal of Sports Medicine.*

Orlando Orthopaedic Center also offers an orthopaedic pediatric surgeon, Tamara A. Topoleski, M.D. She is committed to an open line of communication with parents who want the best treatment advice for their children's handicaps or injuries.

General maintenance to the foot is important to everyone, and Joseph D. Funk, D.P.M., specializes in both medical and surgical podiatry. Funk educates community athletes and seniors on many aspects of the foot and proper care for injury prevention.

As a native to the Orlando area, Samuel E. Murrell, M.D., a graduate of Harvard and Vanderbilt universities, serves OOC as an additional spine surgeon. Murrell works with the community he knows

well to focus on prevention and education.

Hand injuries are a common problem to the Central Florida area. OOC's Alan W. Christensen, M.D., is an expert in reconstructive hand surgery and microsurgery, allowing complete treatment of the injured hand.

DOWN TO BUSINESS
While medical experience is first and foremost in the mind of patients seeking medical care, a medical facility with experienced business management establishes a solid foundation from which patients receive cost-effective and time-efficient services. From maintaining and updating medical records to customer service and quality of care, the operation of this leading medical practice involves commitment at all levels.

The Orlando Orthopaedic Center prides itself on its internal management philosophy, corporate goals, corporate responsibility, and corporate culture. OOC encourages staff participation in problem solving and involves staff in the development of corporate goals that are never without patient care in mind.

COMMUNITY CARE BEYOND OFFICE DOORS
Individually and as a group, the strength of the Orlando Orthopaedic Center comes from its long-standing commitment to community services, both within the practice and beyond

its office doors. From charitable donations to hands-on involvement, OOC's ongoing community citizenship can be seen throughout Central Florida. The center supports such local organizations as the Arthritis Foundation, Children's Wish Foundation, Jewish Community Center, American Cancer Society, Orlando Area Sports Commission, Florida Medical Association, Orange County Medical Society, Orange County Public Schools, Greater Orlando Chamber of Commerce, Seminole Chamber of Commerce, and many more.

From special events to guest speaker programs, fund-raisers, awareness support programs, and other service efforts, the Orlando Orthopaedic Center notes that rewards, both personal and professional, come directly from the Central Florida people and the community OOC serves.

CLOCKWISE FROM TOP LEFT: DR. SAMUEL BLICK TALKS TO AN OLYMPIC BOBSLED RACER ABOUT A HIP FLEXOR INJURY.

ROBERT C. PALUMBO, M.D., WORKS WITH A RUNNER, EXPLAINING PROPER FOOTWEAR FOR RUNNING.

DAVID D. DOVE, M.D., REVIEWS A BONE DENSITY EXAM WITH A PATIENT.

I N THE EARLY 1960s, FOUR FRATERNITY BROTHERS DREAMED OF BUILDING an underwater restaurant in Mission Bay, California. It was a notion that could not work, but it sparked an idea for something even better. By 1964, Sea World marine life park was a California dream turned into reality, and by 1970, a second park was opened in Cleveland, Ohio. The Sea World company then began to look at Florida for the site of what would become its largest and most sophisticated park to date.

Sea World of Florida was developed from a 125-acre tract of over-run underbrush, dense palmettos, and scrub pines. By its opening day on December 15, 1973, Sea World of Florida featured one of the most extensive marine life collections in the world. For the first time in a theme park setting, visitors were given an up close look at killer whales, stingrays, seals, sea lions, and hundreds of species of fish and birds.

The Sea World concept became a powerful lure to millions of people each year. In its first year of operation, Sea World of Florida's attendance reached more than 1.6 million visitors. Today, Sea World of Florida is the world's most popular marine life park, with more than 4.5 million guests annually.

GROWING OPPORTUNITIES

Constant growth has been a key success factor for Sea World of Florida. For more than 20 years, the park has provided visitors with new and innovative shows and attractions.

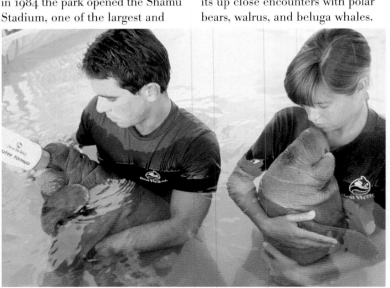

Sea World of Florida has invested millions of dollars in expansion projects that include new stadiums, theaters, several animal feeding pools, habitats, gift shops, and restaurants. In 1974, the park's signature landmark, the 400-foot Sky Tower observation ride, was built to give guests a bird's-eye view of the park and the surrounding city. In 1976, the Atlantis Theater water ski stadium was opened, becoming home to the world-famous Sea World water-skiers. In 1983, the Nautilus Theater debuted, and in 1984 the park opened the Shamu Stadium, one of the largest and finest marine mammal breeding facilities in the world.

Sea World of Florida's largest growth came in the early to mid-1990s. During that time, the park added two new restaurants, a three-acre children's playground, and more than five new shows and attractions, including Terrors of the Deep in 1991, the world's largest collection of dangerous sea predators. In 1995, the park opened its most ambitious project, the Wild Arctic. The award-winning attraction remains one of the park's most popular features, with its up close encounters with polar bears, walrus, and beluga whales.

CLOCKWISE FROM TOP:
SHAMU AND HIS FRIENDS DIVE INTO ACTION DURING *Shamu: World Focus*, A THRILLING KILLER WHALE SHOW COMBINING LIVE ACTION AND STUNNING VIDEO IMAGERY.

SEA WORLD OF FLORIDA'S ANIMAL CARE TEAM NURSES TWO ORPHANED MANATEES IN THE PARK'S STATE-OF-THE-ART RESCUE AND REHABILITATION FACILITIES. THE TEAM RESCUES HUNDREDS OF SEA ANIMALS EACH YEAR.

THROUGH THE MAGIC OF AN IMMENSE SEMICIRCULAR UNDERWATER VIEWING PANORAMA IN DOLPHIN COVE—A HUGE 2.1-ACRE NATURALISTIC LAGOON IN KEY WEST AT SEA WORLD—VISITORS ARE IMMERSED IN THE UNDERWATER WORLD OF THE BOTTLENOSE DOLPHIN.

In 1996, Orlando's Sea World opened a five-acre themed area called Key West at Sea World. The park has plans for several new attractions and park entertainment projects to be introduced to the public, including the upcoming debut of Journey to Atlantis, the largest attraction expansion in the park's history.

Corporately, Sea World has undergone several important changes since its inception. The company opened its parks as a private partnership, but in 1976, its rapid growth caught the attention of publishing giant Harcourt Brace Jovanovich, Inc., which purchased its stock. In 1989, its stock was purchased by Busch Entertainment Corporation, the family entertainment subsidiary of Anheuser-Busch Corporation. Today, Orlando's Sea World is among the family of Anheuser-Busch theme parks that include Sea World parks in San Diego, San Antonio, and Cleveland; Busch Gardens and Adventure Island in Tampa Bay and Williamsburg; Water Country USA in Williamsburg; and Sesame Place in Longhome, Pennsylvania.

Nationwide, Anheuser-Busch Theme Parks employ more than 15,000 people. Sea World of Florida has grown in its role as an Orlando economic development leader, and is recognized for its senior citizen employment opportunities and the many jobs it makes available to area students.

More Than a Theme Park

While entertainment is Sea World's most visible side, it is only half of the park's true mission: "To provide world-class entertainment experiences while expanding global leadership in environmental education, conservation, and research." With the park's unique location and climate, Central Florida provides the ideal conditions for Sea World of Florida's Beached Animal Rescue and Rehabilitation Program. Since 1973, animal care specialists within the program have responded to hundreds of calls to aid sick, injured, or orphaned manatees, dolphins, whales, otters, sea turtles, and a variety of birds.

Sea World of Florida continues to bear all costs associated with this program, which shares valuable data with scientists and researchers worldwide. One of the park's own leading researchers, Dr. Daniel K. Odell, was presented with a Point of Light award by President George Bush for his volunteer efforts in the research, rescue, and rehabilitation of stranded and beached marine life along the nation's southeastern coast. Sea World's award-winning staff also includes its growing team of animal care specialists, handlers, trainers, and marine biologists.

Perhaps most important, Sea World of Florida is home to one of the most successful marine life breeding programs in the world. The program resulted in more than 1,000 animal births in 1996, adding to the populations of endangered or threatened birds, mammals, and fish. Its greatest success has been the births of seven killer whales, including the 1985 birth of Baby Shamu (Kalina), the first killer whale to be born and thrive in the care of man.

Education, conservation, and research have been integral parts of Sea World of Florida since its opening more than 20 years ago. These essential components of its mission will continue to guide its growth well into the new millennium.

CLOCKWISE FROM TOP:
SEA WORLD OF FLORIDA'S CELEBRITY POLAR BEAR CUBS, KLONDIKE AND SNOW, TAKE TIME OUT TO RELAX ON A BRIDGE INSIDE THE PARK'S WILD ARCTIC POLAR BEAR HABITAT.

WAITING FOR A WAVE AT SEA WORLD OF FLORIDA'S PACIFIC POINT PRESERVE, FAST-FLIPPERED CALIFORINA SEA LIONS EXPLORE THEIR 2.5-ACRE HOME.

TWO YOUNG GUESTS COME FACE TO FACE WITH AN ATLANTIC BOTTLENOSE DOLPHIN AT SEA WORLD OF FLORIDA'S DOLPHIN COVE.

C HURCH STREET STATION'S JOURNEY INTO ORLANDO ENTERTAINMENT FAME began with a mission: to preserve history while making history. It began with the restoration and renovation of several downtown buildings and abandoned hotels. The complex was gradually built adjacent to the site of the city's first train station, one of only two sites in Orange County registered in the National Register of Historic Places. Historic value and authenticity

TOP: ROSIE O'GRADY'S WORLD-FAMOUS DIXIELAND REVUE FIRST DEBUTED IN 1974.

MIDDLE LEFT: THE AWARD-WINNING CHEYENNE STAMPEDE PERFORMS NIGHTLY IN THE CHEYENNE SALOON & OPERA HOUSE.

MIDDLE RIGHT: THE LATEST ADDITION TO CHURCH STREET STATION IS THE PRESIDENTIAL BALLROOM, ORLANDO'S MOST ELEGANT PRIVATE EVENT FACILITY.

BOTTOM: WITH PHINEAS PHOGG'S DANCE CLUB (ON RIGHT) AND THE HISTORIC BUMBY BUILDING (ON LEFT) CHURCH STREET STATION IS A TOP-NOTCH TOURIST ATTRACTION.

are two factors that continue to set this complex apart from the competition.

In 1974, Rosie O'Grady's Goodtime Emporium was the first leg of the project to be completed, and it became the center's signature showroom. It featured entertainment that was new and exciting to the growing city: strumming banjos, Dixieland jazz, singing waiters, cancan girls, and acts such as the Last of the Red Hot Mamas and the Baron of Bourbon Street. The shows are flamboyant, foot-stomping fun.

In 1976, Apple Annie's Courtyard opened next to Rosie O'Grady's, serving fresh fruit drinks in a gar-

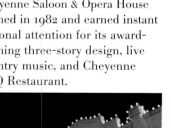

den setting; and in 1977, Lili Marlene's Restaurant opened for fine-dining service. It was the first of three themed restaurants to open at Church Street Station.

Phineas Phogg's Dance Club rounded out the north side of the complex when it opened in 1978. The club is uniquely designed with vintage flying machines and other memorabilia honoring famous balloonists and their historic journeys.

KEEPING THE DREAM ALIVE

Rosie O'Grady's Goodtime Emporium grew to become known as Church Street Station, and its entertainment offerings continued to add diversity to the mix. The Cheyenne Saloon & Opera House opened in 1982 and earned instant national attention for its award-winning three-story design, live country music, and Cheyenne BBQ Restaurant.

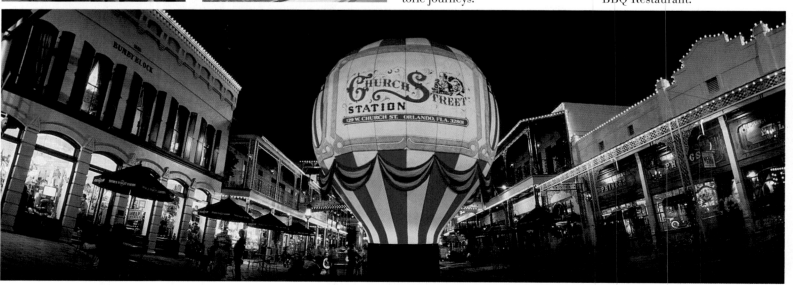

Church Street Station soon stretched more than four city blocks. In 1986, it expanded to include Crackers Seafood Restaurant and an underground wine cellar. The live entertainment venues were completed later that year with the addition of the Orchid Garden Ballroom. The Orchid Garden was designed as a Victorian-style rock 'n' roll palace featuring live music from the 1960s to the 1990s. In 1988, the $20 million Exchange Shopping Emporium, a three-level shopping center featuring more than 50 specialty shops, was added.

Under the leadership of its current president, Bob Windham, Church Street Station continues to thrive. In 1994, Windham unveiled Church Street Station's crown jewel, the Presidential Ballroom. The addition of this grand meeting and banquet facility has brought Church Street Station's total banquet and meeting space to more than 25,000 square feet and growing.

COMMITMENT TO SERVICE

Church Street Station has long been regarded as a place of quality and service. The mission of Church Street Station and its employees is to carry on its proud tradition of good times for the more than 2 million guests that visit each

year. Each restaurant, dance club, or shop at Church Street Station continues to uphold the original salute to historic Orlando through an array of antiques and artifacts from around the world. Church Street Station has been successful in both design and customer service, earning it the title of Orlando's number one nighttime dining, shopping, and entertainment complex.

ABOVE: THE HISTORIC RAILROAD DEPOT IS ON THE NATIONAL REGISTER OF HISTORIC PLACES.

CLOCKWISE FROM TOP LEFT: THE CHEYENNE SALOON & OPERA HOUSE, BUILT IN THE SPIRIT OF THE OLD WEST, WAS COMPLETED IN 1982.

THE RESTAURANTS OF CHURCH STREET STATION OFFER EXCELLENT CUISINE COUPLED WITH ONE-OF-A-KIND ATMOSPHERE.

CHURCH STREET STATION OFFERS GOOD FOOD AND GREAT TIMES AT SUCH ESTABLISHMENTS AS ROSIE O'GRADY'S GOODTIME EMPORIUM (ON LEFT) AND THE CHEYENNE SALOON & OPERA HOUSE (ON RIGHT).

H

OW CAN A HEALTH CARE ORGANIZATION MANAGE ITS INFORMATION systems technology effectively throughout its entire health enterprise? As the top provider in the $15 billion health care informatics industry, HBO & Company (HBOC) has the solution. HBOC is a health-based organization that sells, installs, and services a comprehensive range of computer-based information systems for hospitals, managed care organizations, and health care enterprises.

Founded in 1974, HBOC's client base today includes more than half of the nation's 6,000 hospitals, and its products and services are sold internationally through its subsidiaries in Israel, the United Kingdom, and Canada, and through distribution agreements in Australia, Puerto Rico, and New Zealand.

From offices in Central Florida and Atlanta, as well as from sites across America, HBOC and its staff of more than 5,000 employees develop and implement software support networks. HBOC's information systems are widely used for patient care, clinical, financial, and strategic management services at health care enterprises and related businesses worldwide.

HEALTH CARE INFORMATION AUTOMATION

When HBOC founders Walter Huff, Bruce Barrington, and Richard Owens organized their company nearly 25 years ago, few people knew how this team from Peoria, Illinois, could harness the new world of microchips and software innovations. However, the seeds of the company got a healthy start. With a $2 million federal grant in hand, HBOC's founders installed their first shared patient-accounting system in three Illinois hospitals. Their services were quickly picked up by 30 other area hospitals in need of information automation.

This new form of hospital communications through shared patient-accounting systems was spreading. In 1970, the system was sold to St. Louis-based McDonnell-Douglas, an aerospace company that incorporated the system into its own automation company. Under HBOC leadership, the system's customer base increased by more than 145 hospitals. As each year passed, more hospitals and related health care businesses discovered HBOC's new high-tech informatics system.

The company grew quickly, with a growth spurt in the mid-1980s and again in the mid-1990s, triggered by the firm's acquisition of two industry-leading mainframe companies: Mediflex Systems, a firm that brought IBM mainframe technology to HBOC, and Amherst Associates, a Massachusetts-based firm with an innovative product support line known as TRENDSTAR.

In 1991, under the new leadership of former CompuServe executive Charles W. McCall, HBOC repositioned itself with additional corporate acquisitions, including the Longwood, Florida-based IBAX, a company specializing in mainframe and minicomputer information systems.

The acquisitions of the 1980s and early 1990s expanded the firm's depth of product offerings and extended its reach into new markets such as physicians' offices, reference laboratories, home care, and international health care systems. Hospitals wanted the new customization and speed offered by microcomputers, which now enabled them to develop in-house information systems.

HBOC PROVIDES SOFTWARE SOLUTIONS AND SERVICES TO HEALTH CARE ORGANIZATIONS THROUGHOUT THE WORLD.

INNOVATIONS IN PRODUCTS AND SERVICES

HBO & Company is committed to ongoing research and development to discover new ways to improve health care information communications. The company's products and services are based on a strategic mix of applications and technologies that support today's restructuring of health care markets. The HBOC portfolio of products is organized into three areas: Infrastructure, Enterprise Management, and Improved Clinical Practice.

The firm's Infrastructure Program is similar to that of a cityscape: Each health care unit adds to the strength of the entire system. The program is designed to provide key elements for integrating providers across the continuum of patient care. By bringing various health care systems together through computer technologies, HBOC works to provide management solutions and establish lifelong patient records.

Through its Pathways 2000® family of client/server applications, HBOC provides clients with the ability to collect, manage, and disseminate clinical information organized on the basis of a patient's entire medical history. In addition, Pathways 2000 provides access to patient data from any point within the computerized information delivery system.

HBOC's Enterprise Management Program includes Pathways Managed Care, Pathways Contract Management, and the QUANTUM Enterprise Information Systems. These units provide the critical business functions necessary to manage today's new and emerging health networks.

HBO & Company offers hospital information systems such as STAR and SERIES 2000. Its TRENDSTAR software assists in the area of decision support, while its Pathways Care Manager and Pathways Coordinated Care help to streamline treatment and evalu-

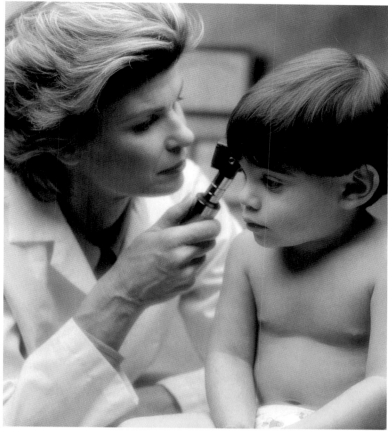

ate the health status of patients through long-term care services.

HBOC's outsourcing teams encompass strategic management services and assist clients in the areas of systems planning, receivables management, business office administration, major systems conversions, and computing services. The firm has been in the outsourcing business for more than 20 years in the United States and has recently begun offering its services in the United Kingdom.

A HEALTHY MISSION

HBO & Company is committed to designing strategies that fit clients' growth, providing health care businesses with access to technology, highly skilled employees, and improved information technology for creative health care computing solutions.

Throughout its history, HBOC has sought to improve and expand its product portfolio through internal development, the acquisition of complementary products, and

partnerships with other leading high-tech vendors. By adhering to its build, buy, and partner strategy, HBOC is well positioned to maintain its leadership in the health care information systems industry today, tomorrow, and well into the future. Its mission is to remain synonymous with quality software products and related services, outstanding customer support, innovative thinking, and successful information technology solutions.

HBOC IS THE INDUSTRY LEADER IN GIVING ORGANIZATIONS THE ABILITY TO MANAGE HEALTH CARE COST AND IMPROVE THE QUALITY OF DELIVERING PATIENT CARE.

POST, BUCKLEY, SCHUH & JERNIGAN, INC.

FROM INTERSTATE TOLLED EXPRESSWAYS TO WETLAND TREATMENT systems, and from master infrastructure systems for mixed-use developments to parks on closed landfills, the works of Post, Buckley, Schuh & Jernigan, Inc. (PBS&J) touch the lives of virtually all Central Florida residents. Over the course of its nearly 40-year history, PBS&J has evolved into one of the nation's largest engineering consulting firms, offering high-quality services worldwide in the areas of civil engineering, transportation planning and design, environmental engineering and sciences, land use planning, landscape architecture, architecture, program management, and construction management, as well as leading-edge analytical laboratory and surveying capabilities.

Today, PBS&J is the largest engineering consulting firm based in the state of Florida and is consistently ranked among the top 10 percent of design firms in the nation. The firm's steady growth and success are attributed to close attention to client service, the technical excellence of its staff, and their ability to provide innovative solutions to challenging projects.

PBS&J began its partnership with the Orlando area in the 1970s, when the firm first established an office in the city. The region was facing explosive population growth and needed an improved infrastructure to accommodate that growth. As general engineering consultant to the Orlando-Orange County Expressway Authority since 1979 and Florida's Turnpike since 1989, PBS&J has assisted in the expansion and modernization of the area's tolled expressway system, including development and implementation of the Expressway Authority's E-PASS electronic toll collection system.

Beginning in the early 1980s and continuing today, PBS&J has provided consulting services to the City of Orlando's Iron Bridge Water Pollution Control Facility, a facility vital to accommodating the rapid growth of Orlando's northeastern communities. Among these services has been the design and construction of the 24 million-gallons-per-day (mgd), state-of-the-art, biological nutrient removal portion of the plant and the Orlando Easterly Wetlands Reclamation Project, an award-winning, man-made wetland able to treat up to 20 mgd of reclaimed water from the Iron Bridge plant before sending it to the St. Johns River system. After more than a decade of operation, this successful system continues to serve as a model of wetland treatment systems technology for the world.

PBS&J also delivers much of what public and private developers need to realize their projects. From civil engineering and regulatory permitting to land use planning and landscape architecture, PBS&J has assisted in some of the area's most prominent office and residential developments. Highlighting these is Walt Disney Imagineering's new town of Celebration, for which PBS&J has continuously provided services since the project's preliminary design stage.

With an annual local payroll in excess of $13 million, PBS&J is a significant economic force in the community. More than 300 PBS&J employees now live and work in the Orlando area, and they are proud of their roles in building the quality of life unique to Central Florida. Combining an unparalleled depth of local resources and local experience with broad-based, internationally recognized expertise, PBS&J continues to be Central Florida's source for engineering excellence.

PBS&J ASSISTED IN THE DEVELOPMENT OF WALT DISNEY IMAGINEERING'S TOWN OF CELEBRATION, FOR WHICH PBS&J HAS CONTINUOUSLY PROVIDED SERVICES SINCE THE PROJECT'S PRELIMINARY DESIGN STAGE (LEFT).

THE FIRM'S SUCCESS CAN BE ATTRIBUTED IN PART TO THE TECHNICAL EXCELLENCE OF ITS STAFF AND THEIR ABILITY TO PROVIDE INNOVATIVE SOLUTIONS TO CHALLENGING PROJECTS (RIGHT).

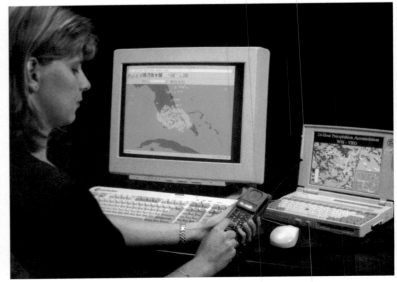

W ITH AS MANY AS 43 MILLION VISITORS TO THE STATE OF FLORIDA each year, the Greater Orlando Aviation Authority (GOAA) is internationally renowned as a leader in world travel. For more than 20 years, GOAA has administered all aviation activities of the City of Orlando, including an airport system that serves commercial, charter, and cargo flights through the Orlando International Airport and Orlando Executive Airport. As the aviation industry is changing to respond to advances in air traffic technology and travel industry reform, so too is this organization of more than 600 full-time employees that is governed by a seven-member board.

SUPERLATIVE CUSTOMER SERVICE

The airport reflects Central Florida's character inside and out, from the ground and from the air. The modern, high-tech terminal has a unique architectural style. Constructed of cement and stone, the linear structure seems to grow out of the lush, tropical landscape. The terminal occupies 450 acres of carefully preserved natural land, dotted with lakes and islands. Passengers immediately feel a relationship with the beauty of the natural Florida environment. Its advanced planning and architectural approaches make Orlando International Airport the first environmentally responsive airport in the world, with the flexibility and expansion potential to serve into the 21st century.

Orlando International Airport is an award-winning facility in the area of customer service, placing its focus on the unique needs of the origination and destination of the passenger. Efforts were made to minimize passenger walking and maximize convenience by providing the land-side terminal's three floors, which were designed for efficient traffic flow.

The Airport occupies approximately 15,000 acres and is located eight miles from downtown Orlando. The Airport includes about 1,400 acres that are being developed for commercial and industrial activities related to aviation.

The Airport is the 16th-largest airport in the United States and the 25th-largest airport in the world. In 1996, Orlando International Airport was ranked as the fastest-growing major airport in the world by Airports Council International, and served 25,587,773 travelers, of which more than 2.5 million were international passengers.

GATEWAY FOR GLOBAL COMMERCE

GOAA's mission is "To advance Orlando and Central Florida as the premier intermodal gateway for global commerce." To accomplish its mission, GOAA has established partnerships with local, state, and federal agencies, and works closely with its business partners—such as airlines and concessions—to continue its success as an industry leader.

With 97 airlines—41 scheduled, 41 charter, and 15 cargo—Orlando International Airport provides more scheduled service to domestic des-tinations than any other airport in Florida, and service to more than 100 cities worldwide. Through facility expansion and service innovations, GOAA continues to promote Orlando and its airports as key international and domestic centers of commerce, and to maintain Orlando as the world's top travel destination.

AN AERIAL VIEW REVEALS THE ORLANDO INTERNATIONAL AIRPORT'S TERMINAL COMPLEX (TOP).

THIS ATRIUM AREA NEAR THE HYATT REGENCY ORLANDO INTERNATIONAL AIRPORT IS LOCATED ON TOP OF THE AIRPORT'S MAIN TERMINAL BUILDING (BOTTOM).

HEN JOE ALBERTSON OPENED HIS FIRST GROCERY STORE IN 1939 in Boise, Idaho, he changed the rules in the grocery business. Introducing innovative services such as a scratch bakery, magazine racks, homemade ice cream, popcorn, nuts, and an automatic donut machine, Albertson based his store on high quality, good value, and excellent service. ✳ Built on a philosophy of "giving customers the merchandise they want at a price they can afford, in clean stores with great service from friendly personnel," Albertson's is now the fourth largest among retail food-and-drug chains in the United States.

NATIONAL CHAIN, NEIGHBORLY ATMOSPHERE

Joe Albertson's original philosophy set the stage for success at Albertson's Inc. In those early days, food stores were typically small and offered limited food choices. Albertson had a vision of a market that would offer customers convenience and lower prices while still generating profits for the company. In the words of Warren E. McCain, former CEO of Albertson's Inc., "Once in a while a person comes along who has the vision to revolutionize an entire industry. Joe Albertson was such a man."

Today, Albertson's Inc., which remains headquartered in its founding city of Boise, operates more than 846 stores in 20 western, midwestern, and southeastern states. The company's Best Supermarket in Your Neighborhood and Albertson's: It's Your Store campaigns have made it one of the country's most popular supermarket chains. In 1993, sales reached more than $10 billion; by February 1, 1996, the company's 27th consecutive year of increased sales and earnings, sales had reached nearly $14 billion. Its stock is currently traded on the New York and Pacific stock exchanges under the symbol ABS.

All Albertson's stores are supplied by the company's 11 distribution centers located in Plant City,

Florida; Boise, Idaho; Salt Lake City, Utah; Portland, Oregon; Houston and Fort Worth, Texas; Denver, Colorado; Sacramento and Brea, California; Ponca City, Oklahoma; and Tolleson, Arizona. Its Florida division office is headquartered in Orlando.

Convenient local access has been a key to the company's growing market share. By pursuing its goal of being the performance leader, Albertson's continues to earn increasing customer loyalty and industry recognition. The company's Neighborhood Marketing system provides demographic information on each store, enabling it to design the best product selection and display space for each store. Albertson's uses telephone surveys, focus groups, one-on-one interviews, and customer comment cards to stay in touch with its shoppers.

Such customer service programs have not gone unrecognized by national watchdogs. In 1996, *Fortune* ranked Albertson's Inc. number one in the food-and-drug industry for the third consecutive year on its America's Most Admired Companies list.

GROWTH AND INNOVATION

While the original Albertson's philosophy has remained constant during its nearly six decades in business, the company has changed to meet the diverse needs of its customers. In order to facilitate one-stop shopping, Albertson's stores average more than 48,000 square feet of shopping space and include a wide selection of perishable, grocery, and general merchandise. Its stores offer prescription drugs and an expanded section of cosmetics and nonfood items, as well as specialty departments featuring video rentals and floral services.

During 1995, Albertson's partnered with local banks to open 82 in-store bank branches and more than 560 automated teller machines for customer safety and convenience. Currently, Albertson's operates more than 340 in-store banks. The company also created a new front end manager position to increase customer service and convenience at the checkout.

In an effort to better serve its customers, Albertson's has instituted a new employee training program. All entry-level employees must complete part of their initial orientation on multimedia computers. The training by computers is said to improve employees' thoroughness, consistency, and retention.

Albertson's also works to "grow its own leadership" by developing managers from within the company, and by offering career advancement and training opportunities for all employees. The company also works with schools, government agencies, and other organizations to help hire and train disabled employees. Albertson's is an equal opportunity employer.

COMMUNITY DRIVEN

Each year, thousands of Albertson's employees make a difference in the lives of others by volunteering for countless community projects. Albertson's recognizes an employee from each of its divisions nationwide for his or her outstanding

community work by presenting each person with its Warren E. McCain Community Volunteer Award. The company donates $500 in each honoree's name to a charity of his or her choice.

Many Albertson's employees sign up for payroll deductions to assist charities under the United Way umbrella. More than 32,000 employees participated in 1996, raising more than $1.3 million for hundreds of community service organizations.

Each Albertson's store is given the discretion to make in-kind donations to community efforts. These types of donations help groups such as youth athletic leagues, parent-teacher organizations, and community service groups. In 1995, some $2.5 million in cash and in-kind corporate donations was given to more than 2,100 charitable nonprofit organizations, as well as education, arts, and senior citizen programs.

When disaster strikes the communities Albertson's serves, the company helps with donations of food, fresh water, and basic necessities. The company has also been an active supporter of the environment and has been recognized by

the Environmental Protection Agency for its energy conservation and efficient lighting programs, as well as for its recycling and food safety programs. In locations where counties have enacted air pollution control programs, Albertson's offers incentives to encourage employees to carpool or use alternative modes of transportation. Customers are offered a five-cent discount for each grocery bag they bring from home and reuse during store visits.

For more than two decades of operation, Albertson's Inc. has provided Orlando with fresh foods, convenient locations, and excellent customer service.

FOR MORE THAN TWO DECADES OF OPERATION, ALBERTSON'S HAS PROVIDED ORLANDO WITH FRESH FOODS, CONVENIENT LOCATIONS, AND EXCELLENT CUSTOMER SERVICE (TOP).

BY PURSUING ITS GOAL OF BEING THE PERFORMANCE LEADER, ALBERTSON'S CONTINUES TO EARN INCREASING CUSTOMER LOYALTY AND INDUSTRY RECOGNITION. THE COMPANY IS NOW THE FOURTH LARGEST AMONG RETAIL FOOD-AND-DRUG CHAINS IN THE UNITED STATES (BOTTOM).

WLOQ

WLOQ HAS BEEN PRAISED BY MANY AS ONE OF THE BEST JAZZ AND adult contemporary radio stations in the nation. It's not just any jazz that is placed over these airwaves—it's Smooth Jazz. But there is more to this Central Florida institution than top-rated sounds. There is also a story of a family business in one of the country's fastest-growing towns, Orlando, and in one of the most competitive industries: radio. WLOQ is the birthplace of the Smooth Jazz format now heard in numerous markets throughout the country. The story on how a local family created a format now heard in most cities is one of dedication to an ideal.

Since WLOQ began programming jazz in 1977, every effort was dedicated to improving the musical quality of life and the radio environment of the Greater Orlando area. The WLOQ mission became one of dedication not just to jazz, but to its community overall: Grow a radio station of people committed to a vision of radio at its best with programming that demonstrates integrity, passion, and support for the community.

First Family of Music

Everything the station does can be traced back to the guiding principles of its first family of music, Herbert P. and Margaret Gross, a husband-and-wife team who believe strongly in the station's responsibility its to listeners. WLOQ 103.1 is widely known for supporting Orlando's most popular community events.

The station's commitment to community involvement includes providing the area's most complete agenda of free concerts. During the past 10 years, WLOQ has helped support and present the Winter Park Sidewalk Art Festival's widely regarded concert program, which is among the most successful in the nation. Each year thousands enjoy free concerts from artists like Ramsey Lewis, The Rippingtons, Richard Elliot, Larry Carlton, Warren Hill, Grover Washington Jr., and others. Jazz legends and rising stars alike have made the Winter Park Sidewalk Art Festival's concerts an Orlando tradition. The staff and management of WLOQ have helped to make this tradition one of Orlando's finest outdoor events. In addition, WLOQ consistently donates time and services to area charities and service projects, including the Metropolitan Orlando Urban League scholarship program, the United Way, and others.

As a business, the company has grown into a communications

CELEBRATING 20 YEARS AS THE BIRTHPLACE OF SMOOTH JAZZ, WLOQ'S MAY 31, 1997, BIRTHDAY PARTY FEATURED A WORLD-CLASS JAM AT WALT DISNEY WORLD'S ATLANTIC DANCE. ATTENDEES INCLUDED NESTER TORRES, DAVID BENOIT, LARRY CARLTON, JOHN TESH, RICKY PETERSON, KIRK WHALUM, JEFF KASHUWA, MICHAEL PAULO, RUSS FREEMAN, CHARLIE BISHARAT, BOB JAMES, AND GEORGE DUKE.

leader. Today, the Gross Communications Corporation owns and operates WLOQ under the vision of owners Herbert and Margaret Gross. Sons John and Jim have taken the reins as WLOQ's general manager and general sales manager, respectively.

The family's award-winning style earned the station two of the industry's top rankings: the Gavin Award for Station of the Year and Steve Huntington's Program Director of the Year, both for 1995. In 1996, WLOQ was named by industry leaders as the number one Smooth Jazz radio station in America. And, in 1997, the station was nominated for the prestigious Marconi Award as Jazz Station of the Year, presented by the National Association of Broadcasters.

PURE MUSIC PIONEERS

The center of WLOQ's commitment to the community has always been its innovative, consistent, and customer-oriented delivery of quality jazz programming. The station was the first radio station in the country to program the format the radio industry now calls Smooth Jazz or New Adult Contemporary. The original scope of the company began with some of Orlando's most prominent announcers, including Russ Wheeler, Joe Francis, Bob Church, and Don Kirby, all trade-

mark voices and icons of WLOQ for more than 20 years. A whole generation of Orlando residents has grown up with the voices of WLOQ.

The station prides itself on calling Orlando its home. Says John Gross, "We are very much a part of Orlando's history. We began this format in Orlando when it was a much smaller town. WLOQ and Orlando have grown together. I have always been proud to be a part of this truly great city."

A NEW BEAT

In November 1995, WLOQ launched *Pure Music* magazine, which features a mix of arts and entertainment news, thus joining a new trend of radio station publications. Within its first several years in circulation, the artist interviews, music reviews, and lifestyle information of *Pure Music* magazine earned it more than 50,000 subscribers. It is currently one of the most widely circulated publications in Orlando.

WLOQ has expanded its magazine format and developed new communications outlets to reach its listeners. For example, the station now can be reached via the Internet. Its parent company, Gross Communications, is working to expand its popular products and services for listeners and for its local advertisers. "We view every contact with the advertiser as an

opportunity to help reach their business goals," says General Station Manager Jim Gross. "Only through their success can we continue to serve our listeners with the best possible jazz."

WLOQ's loyal listener numbers continue to climb the charts. The station's cross section of consumers is ideal and mirrors Orlando with white-collar professionals, Hispanics, African-Americans, and baby boomers.

"Orlando is our home," Gross explains. "We're fortunate enough to have the opportunity to be in business in one of the country's best markets." Through quality broadcasting, consistent programming, and customer-oriented services that matter to Central Florida, WLOQ enjoys an unmatched standing in its community and its industry, and is looking forward to a great future.

CLOCKWISE FROM TOP LEFT: RAMSEY LEWIS ENTERTAINS WLOQ LISTENERS AT LAKE NONA FOR ONE OF THE STATION'S LISTENER APPRECIATION CONCERTS.

THIRTEEN YEARS OF FREE JAZZ JAMS CONCERTS HAVE PACKED CENTRAL PARK IN WINTER PARK EACH SUMMER SEASON FROM MAY THROUGH OCTOBER.

HERB AND MARGARET GROSS ARE THE FOUNDERS OF WLOQ.

◆ EVERETT & SOULÉ

1978-1997

1979   BAKER & HOSTETLER LLP, COUNSELLORS AT LAW

1980   DEAN, MEAD, EGERTON, BLOODWORTH, CAPOUANO & BOZARTH, P.A.

1982   FISERV CBS WORLDWIDE

1982   FMC AIRPORT PRODUCTS AND SYSTEMS DIVISION

1983   CBIS

1983   YESAWICH, PEPPERDINE & BROWN

1984   CHRISTINI'S RISTORANTE ITALIANO

1984   FISHER, RUSHMER, WERRENRATH, WACK & DICKSON, P.A.

1984   HARCOURT BRACE & COMPANY

1984   ORLANDO/ORANGE COUNTY CONVENTION & VISITORS BUREAU, INC.

1986   FORUM ARCHITECTURE & INTERIOR DESIGN, INC.

1986   THE PEABODY ORLANDO

1989   FLORIDA EXTRUDERS INTERNATIONAL, INC.

1989   GREAT WESTERN FINANCIAL CORPORATION/GREAT WESTERN BANK

1989   RECOTON CORPORATION

1990   HARD ROCK CAFE

1990   UNIVERSAL STUDIOS FLORIDA

1991   CAMPUS CRUSADE FOR CHRIST INTERNATIONAL

1991   EMBASSY SUITES OF ORLANDO

1991   MATRIXX MARKETING INC., SOFTWARE SUPPORT DIVISION

1992   FIDELITY NATIONAL TITLE INSURANCE COMPANY

1992   SIGNATURE FLIGHT SUPPORT

1993   SPLENDID CHINA

BAKER & HOSTETLER LLP, COUNSELLORS AT LAW, WAS FOUNDED IN 1916 in Cleveland, Ohio, by Newton D. Baker, who served as secretary of war in President Woodrow Wilson's cabinet, and his contemporaries, Joseph C. Hostetler and Thomas L. Sidlo. Since its founding more than 80 years ago, Baker & Hostetler has grown into a national law firm with approximately 500 lawyers and with offices in 10 cities: Orlando, Florida;

Cincinnati, Cleveland, and Columbus, Ohio; Denver, Colorado; Houston, Texas; Long Beach, Los Angeles, and Los Gatos, California; and Washington, D.C.

The Orlando office of Baker & Hostetler was formed through a series of mergers with local firms beginning in 1979 and has grown steadily to its present size of 50 lawyers. The Orlando attorneys maintain a full-service civil law practice in order to meet the diverse needs of the firm's clients and their businesses. "Our national scope enables us to provide clients with the full resources of one of the country's leading law firms," says G. Thomas Ball, Orlando office managing partner.

"Access to the people, knowledge, and technology of the entire firm—from Washington, D.C., to Los Angeles—enables our Orlando office to counsel and represent clients in Central Florida and throughout the world," Ball explains. "At the same time, our knowledge of Orlando's and Florida's businesses, industries, and legal issues gives clients the opportunity to work

closely with Baker & Hostetler attorneys who understand their needs."

PRACTICE AREAS

Baker & Hostetler's Orlando business law practice includes general corporate law; national and international transactions involving public and private equity, debt, and mergers and acquisitions; structured finance; consumer finance; reorganizations; and workouts. Baker & Hostetler's business lawyers also offer a full spectrum of legal counseling and experience in the area of public offerings of

equity and debt securities. The firm regularly counsels clients in connection with the federal and state securities laws that regulate public and private companies.

The real estate practice ranges from handling complex land-use projects to meeting the unique needs of Florida's booming resort and leisure industries, as well as negotiating commercial loans and joint venture arrangements, commercial development activities, and industrial development revenue bond financing. Baker & Hostetler's national Hospitality Industry Team,

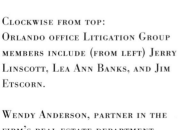

CLOCKWISE FROM TOP:
ORLANDO OFFICE LITIGATION GROUP MEMBERS INCLUDE (FROM LEFT) JERRY LINSCOTT, LEA ANN BANKS, AND JIM ETSCORN.

WENDY ANDERSON, PARTNER IN THE FIRM'S REAL ESTATE DEPARTMENT (SEATED), WITH CLIENT BANCO POPULAR, N.A. (FLORIDA) PRESIDENT MERCEDES MCCALL

ORLANDO OFFICE MANAGING PARTNER G. THOMAS BALL (LEFT) AND PARTNER JOEL H. SHARP JR.

headquartered in Orlando, has been serving the legal needs of the leisure industry worldwide for more than a decade.

The Litigation Group of the Orlando office represents businesses, industries, and individuals in commercial litigation settings. The 20-lawyer Orlando Litigation Group has experience in litigation cases including contract disputes, securities litigation, construction litigation, employment law issues, intellectual property, product liability, health-care-related litigation, and entertainment industry litigation. The group handles cases in both federal and state courts, and represents clients involved in litigation throughout Florida and the Southeast. Its lawyers are experienced in evaluating litigation problems, in assisting the client in deciding the strategic and tactical handling of litigation matters, and in resolving such matters on a businesslike basis or aggressively litigating to protect its clients' interests.

The Tax and Personal Planning Group handles international, federal, state, and local tax matters, and represents corporations, partnerships, individuals, trusts, and estates. In conjunction with Baker & Hostetler's Washington, D.C., office, the Orlando office is able to monitor legislation and provide opportunities for Central Florida's business leaders to make their views on legislative matters known to lawmakers in the nation's capital.

Employment and labor law attorneys in Orlando counsel and represent employers on employment law issues, ranging from contract negotiation through personnel policy and procedure development. The firm represents employers before administrative bodies, and works closely with clients to address their human resources issues.

Many of Central Florida's health care providers have worked with members of Baker & Hostetler's national Health Care Team through the Orlando office. The firm's attorneys have experience in represent-

ing hospitals, insurers, nursing and convalescent facilities, physician practices, and medical equipment ventures. They remain abreast of legislative developments to help health care providers anticipate, prepare for, and respond to changes in the industry.

Business leaders ranging from the hospitality and leisure industries to health care and high technology work with the firm's Orlando attorneys, its industry teams, and its national practice groups to address legal issues beyond practice-area and geographic boundaries.

The firm provides legal counsel and representation in the restaurant and food, cable television and wireless cable, broadcasting and print media, international law, transportation, construction, and insurance defense industries.

CLIENTS

Baker & Hostetler's clients include ▶ public and private companies, financial institutions, individual entrepreneurs, institutions of higher learning, physicians, health care providers, print media, broadcasters, cable and wireless operators, and developers and syndicators involved in all areas of business, commerce, and litigation. The Orlando office has a substantial international clientele, including clients from Latin America, Canada, the Middle East, Great Britain, India, Finland, China, and Japan.

COMMITMENT TO COMMUNITIES

In addition to Baker & Hostetler's commitment to its clients and to the legal profession, the firm is also dedicated to the communities in which its people live and work. In Orlando, the firm's community involvement includes active participation in addition to financial support. Members of the firm serve on the boards of directors for more than 50 community organizations. The Orlando office is proud to play an active role through a scholarship fund and participation in the

Orlando/Orange County COMPACT Program, which helps at-risk students by providing internships and mentoring programs. This is one of the many worthwhile charitable, civic, and cultural organizations Baker & Hostetler supports in the Orlando community. "Our community is expanding by the moment," says Orlando Partner Tico Perez. "Orlando is the city of the future, and we consider it part of our responsibility to help the community grow in the best way possible."

THE FUTURE

The firm is proud to continue the Baker & Hostetler tradition of long-standing relationships with clients and community involvement. In Orlando, Baker & Hostetler is proud to help the City Beautiful continue to thrive and grow throughout the next century.

DANIEL LEVIN PHOTOGRAPHY 1997

DANIEL LEVIN PHOTOGRAPHY 1997

DEAN, MEAD, EGERTON, BLOODWORTH, CAPOUANO & BOZARTH, P.A.

S TEPHEN T. DEAN WAS THE FIRST TAX ATTORNEY IN THE ORLANDO AREA when he arrived in the city in 1961. He joined an existing law practice, charting the early course of what would one day evolve into the law firm of Dean, Mead, Egerton, Bloodworth, Capouano & Bozarth, P.A. The firm's policy of personal and professional services has helped Dean Mead develop a clientele that includes many of Central Florida's leading businesses.

Dean Mead first opened its doors in May 1980, when nine attorneys who had practiced together in the Orlando office of a large state-wide law firm left to form the firm. From its inception, Dean Mead has provided services to its clients in the areas of corporate and business law, tax law, real estate, commercial lending, litigation, creditor and debtor representation, employee benefits, estate planning and administration, health law, securities law, environmental and land use law, agricultural law, legal research, and counseling. The scope of the firm's practice was expanded in the early 1990s to include representation in the area of family law.

From the original nine lawyers who started the firm, Dean Mead

has more than quadrupled in size. Although becoming a large firm has never been a goal of Dean Mead, the firm is committed to growth that will meet the changing needs

of its clients due to the rapid commercial and economic development of Central Florida. Now, as always, outstanding legal representation remains the firm's priority. In a written statement in 1980, founding partner Stephen Dean outlined the qualities that the lawyers at Dean Mead strive to achieve: "The founders of the firm are convinced that a combination of their different skills, plus hard work, will provide an intelligent and strong response to the needs of our clients. We believe that a successful legal result requires careful research, thorough investigation, imaginative analysis, prompt action, and good communication with the client. As we grow in size, these are the attributes we will seek in the selection of new attorneys. They reflect the attitudes that motivate our entire firm."

Dean Mead continues to serve the changing needs among hundreds of area businesses, individuals, and service organizations. To better serve clients statewide, the firm opened offices in Fort Pierce, Merritt Island, and Viera. In 1989, Dean Mead's Orlando office was relocated to Olympia Place, now known as One City Centre, where it occupies the 15th floor and a portion of the 16th floor of the downtown Orlando office center.

SERVICE AND LEADERSHIP ARE PARAMOUNT
While Dean Mead's founders believe that experience within each area of practice is essential, there are no rigid barriers between departments. The firm often uses the team concept, with lawyers who concentrate in different fields working together on a particular

WHILE DEAN MEAD'S FOUNDERS BELIEVE THAT EXPERIENCE WITHIN EACH AREA OF PRACTICE IS ESSENTIAL, THERE ARE NO RIGID BARRIERS BETWEEN DEPARTMENTS.

case. Over the years, the firm has found that many clients appreciate the team concept, but want one lawyer as their responsible attorney. Responding to that need, the firm provides individual attorneys who maintain an overview of a client's entire legal needs, including a concern for future problems caused by legislative changes, court decisions, or new issues arising out of the developments in the client's business or personal situation.

Dean Mead's business clients include some of the area's major banks, several large construction companies, casualty and life insurance companies, a national stock brokerage firm, one of the largest agricultural companies in the world, several of the state's leading trade associations, numerous medical and other professional organizations, individuals, trusts, and estates. Dean Mead also serves companies involved in manufacturing, real estate development, finance, agriculture, energy, communications, assisted living, and consulting.

Dean Mead has one of the largest tax practices in the state of Florida. Its services include tax issues at all levels of trial and appeal. The firm also offers tax planning and advice in general business matters, real estate transactions, and informational issues related to corporations and professional

associations. Dean Mead's tax attorneys regularly serve as lecturers at tax institutes and seminars on the national, state, and local levels.

Firm members serve or have served as adjunct professors at state universities and as members of professional committees and associations, such as the American Bar Association, Florida Bar, Florida Bar Foundations, University of Florida College of Law, American College of Trust and Estate Counsel, American College of Tax Counsel, and Orange County Planning and Zoning Commission. In addition, many of the firm's lawyers serve or have served as community leaders, including service as board members

in civic organizations such as the American Red Cross of Central Florida; Community Foundation of Central Florida, Inc; Jewish Federation of Greater Orlando, Inc.; Tampa-Orlando-Pinellas Jewish Federation, Inc.; Resurrection Housing of Central Florida, Inc.; National Kidney Foundation; and Florida 4-H Foundation, Inc. Its lawyers are also active in the field of continuing legal education, having lectured at numerous institutes and contributed to many legal periodicals.

Dean Mead strives to provide excellent legal service without forgetting the specific needs of its clients and the community.

DEAN MEAD STRIVES TO PROVIDE EXCELLENT LEGAL SERVICE WITHOUT FORGETTING THE SPECIFIC NEEDS OF ITS CLIENTS AND THE COMMUNITY.

Fiserv CBS Worldwide

THE SOFTWARE AND SERVICES OF FISERV CBS WORLDWIDE TOUCH THE lives of consumers and businesses across a wide spectrum—from a small community bank in the Midwest to a large money center bank in the Northeast, and from the remarkable first steps into capitalism by customers in Poland, Russia, and other markets in eastern Europe to the aggressive expansion of large, multinational customers in Europe, Latin America, and Asia. CBS Worldwide technology helps make it all possible, improving the lives of more than 50 million consumers and businesses all over the world. Fiserv CBS Worldwide is a rapidly growing division of Fiserv, Inc., the largest data processing provider for banks and savings institutions in the United States. With revenues reaching nearly $800 million and employing more than 8,500 professionals, the company is also the largest check processing provider for U.S. banks and savings institutions.

Orlando-Based, Global Perspective

Since its inception in 1982, the CBS Worldwide division of Fiserv has called Orlando its home. Fiserv CBS Worldwide develops, sells, and supports software for banks and other types of financial institutions in the United States and in 42 countries worldwide. The division also has sales and support offices in London, Lisbon, Warsaw, Singapore, Bangkok, Jakarta, Sydney, Mexico City, and Bogotá.

In addition, CBS Worldwide operates a large data center in Chicago, responsible for processing the accounts of more than 70 banks. CBS Worldwide offers the option of managing account processing services at the Chicago data center, or in the client banks' facilities.

The division's headquarters in Orlando is predominantly responsible for development of CBS and ICBS—complete bank automation solutions for 350 banks worldwide, whose assets range from approximately $100 million to more than $20 billion.

CBS Worldwide develops powerful and comprehensive customer relationship servicing software for use in bank call centers. The Fiserv CRS (customer relationship servicing) system enables representatives to deliver extremely personalized customer service through access to a database containing all customer accounts and contact history. Fiserv Workflow helps standardize and track processes and remind representatives of important tasks, while Fiserv CTI (computer telephony integration) brings the power of computers to call center telephone systems, enabling them to deliver both voice and data to call center operators quickly and efficiently.

CBS Worldwide also develops ATM card management and teller transaction processing systems, as well as telephone banking and other electronic delivery solutions.

These integrated systems share information from a common database, built on an advanced technology architecture that links every aspect of the bank's systems.

A History of Growth and Prosperity

CBS Worldwide has enjoyed a rich history of growth and expansion since its inception. Originally a small start-up formed in 1982, the company—then called Smith, Weiss, Delker—was dedicated to the development and support of community banking software in the United States. The company underwent a series of expansions before being acquired by Fiserv in 1991. With this acquisition, Fiserv obtained two powerful retail banking systems—CBS and ICBS—which added new capabilities to the corporation's variety of financial services. Employing more than 240 programmers, banking consultants, project managers, trainers, and technical writers,

BASED IN ORLANDO SINCE ITS INCEPTION IN 1982, FISERV CBS WORLDWIDE DEVELOPS SOFTWARE FOR 350 FINANCIAL INSTITUTIONS IN THE UNITED STATES AND 42 COUNTRIES WORLDWIDE.

CBS Worldwide continually takes advantage of the rich pool of talent found in the Orlando area.

CBS Worldwide's offices in Orlando, London, and Singapore provide locally specific sales, training, support, customization, translation, and implementation expertise. In total, CBS Worldwide employs more than 500 professionals.

Listening to the conversations in the halls, one gets a sense of the company's global flavor—employees from all over the world, speaking Thai, Spanish, Hindi, Polish, and many other languages.

A Commitment to Quality

In 1994, the British Standards Institute (BSI) granted ISO 9000 certification to Fiserv CBS Worldwide, making it the first U.S.-based banking software and services provider to be recognized by the International Organization for Standardization (ISO). The globally adopted standard provides a framework to establish an effective quality system that meets industry standard quality principles.

Focus on Community

Fiserv is also committed to building relationships in the communities where its employees live and work. The company contributes to a wide range of community and professional service programs such as the United Way, March of Dimes, Central Florida Blood Bank, Coalition for the Homeless, Second Harvest Food Bank, Leukemia Society, U.S. Marine Corps Toys for Tots, Toastmasters International Club, Association of Computer Professionals, Association of Certified Data Processors, and more.

CBS Worldwide has provided aid to its larger community of diverse clients in a variety of relief efforts in times of need. Employees organized a drive to send a truckload of food and clothing for hurricane victims in south Florida. Customer Support representatives provided specialized support sessions for a

THE FINANCIAL SERVICES INDUSTRY IS IN A STATE OF CONSTANT TRANSFORMATION. FISERV CBS WORLDWIDE IS LEADING THE INDUSTRY WITH ITS SOFTWARE AND SERVICES (TOP).

FISERV CBS WORLDWIDE DEVELOPS SOPHISTICATED SYSTEMS THAT HELP ITS CUSTOMERS DELIVER EXTREMELY PERSONALIZED SERVICE USING A RICH DATABASE OF CUSTOMER INFORMATION (BOTTOM).

flood-ravaged client bank in North Dakota, helping to ensure that the bank's business customers could meet payroll and flood victims could access their accounts.

Financial Automation Solutions for the New Millennium

With new technologies emerging every day, the financial services industry is poised for consistent and exciting breakthroughs that will forever transform the nature of money throughout the world. Smart cards, electronic cash, larger and more flexible payment networks, and the continual stream of more powerful computers are just a part of the technologies that will be influenced by Fiserv.

The company promises a continuing reach into new markets in the United States and all over the world, ultimately bringing convenience and financial control to consumers and businesses worldwide.

FMC Airport Products and Systems Division designs, manufactures, and markets automated guided vehicle systems, cargo loaders, deicers, passenger boarding bridges, and other aviation ground support systems worldwide. Industrial manufacturers, warehousers, hospitals, publishers, air carriers, airport authorities, municipalities, and governments rely on FMC equipment daily for efficient, cost-effective operations. The Airport Products and Systems Division is composed of three business units: Airline Equipment, Jetway Systems, and Automated Material Handling Systems. Today, the Division boasts more than 1,200 employees and generates more than $270 million in annual sales. With more than 40 years of material handling and airline equipment experience, FMC has been able to creatively meet the unique challenges presented by its customers on a global basis. Through leading-edge technology for its industries, FMC Airport Products and Systems Division has consistently been able to provide its clients with unique and cost-saving solutions to maximize their profits and services. Having business centers in Orlando; Ogden, Utah; Chalfont, Pennsylvania; Madrid, Spain; Singapore; and the United Kingdom has allowed FMC to grow into what industry experts are calling "the leading supplier of ground support equipment and automated guided vehicle systems in the world."

A Firm Foundation

FMC Airport Products and Systems Division is a unit of the FMC Corporation. As one of the world's leading producers of chemicals and machinery for industry, agriculture, and government, FMC participates on a worldwide basis in three broad markets: performance chemicals, industrial chemicals, and machinery and equipment. FMC operates 110 manufacturing facilities and mines in 29 countries with more than 15,000 employees.

FMC Corporation was founded more than 100 years ago by inventor John Bean, who built the first continuous-flow spray pump for California growers in the late 1800s. In 1928, the Bean Spray Pump Company introduced a new product line of food machinery for canning fruits, and changed its name to the Food Machinery Corporation to reflect the new line. By 1961, the familiar corporate initials FMC were chosen to designate a new and diversified corporation.

Today, FMC Corporation earns more than $5 billion in annual sales. The company's mission is to grow and become a $7 billion global com-

CLOCKWISE FROM TOP:
FMC AIRPORT PRODUCTS AND SYSTEMS DIVISION IS HEADQUARTERED IN ORLANDO'S CENTRAL PARK AT 7300 PRESIDENTS DRIVE.

FOR OPERATORS AND MAINTENANCE PERSONNEL ALIKE, THE TRUMP/SMD-1200 IS THE ULTIMATE USER-FRIENDLY DEICER.

THE COMMANDER 15 CARGO LOADING SYSTEM HANDLES ALL AIRCRAFT LOADING NEEDS. ITS VERSATILITY, DURABILITY, EASE OF MAINTENANCE, AND OPERATIONAL RELIABILITY ARE THE REASONS COMMANDERS ARE THE BEST-SELLING LOADERS IN THE WORLD.

pany. FMC intends to accomplish its goals by getting, developing, and keeping more than its fair share of the best people; continuing to run its businesses superbly; and increasing its focus on growth through acquiring business and technologies in markets FMC understands, developing new products and markets, and continuing to globalize its businesses.

The FMC Airport Products and Systems Division has been a major producer of airline equipment for more than four decades. With the introduction of jet passenger and cargo aircraft in the 1950s, there arose a need for more efficient ground-handling equipment. The Division's Airline Equipment business responded to the challenge, and it has kept pace with increasing demands throughout the years, becoming the leader in the production of cargo loaders, deicers, and transporters.

In 1982, with anticipated growth and changing industry requirements, Orlando was chosen as the headquarters for the business, and a new facility was built. Orlando was selected for its climate, flexible workforce, natural proximity to major shipping ports, closeness to European markets, and attractiveness to both customers and employees. With 1982 sales of approximately $40 million, FMC has had a strong return on its investment, with a significant increase in sales and production.

In 1994, FMC Airport Products and Systems Division acquired Jetway Systems and expanded FMC's exist-

ing line of products. Jetway Systems is located in Ogden, and is the largest manufacturer of passenger boarding bridges in the world. Jetway is known globally for its Smart Bridge technology. The business is on a path toward strong growth, especially in Asian and European markets, where the development of new airports is growing substantially.

The Automated Material Handling Systems business has been a part of FMC for nearly 30 years. FMC offers automated vehicles, which make it easy for its customers to move, load, store, and retrieve materials throughout their facilities in a cost-efficient manner. The Automated Material Handling Systems business utilizes state-of-the-art software engineering concepts to design, build, install, and control all of its vehicles. FMC's trademark of ingenuity and service makes this business poised for future growth.

Maintaining Leadership

In order to meet the changing needs of its industry, customers, and internal team of professionals, FMC is currently refocusing its working relationships. New programs provide a distinct, competitive edge while emphasizing core values that create a work environment that values diversity and encourages teamwork.

"We can't accomplish our business objectives without changing our culture. And the most fundamental part of that change is creating

an environment that allows us to attract, develop, and keep the best people," says Bob Burt, FMC chairman and chief executive officer.

In addition to streamlining the decision-making process, FMC is committed to implementing new strategies that put in place new operating systems focusing on key success factors: customer satisfaction, productivity, innovation, and finance operations.

"These changes in culture supplement our traditional values of maintaining the highest ethical standards; protecting health, safety, and the environment; and acting as a responsible corporate citizen," says FMC President Larry Brady.

Increasing emphasis on cost efficiency and improved cycle times has led to breakthroughs in technology at all levels at FMC. The firm credits its high-tech success to the company's ongoing research and development innovations designed to develop new solutions, refine existing products and processes, and otherwise help customers to profit. Recent technological advancements include FMC's glass-walled passenger bridges. At FMC, serving the customer is the most important goal.

CLOCKWISE FROM TOP LEFT: JETWAY SYSTEMS PROVIDES PASSENGER BOARDING BRIDGES TO AIRPORTS ALL OVER THE WORLD.

TUGGERS PROVIDE A COST-EFFECTIVE MEANS TO MOVE LARGE VOLUMES OF PRODUCT. FMC CAN DESIGN AND BUILD VEHICLES TO TRANSPORT, TRANSFER, LIFT, OR TOW MATERIAL OVER VIRTUALLY ANY TYPE OF FLOOR IN MOST INDUSTRIAL ENVIRONMENTS.

FMC'S SELF-PROPELLED SMART STEP PASSENGER BOARDING STEPS ARE RECOGNIZED FOR THEIR PERFORMANCE AND INNOVATIVE MODULAR DESIGN.

FMC HAS DESIGNED SELF-GUIDED FORKLIFT VEHICLES TO CARRY UP TO 8,000 POUNDS.

CBIS

THE WORLD'S LARGEST TELEPHONE, CABLE, AND WIRELESS SERVICES providers turn to one company for solutions to their customer care and billing needs: CBIS (Cincinnati Bell Information Systems Inc.). With offices around the world—including Orlando and Sunrise, Florida; Cincinnati, Ohio; and Chicago, Illinois—CBIS is the world leader in the provision and management of customer care and billing solutions for the communications industry. But there is more to CBIS than high-powered communications software systems.

Since its inception in 1983, CBIS has consistently demonstrated its ability to develop innovative software solutions to support the ever changing needs of communications providers. "Our mission is to be the global leader in the provision and management of customer care and billing systems for companies in communications. We already are the leader in billing services for wireless carriers, and we intend to take a leadership position across the communications industry," says Robert J. Marino, CBIS president and chief executive officer.

HERITAGE, FOCUS, SYNERGY

CBIS, a subsidiary of Cincinnati Bell Inc. (CBI), attributes much of its success to the heritage, focus, and synergism it derives from being part of Cincinnati Bell. CBIS draws its experience from a communications industry heritage that dates back more than 100 years to when its parent company first developed telephone service for area homes and businesses. CBIS' industry-specific focus allows the firm to understand each client's unique set of customer care and billing needs, and the core technology required to support those needs. Additionally, CBIS provides added value to its clients by capitalizing on the many strengths of its sister companies. "We derive tremendous synergism through our unique relationship with the various subsidiaries, primarily with Cincinnati Bell Telephone and MATRIXX Marketing," Marino notes.

CBIS clients cover a wide range of domestic markets, including cellular telephone providers and their resellers, personal communications service (PCS) providers, cable television operators, interexchange carriers, independent telephone companies, and emerging communications services providers. Its international markets include post, telegraph, and telephone (PTT) organizations; wireless communications providers and their resellers; and cable television companies providing cable and telephony services.

CALLING ORLANDO HOME

Although its headquarters is in Cincinnati, Orlando is home to CBIS' second-largest office. In 1996, CBIS successfully completed the largest move in its history, relocating its Florida data center operations and more than 500 local employees from Maitland to Lake Mary, Florida. Construction of the new CBIS Orlando Data Center and office complex in Lake Mary represents the firm's investment of more than $80 million to further strengthen its overall data center architecture and to provide its clients with the most reliable and responsive service available.

This investment reaffirms CBIS' position as one of Greater Orlando's leading employers. "We are one of the largest data

IN JUNE 1996, CBIS' 500-PLUS ORLANDO-AREA EMPLOYEES MOVED TO A NEW, STATE-OF-THE-ART DATA CENTER AND OFFICE COMPLEX IN LAKE MARY, FLORIDA (LEFT).

ROBERT J. MARINO, PRESIDENT AND CEO (RIGHT)

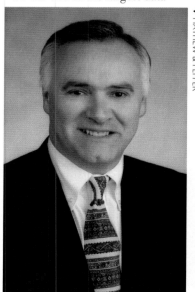

MAYHEW & PEPPER

centers in the state in terms of the amount of processing we do. Both of our data centers, in Orlando and Cincinnati, were designed by experts in the field to deliver the utmost in capacity, efficiency, compatibility, security, and expansion potential," says Dan Cornely, CBIS vice president. "Combined with CBIS' round-the-clock operation of mission-critical systems, the centers offer our clients the most modern facilities available in the communications industry." Today, CBIS solutions and data centers produce more than 300 million bills for cable television, wireless and wireline telephone systems, and convergent services each year.

Orlando has become home to new and emerging technologies generated by CBIS. Notes CBIS Vice President Jeff Karakoosh: "We are developing the next-generation systems of customer care and billing services for the personal communications industry here." Among CBIS' flagship systems is the Precedent 2000® wireless business management solution, which is based on client/server distribution technology.

MEASURING SUCCESS

"We measure success by looking at our four constituencies: our clients, our shareholders, our employees, and our hometown communities," says Marino. "We are constantly communicating

with our clients and certainly a key source of their feedback is receiving contract extensions for critical customer care and billing services. For our shareholders, we focus on growing revenue and operating income. Although we represent less than one-third of CBI's revenue, we take pride in knowing that our performance is a key contributor to the value of CBI's stock today and in the future." Marino adds that the firm measures success with its employees in a number of ways, from regular employee surveys to special feedback sessions.

Finally, CBIS measures success by its level of community involvement. Even with its worldwide interests, CBIS has remained committed to serving its hometown communities. The CBIS Community Action Team coordinates employee community projects that support area schools and the local environment. From community cleanup days to local fund-raisers and support programs for cultural organizations, CBIS employees and management actively donate hours of community service and communications technology in the neighborhoods where they live and work. CBIS is also founder of the Hispanic Scholarship Council of Central Florida. CBIS initiated the Hispanic Scholarship program in 1994 after reviewing the educational resources available to

Hispanic students from public high shools in Osceola, Orange, and Seminole countries, and determining that such a scholarship program would be an important and much-needed local adjunct to existing national programs. CBIS then solicited support from other area businesses to form a council to increase the scope and impact of the scholarship initiative. In 1997, CBIS and the 23 other companies that constitute the council selected seven students to receive college scholarships totaling $33,300.

"We have long realized that success comes in many shapes and sizes," says Marino. "We realize that by satisfying our clients, our shareholders, and the people and communities that support us, we create new opportunities for employees and make CBIS a better place to work."

CLOCKWISE FROM TOP LEFT: EACH OF THE 10 TAPE SILOS IN THE ORLANDO DATA CENTER STORES UP TO 5,000 CUSTOMER TAPES, WHICH CAN INSTANTANEOUSLY PULL CUSTOMER INFORMATION. NEW TAPES CAN BE MOUNTED IN LESS THAN 20 SECONDS.

CBIS FOUNDED THE HISPANIC SCHOLARSHIP COUNCIL OF CENTRAL FLORIDA. IN 1997, CBIS AND THE OTHER 23 COMPANIES THAT CONSTITUTE THE COUNCIL SELECTED SEVEN LOCAL STUDENTS TO RECEIVE COLLEGE SCHOLARSHIPS.

CBIS COMMUNITY ACTION TEAM MEMBERS HELPED HABITAT FOR HUMANITY DURING ITS BLITZ BUILD OF TWO HOUSES IN SANFORD.

CBIS EMPLOYEES SHARED THEIR TECHNICAL EXPERTISE AT A SEMINOLE COUNTY TEACHERS' WORKSHOP THAT FOCUSED ON TECHNOLOGY FOR THE FUTURE AND EXERCISES FOR LEARNING REINFORCEMENT.

recipes. His patrons must agree with his selections, as more than 93 percent of his customers are repeat clientele.

Yesawich, Pepperdine & Brown (YP&B) is Orlando's premier full-service marketing, advertising, and public relations agency specializing in serving the travel and leisure industry. From the rolling

Florida Extruders International, Inc.

After more than 30 years in the public accounting and metalworking industries, Joel G. Lehman wanted a change from the working environment of a large conglomerate. In 1989, with the help of an investment group and with his personal assets as collateral, the 54-year-old Lehman started over by purchasing an aging aluminum plant on the outskirts of Orlando. After refurbishing the building, upgrading

Florida Extruders International, Inc.'s operations include (clockwise from top left) Milestone® window and sliding glass door manufacturing, a 2,300-ton aluminum extrusion line, and the Hot Top aluminum billet casting system.

the equipment, and purchasing painted patio shapes from other aluminum extruders, Lehman launched Florida Extruders International, Inc. in 1991 and began manufacturing profiles and unique patio screen doors for patio and pool enclosure applications.

Through Lehman's innovative approach to business, Florida Extruders rose from virtual obscurity to become the talk of the industry. Historically, patio extrusions were warehoused by stocking distributors and sold to specialty structure contractors. Since Lehman knew how to manufacture these products cost effectively, he recognized a void in the marketplace. He chose to bypass the distributor and sell directly to the contractor, therefore becoming a mill direct distributor. Florida Extruders penetrated the market by passing the savings on to end users and providing them with the highest-quality products in the industry. Today, the company is a dominant supplier of these products in Florida and beyond. In addition to large contractors, many of the firm's competitors in distribution have recognized the value of buying from Florida Extruders.

Manufacturing Integration

"Quality, quality, quality," says Lehman, describing Florida Extruders' philosophy. "It all goes back to being fully integrated and having total control over products and service. We entered an established market that had been in existence for 30 years. It was an industry well serviced by our competitors, yet we carved out our niche. We capitalized upon our manufacturing strengths to supply the best products, offer the widest variety of stocked lengths, and maintain reliable inventory levels, all of which has enabled us to provide the best service the industry has ever experienced."

The company's integration, which includes making its own raw material in a state-of-the-art aluminum billet casting facility with a 40 million-pound annual capacity, has resulted in the ability to offer the best product proposition. Like quality, the words "low-cost leader" are emblazoned in the mission statement of Florida Extruders. Human Resource Manager Kim Lehman emphasizes, "This mission includes being recognized as the best in the business, and is shared with employees and customers alike as a reflection of the company's commitment to being the low-cost producer, controlling quality from raw materials to the finished product, providing dependable service, and being flexible to satisfy the needs of our customers."

"Here's an example," says Operations Manager Dana Lehman: "We put powder paint on our products. This finish is two to three times thicker than the typical liquid-painted extrusions. Our products are more durable and weather better in the hot Florida sun. Also, we are able to recycle the paint that does not get on our product, which ensures 98 percent material utilization." In addition to this powder recovery system, the company's powder-coating technology features an automated photo eye operating system to optimize efficiency; a climate-controlled application area to ensure the best coating quality and appearance; an environmentally friendly, nonchrome pretreatment process for true conversion coating; and a spraying system engineered to optimize coverage based on the end application.

PRODUCT SPECIALIZATION

Marketing Manager Barry Dombchik says, "Florida Extruders prides itself on being applications oriented versus commodity driven. This operating philosophy ensures that both sales and manufacturing personnel understand where our products are used, and enables us to do the best job of providing the highest-quality products and servicing our customers. We have earned a reputation for excellence."

The company has focused heavily on manufacturing specialized products and marketing them to targeted industries, such as patio and pool enclosure, railing, shutter, and fenestration. The product line features blank and prehung patio screen doors, shutter systems, mechanical and welded handrail extrusions, windows, and sliding glass doors. The company plans to expand its business significantly by extruding standard industrial and custom shapes and selling them to a broader range of customers.

In 1995, Florida Extruders introduced Milestone® Quality Windows and Sliding Glass Doors.

Milestone® products have received wide acclaim for their innovative design, stylish appearance, operating performance, and structural integrity, which meets the current and projected stringent building codes enforced in Florida. The success of this aluminum window product line can be directly attributed to the company's strengths, including its extensive integrated manufacturing capabilities, unsurpassed design engineering, automated processes, outstanding powder-coated finishes, and an experienced dealer network with both remodeling and new home construction expertise. "As the name implies, Milestone® products *do* set the standard," says Earl Moore, Window Division operations manager. The Milestone® name is a federally registered trademark of Florida Extruders.

GROWING TO THE TOP

With unparalleled quality, service, technology, and growth, Florida Extruders has increased its workforce from a staff of 18 people to more than 300 employees. Sales have grown from $5 million in 1991 to more than $30 million in 1997. Revenues are projected to exceed $50 million by the year 2000. As sales continue to break records, the company will have expanded in 1997 from its original, 140,000-square-foot facility to nearly 400,000 square feet of total manufacturing and warehouse space. Says Plant Engineering Manager Ed Gresh, "We're continuing to expand in every way. We're adding extrusion capacity; a new, high-speed, more efficient powder paint line; a larger warehouse facility with many more loading docks; and additional delivery vehicles to better service our ever-increasing domestic and export customers."

Recognition is nothing new to Lehman-run manufacturing operations. For example, the company he previously managed received such honors as the President's E Award for excellence in exporting

and the Ford Motor Company Q1 Preferred Quality Award, which was awarded to fewer than 30 percent of Ford's suppliers. In addition, Florida Extruders has been recognized locally in the *Orlando Business Journal*'s Golden 100 and Silver 50 lists of top privately held companies in the area, and as one of the largest employers among manufacturing companies. A further tribute from the business and financial community to corporate founder Joel Lehman and his dedicated employees has been his repeated nomination as Florida's Entrepreneur of the Year in the manufacturing category.

But with future growth, some things will never change: Florida Extruders will maintain, in the words of Production Control Manager Nina Lehman-Wilson, "its commitment to be the low-cost producer, as well as the most dependable, quality-conscious, customer-oriented aluminum extruder and fabricator in the industry."

TOP: FLORIDA EXTRUDERS HAS AN ELECTROSTATICALLY APPLIED (ESP) POWDER PAINT OPERATION.

BOTTOM: JOEL LEHMAN AND STAFF REVIEW EXPANSION PLANS. PICTURED HERE ARE (SEATED, FROM LEFT) NINA LEHMAN-WILSON, KIM LEHMAN, BETTY BEERS, (STANDING, FROM LEFT) ED GRESH, DANA LEHMAN, JOEL LEHMAN, EARL MOORE, AND BARRY DOMBCHIK.

GREAT WESTERN BANK IS THE LEGACY OF A SMALL BAND OF FINANCIAL visionaries who, in the glow of national optimism, organized the Great Western Building and Loan Association. Largely made up of Czechoslovakian immigrants, the 32-member group started the company in a rented office of the Los Angeles Stock Exchange shortly after Independence Day in 1925. Its goal was to "encourage industry, frugality, and the accumulation of savings among shareholders, and to help customers purchase and improve real estate holdings."

Over the years, Great Western, which both fulfilled and exceeded its goal, continued to maintain strong capital levels despite an unstable stock market. Company growth came in the form of acquisitions and mergers. Great Western quickly shaped its industry and, in the process, established the foundation for what would become one of nation's largest financial service companies.

Events in 1997 have made Great Western's future even brighter. On July 1, two industry giants, Great Western and Seattle-based Washington Mutual, effected a merger that has created a bicoastal banking behemoth, with total assets of $93.5 billion and shareholders' equity in excess of $5 billion. The combined company has a dominant market presence in the Pacific Northwest and a major (and growing) presence in two of the country's best banking markets—California and Florida.

INNOVATION EARNS RESULTS

From the spirit of its founding fathers through the struggles of a fickle economy, Great Western has shown that innovation earns results. In 1942, Great Western Building and Loan Association officially became Great Western Savings and Loan, and nearly a decade later, the company went public, forming Great Western Financial Corporation. The corporation was one of the first savings and loan holding companies; one of the first lenders to be underwritten by Wall Street; one of the first industry leaders to issue debentures, or bonds; and the first to be listed on a national stock exchange. As a result, it is today called the parent of the public savings and loan business.

Concerned about the need for additional inner-city urban lending, Great Western has also emerged as a leader of reform efforts. In the 1960s, the company adopted a non-discrimination policy that called for each mortgage loan application to be judged solely on mortgage underwriting standards without regard to geographic location. This action has since become an industry standard. In addition, Great Western has earned outstanding

GREAT WESTERN CONTINUES TO TAKE MAJOR STEPS TO PROVIDE A FULL RANGE OF HIGH-QUALITY SERVICES AND PRODUCTS FOR ITS CUSTOMERS.

▼ JUDY W. TRACY

ratings from the U.S. Office of Thrift Supervision for its consistent lending and outreach efforts in low- to moderate-income communities.

GROWING IN NEW DIRECTIONS

The combination of Washington Mutual and Great Western creates a company with assets of $93.5 billion. Together, they employ more than 20,000 people and operate nearly 1,700 mortgage lending, retail banking, and consumer finance offices nationwide. A Fortune 500 company, Washington Mutual has earned recognition as one of the nation's leading real estate lenders and the nation's largest thrift.

Great Western Bank is a full-service consumer bank, operating branch networks in California and Florida. It began its expansion into the Florida market in 1986 with a single start-up real estate lending office in Boca Raton and opened its first Orlando office in 1989. One year later, during its most aggressive growth period, Great Western acquired a dozen more branches—seven in Florida and five in California—bringing its total to more than $14 billion in retail deposits and nearly 400 branches.

With growth comes service expansion, and leading Great Western's effort is IQ, an unsecured business line of credit that uses state-of-the-art credit-scoring technology and a one-step application to process loans in 24 hours at a low overhead cost. The unit will build on Great Western's existing 96,000 small-business accounts and will include special mortgage loan programs in conjunction with Fannie Mae, the nation's largest source of home mortgage funds, to help low- and moderate-income home buyers.

GREAT WESTERN AND ITS COMMUNITIES

Since it began, Great Western has worked aggressively to strengthen the fabric of life in its communities

through financial investments, philanthropy, and the personal participation of its employees and executives in neighborhood programs. One such mission is to advance educational opportunities through grants to area colleges and universities. Great Western also assists community development programs, including those aimed at overcoming unemployment, drug abuse, and gang violence.

As part of Great Western's long-standing commitment to promote affordable housing, the com-

pany awarded a $25,000 grant to the Orlando Neighborhood Improvement Corporation, a nonprofit housing organization. And since 1987, it has donated more than $1.8 million in cash grants to 34 nonprofit housing organizations in Florida and California.

From its first day forward, Great Western has been on a mission. Today, following the merger with Washington Mutual, its mission is to be one of the premier financial services organizations in the United States.

WASHINGTON MUTUAL AND GREAT WESTERN BANK EMPLOY MORE THAN 20,000 PEOPLE AND OPERATE NEARLY 1,700 MORTGAGE LENDING, RETAIL BANKING, AND CONSUMER FINANCE OFFICES NATIONWIDE.

T HE RECOTON NAME MAY NOT BE EASILY RECOGNIZABLE, BUT IT IS likely that nearly every American currently owns at least one of the company's more than 3,750 consumer electronic accessories, high-fidelity speakers, home theater speaker systems, or automotive audio products. Recoton products are sold worldwide under 20 widely recognized and highly respected brand names, including the accessory labels

Ambico®, Ampersand®, Calibron®, Discwasher®, InterAct®, Parsec®, Recoton®, Rembrandt®, Ross™, SoleControl®, SoundQuest®, and STD®. Organized in 1996 as the Recton Audio Group, the company is one of the world's foremost developers and manufacturers of high-quality, high-performance loudspeaker products marketed under the Advent®, AR®/Acoustic Research®, HECO™, Jensen®, MacAudio™, Magnat™, NHT™, and Phase Linear® names.

Since its founding in 1936 as a manufacturer and marketer of phonograph needles, Recoton has set new standards in consumer electronics accessories through the development, manufacturing, and marketing of timely, unique, and affordable products. The company

offers the industry's broadest array of highly functional accessories used to install, connect, enhance, modify, store, clean, and maintain virtually every type of electronic product, including TVs, VCRs, home and automotive sound systems, home theater, computers, multimedia and video game systems, cellular phones, DSSs, (digital satellite systems) and much more. For home entertainment and car audio customers, it offers a complete range of speakers and car amplifiers, as well as CD and cassette receivers.

Recoton remains committed to its mission to bring to market innovative and user-friendly aftermarket products for both popular and emerging consumer electronics products. The company's internal research and development efforts have resulted in the successful introduction of many proprietary and patented products, and the creation of new product categories that bridge the market between accessories and hardware. Its diverse offerings include a patented family of wireless audio and video products based on 900

MHz technology that allows for the transmission of audio and video signals through walls and floors 150 feet or more from the original source; universal remote controls; and video game joysticks and controllers.

WHAT CONSUMERS NEED, EVERYWHERE THEY SHOP

Recoton serves as a one-stop shopping source to most of North America's leading retailers and, increasingly, to customers in the global marketplace. Recoton is also a leading creator and supplier of many products under private label and OEM agreements for multinational consumer electronic companies and retail merchandisers throughout the world. "If we don't have an accessory or product you want, chances are you don't need it," says Robert L. Borchardt, president of Recoton.

Under Borchardt's guidance, the company went public in 1969, and in 1984 listed on the NASDAQ National Market under the symbol RCOT, where it has enjoyed a track record of growth. Borchardt also implemented the company's aggressive acquisition program, completing 12 acquisitions since 1989, which have expanded Recoton's global presence and product offerings.

BRINGING GROWTH TO FLORIDA

As part of the 1989 purchase of Lake Mary, Florida-based Calibron Inc., a manufacturer and marketer of stereo headphones and CD accessories, the company acquired eight acres of land with a 40,000-square-foot manufacturing facility. After expansions in 1991 and 1993 brought the facility to 200,000

square feet, Recoton relocated its U.S. operations to Lake Mary from New York. Recoton subsequently purchased 31 acres of vacant land close to its current facility, and built a 245,000-square-foot warehouse and distribution plant to accommodate the company's growth and consolidate acquisitions for maximum operating efficiencies. With the addition of a contiguous, 318,000-square-foot facility, Recoton's Lake Mary complex exceeds 750,000 square feet and now employs more than 900 Florida residents.

A Timeless Formula for Success

At age 91, Recoton founder and Co-Chairman Herbert H. Borchardt remains active in company operations. He has imparted his experience and knowledge to his son Robert Borchardt, Recoton's president, who joined the company in 1961 and actively guides the company's operations, acquisitions, and expansion. "The secret to Recoton's

61-year success story lies with the timeless practice of relationship marketing and partnerships built between our company and its customers, and between our customers and the users of our products," notes Robert Borchardt. Recoton has revolutionized its market with a number of new service concepts, including its innovative computerized sales information system and completely self-contained and self-explanatory outer packaging. Recoton's products are supported by promotional advertising and by hot- and help-lines for retailers and consumers.

A key ingredient of Recoton's success has been its family relationship with its employees. Many senior executives and employees have been with the firm for more than 25 years, and as acquisitions take place, new employees find a support system that delivers loyalty and growth opportunities. With approximately 2,500 employees and operations worldwide, the company has the breadth of experience and glo-

bal presence to stay ahead of the curve of new technologies.

Positioned for the Digital Revolution

Over the next several years, Recoton believes the consumer electronics industry will continue to expand as the digital age brings many exciting new products, including DVD (digital versatile disk), HDTV (high-definition television), flat screen TV, expanded DSS capabilities, continued growth of home theater, and the convergence of audio, video, and the computer. Recoton is prepared to supply the most innovative and in-demand product lines for the digital revolution as it capitalizes on its position as a leading global supplier of consumer electronic accessories and speaker products.

With its strong roots in the Orlando/Lake Mary community and expected growth, Recoton will undoubtedly continue to expand its contributions to Florida's economic development and employment opportunities.

HARD ROCK CAFE

SINCE ITS 1971 OPENING IN LONDON, HARD ROCK CAFE HAS BECOME A global restaurant industry phenomenon. Combining rock music, memorabilia from top musical artists of the last 40 years, classic American food, and a commitment to widespread altruistic causes, Hard Rock Cafe has continued to successfully grow as a true cultural force around the world. ✳ Hard Rock Cafe Orlando, which opened in 1990, is the largest facility

THE LARGEST OF ITS NAMESAKES, HARD ROCK CAFE ORLANDO IS HOUSED IN A LANDMARK TWO-STORY BUILDING SHAPED LIKE AN ELECTRIC GUITAR AND OUTLINED IN BRIGHT NEON. IT DISPLAYS MORE THAN 500 ITEMS OF MEMORABILIA FROM ROCK LEGENDS OF THE PAST FOUR DECADES (LEFT).

NO VISIT TO A HARD ROCK CAFE IS COMPLETE WITHOUT A STOP AT THE MERCHANDISE STORE, WHERE GUESTS CAN PURCHASE CLOTHING AND OTHER MERCHANDISE BEARING ONE OF THE WORLD'S MOST RECOGNIZED LOGOS (RIGHT).

in the company's 26-year history. Located on the main road into Universal Studios, its landmark, two-story building is shaped like an electric guitar and outlined in bright neon colors. Stretching more than 23,000 square feet, it seats up to 500 diners and is larger in size and scope than any other Hard Rock Cafe in the world.

Hard Rock Cafe Orlando is open seven days a week, 365 days a year, from 11 a.m. to 2 a.m. It is open to the general public free of charge via the front entrance, and

it is also a stop on the Universal Studios Florida tour. In keeping with the Hard Rock Cafe's Love All, Serve All philosophy, reservations are not accepted; patrons are admitted on a first-come, first-served basis.

The Orlando facility houses one of the largest collections of rock-and-roll history displayed anywhere, according to Sotheby's. The Orlando collection includes more than 75 guitars collected from rock music legends such as Eric Clapton, Keith Richards, Elvis Presley, U2, Tom Petty, and Eddie Van Halen. Hard Rock Cafe Orlando also features costumes worn by Jimi Hendrix, Janis Joplin, and Jon Bon Jovi; lyrics written by Bob Dylan; and gold records earned by major music legends from Jim Morrison to Elton John. It displays more than 500 items culled from the original Hard Rock archives, and the company's national memorabilia repository is also located in Orlando.

In fall 1998, Hard Rock Cafe Orlando will again make history, as it will be the first ever Hard Rock Cafe to close. Don't fret,

though—a newer, larger Hard Rock will open the next morning as part of the Universal Studios Florida's CityWalk expansion. The new Hard Rock Cafe Orlando will be the largest in the chain, seating up to 650 guests, and will feature a 2,000-capacity amphitheater for live music performances.

MAKING HISTORY
Hard Rock Cafe has been called "history in the making" by entertainment industry experts. Its founders, Isaac Tigrett and Peter Morton, began their enterprise with a single London café. In 1982, cofounder Peter Morton sold his interest in the original Hard Rock, and both he and Tigrett agreed to develop their own Hard Rock Cafes in various parts of the world. The companies expanded, opening cafés in some of the most popular U.S. cities, including Orlando, Miami, Key West, Los Angeles, San Francisco, Chicago, Boston, Atlanta, Nashville, Houston, and Washington, D.C.

The companies' concept of classic food, music, and one-of-a-kind memorabilia seems unbeatable. Menus feature the trademark Hard Rock hamburger—the sandwich that launched the original café nearly 30 years ago—as well as an array of vegetarian dishes, desserts, and freshly prepared American foods at moderate prices.

Hard Rock's extensive rock music collections have been declared unmatched anywhere in the world, and each restaurant sells merchandise displaying its own brand of history: the famous Hard Rock logo.

Hard Rock around the World

Internationally, Hard Rock has opened in some of the world's most popular destinations. There are more than 76 restaurants in 30 countries around the world in such cities as Toronto, Tokyo, Cancún, Acapulco, Singapore, Reykjavik, and Cape Town.

In 1996, the London-based Rank Organization, Plc., owner of Orlando-based Hard Rock Cafe International, purchased Hard Rock America, Hard Rock Canada, and Hard Rock South Africa, unifying the Hard Rock logo across the globe. Company President and Chief Executive Officer Jim Berk, former executive director for the National Academy of Recording Arts & Sciences Foundation, over-

sees Hard Rock's U.S. and international operations.

There are now company-owned Hard Rock Cafes located in London, Paris, Berlin, Montreal, Copenhagen, Madrid, and other top international cities. Hard Rock Cafe franchises are located in Puerto Vallarta, Cabo de San Lucas, and Mexico City, Mexico; Bangkok; Calgary; San Juan, Puerto Rico; Bali; Dubai; Sydney; Tel Aviv; and other international destinations, making history as one of the fastest-growing restaurants in the world.

Saving the Planet

The Hard Rock Cafe has always been more than a good restaurant. Since its inception, the company has been a leader in a wide variety of humanitarian activities around the world. It has adopted a companywide Save the Planet mission, raising millions of dollars for global service programs and smaller community projects.

In April 1997, general managers from all 76 restaurants worldwide gathered together for the first time in the company's history to pledge their commitment to a $500,000 fund-raising effort for Give Kids the World, an organization that provides magical Central Florida vacations for terminally ill children.

In addition to fund-raising, Hard Rock's pioneering programs

to "give something back" have used music to help raise public awareness of charitable organizations that focus on issues such as AIDS, homelessness, environmental abuse, and education. Its most recent support has gone to such organizations as UNICEF, People for the Ethical Treatment of Animals (PETA), British Red Cross, Elton John AIDS Foundation, Conservation International, Natural Resource Defense Council, Friends of the Earth, and Earth Communications Office.

In 1990, the company launched its Signature Series charity T-shirt line. Celebrity participants in the program have included Yoko Ono, R.E.M.'s Michael Stipe, Sting, and, most recently, Peter Gabriel. Through its Signature Series program, Hard Rock Cafe has raised more than $4.5 million for world charity organizations.

HARD ROCK CAFE ORLANDO FEATURES ONE OF THE LARGEST COLLECTIONS OF MUSIC MEMORABILIA IN THE WORLD, HOUSING HUNDREDS OF PRICELESS ITEMS, FROM GUITARS USED BY ERIC CLAPTON AND ELVIS PRESLEY TO COSTUMES WORN BY JIMI HENDRIX, JANIS JOPLIN, AND JON BON JOVI (LEFT).

WELL KNOWN FOR ITS COLLECTION OF MUSIC MEMORABILIA, HARD ROCK CAFE ORLANDO IS ALSO A GREAT PLACE TO SAMPLE THE BEST IN ALL-AMERICAN CUISINE (RIGHT).

MICHAEL LOWRY

UNIVERSAL STUDIOS FLORIDA PROVIDES MILLIONS OF PEOPLE EACH year with entertainment that is beyond the limits—a unique, behind-the-scenes journey into movies and moviemaking. Since it opened in 1990, Universal Studios Florida has become the most popular movie studio theme park in the world—and the largest motion picture and television production studio outside of Hollywood. ✳ Universal's larger-than-life

approach to theme park entertainment has led to wide praise from guests and travel organizations. Travelers rate Universal tops among their theme park experiences. And even Fodor's *Disney Like a Pro* travel guide author Rick Namey calls Universal "the best theme park in the world."

The reasons are simple. From the start, the goal has been to make Universal Studios Florida a world-class destination offering world-class experiences. The result has been a huge success.

"We use state-of-the-art technology and tremendous creativity to bring guests the theme park experience of a lifetime," said Tom Williams, president and chief executive officer for Universal City Florida. "Our rides continue to get superb reviews and our events—such as Halloween Horror Nights and Mardi Gras—have become a major part of what makes our park popular. Universal has become a must-see in Orlando."

Universal features dozens of incredible rides and shows along with street entertainment, celebrity look-alikes, dining, and shopping

UNIVERSAL STUDIOS FLORIDA

experiences. Its streets look like they're straight out of favorite films—and on any day, guests may have the chance to watch movies and television shows being filmed in one of Universal's soundstages or along one of its streets.

Cutting-edge entertainment is a large part of what makes Universal so successful. It made entertainment history when it opened one of its newest attractions, Terminator 2 3D, in 1996. The attraction features Arnold Schwarzenegger and the original *Terminator 2* cast. At a cost of $60 million, it is the

UNIVERSAL STUDIOS FLORIDA

most elaborate and technologically advanced entertainment experience ever created for Universal Studios Florida. Terminator 2 3D relies on state-of-the-art 3D filmmaking, live action stunt work, and amazing special effects to give guests an experience unlike any other theme park in the world.

Terminator 2 3D has received rave reviews from Universal guests, the theme park industry, and entertainment critics. *USA Today* calls Terminator 2 3D "a 3D extravaganza." *Amusement Business* calls it "the best contemporary film experience ever," and *Variety* calls it "wall-to-wall wonderment" that is "ingeniously written and designed."

But cutting-edge entertainment doesn't end with Terminator 2 3D. At Universal, guests know what it's like to be chased by a giant shark in JAWS! or to take a spectacular journey into the future on Back to the Future . . . The Ride. Other popular attractions include Hercules and Xena: Wizards of the Screen, E.T. Adventure, and A Day in the Park with Barney. And coming in summer 1998 will be Twister, a multimil-

THE MAJESTIC UNIVERSAL STUDIOS GLOBE ROTATES WITHIN A CLOUD OF MIST AT THE MAIN ENTRANCE TO UNIVERSAL STUDIOS FLORIDA.

UNIVERSAL STUDIOS FLORIDA SPANS 444 ACRES IN ORLANDO AND IS THE COUNTRY'S LARGEST FILM AND TELEVISION PRODUCTION FACILITY OUTSIDE OF HOLLYWOOD (LEFT).

MONSTERS EMERGE, READY TO SPOOK THE MASSES FOR HALLOWEEN HORROR NIGHTS AT UNIVERSAL STUDIOS FLORIDA (RIGHT).

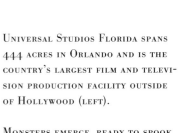

lion-dollar attraction that will allow guests to experience the fury of an actual tornado.

Universal is also in the midst of an extensive expansion project to be called Universal City Florida—a global entertainment destination that will change tourism in Orlando.

Universal City will include the already successful Universal Studios Florida; a new theme park called Universal's Islands of Adventure, set to open in 1999; and Universal CityWalk, a 30-acre entertainment complex opening in 1998 and featuring restaurants, nightclubs, shops, and a 16-screen, 5,000-seat movie megaplex, as well as world-class resort hotel accommodations.

CityWalk will include the largest Hard Rock Cafe in the world—complete with a live entertainment venue—an E! Entertainment Television Production Center, Emeril's of Orlando, a Motown Cafe, a Marvel Mania Restaurant, a Pat O'Brien's of New Orleans fame, a Jazz Center featuring the Thelonious Monk Institute of Jazz Education Academy, the Down Beat Jazz Hall of Fame, and more.

Islands of Adventure will feature five unique islands—all based on themes designed to excite and entertain. The islands include Seuss Landing, Jurassic Park, Toon Lagoon, Marvel Super Hero Island, and Lost Continent: Land of Myths and Legends.

Universal City Florida will attract millions of additional tourists to Orlando each year—giving the local economy a huge boost. Universal currently has about 6,000 employees and has contributed more than $14 billion to the region's economy since opening. Its expansion and continued growth mean that Universal will contribute an additional 14,000 jobs and $37 billion to the economy by 2001.

And beyond economic contributions, Universal works closely with many community groups and agencies to help causes important to Orlando.

Universal City Florida is a joint venture between Universal Studios; a unit of the Seagram Company Ltd., a global beverage and entertainment company; and the Rank Group Plc., a London-based leisure and entertainment company and international provider of services to the film industry. Rank's broad-based leisure and entertainment activities include worldwide Hard Rock Cafes and brand rights.

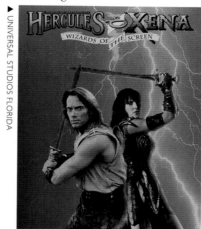

▶ UNIVERSAL STUDIOS FLORIDA

▶ UNIVERSAL STUDIOS FLORIDA

▶▼ UNIVERSAL STUDIOS FLORIDA

I N 1990, CAMPUS CRUSADE FOR CHRIST INTERNATIONAL BEGAN TO LOOK for a new home. Its San Bernardino, California, headquarters had served it well for several decades, but the organization had simply outgrown these facilities and needed a new, dynamic home for the next phase of its ambitious goal of reaching the entire world with the good news of Jesus Christ. Then and now, the goal of Campus Crusade for Christ has always been to give every person on Earth the opportunity to have a personal relationship with Christ.

There were many requirements for the city that would be chosen to house the nerve center of this 46-year-old ministry. After researching the possibilities of 38 cities based on a 56-point set of criteria, the organization's leadership felt that God had led them to Orlando. The international airport, excellent school systems, lovely climate, and generosity of Central Florida's government and civil leaders helped woo the organization to relocate here. Now, more than six years later, Campus Crusade is proud to call Orlando home.

From its Florida headquarters, Campus Crusade for Christ serves and leads more than 14,000 staff members and 163,000 trained volunteers in 167 countries and protectorates worldwide. More than 650 staff members work at the world headquarters, which serves as the hub of the organization's international ministry. The staff directs and administers the plans and strategies of its ministries, which include Athletes in Action, the Campus Ministry (now on 650 U.S. campuses and 470 campuses overseas), and The *JESUS* Film Project. Since this feature film of Christ's life debuted in 1979, it has been translated into 410 languages and viewed by more than 1 billion people.

Campus Crusade for Christ is a nonprofit organization with an estimated budget of more than $270 million. In 1996, Campus Crusade for Christ was recognized by *Money* magazine as America's "most efficient religious group" in terms of the percentage of contributions actually reaching ministry programs.

DR. BILL BRIGHT, WINNER OF THE 1996 TEMPLETON PRIZE FOR PROGRESS IN RELIGION, IS FOUNDER AND PRESIDENT OF CAMPUS CRUSADE FOR CHRIST (TOP LEFT).

▼ GREG SCHNEIDER

▼ JOHN CRONE

PEOPLE REACHING PEOPLE FOR CHRIST
ALL AROUND THE WORLD IS WHAT CAMPUS
CRUSADE FOR CHRIST IS ALL ABOUT.
WHETHER THROUGH SPECIAL EVENTS
SUCH AS CONFERENCES (OPPOSITE RIGHT),
PERFORMANCES BY WORLD-RENOWNED
ILLUSIONIST ANDRÉ KOLE (OPPOSITE,
BOTTOM LEFT), OUTREACHES DURING
SPRING BREAK AND SUMMER VACATIONS
(TOP LEFT), PRESENTATIONS OF THE
JESUS FILM (BOTTOM), OR JUST TALK-
ING ONE-ON-ONE WITH INDIVIDUALS
(TOP RIGHT), IT IS THE DESIRE OF
CAMPUS CRUSADE FOR CHRIST TO
GIVE PEOPLE THE OPPORTUNITY TO
HEAR ABOUT JESUS CHRIST'S GIFTS
OF FORGIVENESS AND ETERNAL LIFE.

IN THE HOTEL AND RESORT INDUSTRY BUSINESS, SUCCESS IS MEASURED BY HOW well the needs of customers are met. With the motto Twice the Hotel, Twice the Value, Embassy Suites in Orlando is on a mission to be the best in the business, providing guests with state-of-the-art amenities, luxury accommodations, and award-winning customer service. ✳ Since the opening of its three Orlando-area properties, Embassy Suites has remained committed

exclusively to quality guest service and customer relations. Today, the combined properties consist of the Embassy Suites Resort at Lake Buena Vista, the Embassy Suites Orlando South on International Drive, and the Embassy Suites Orlando North in Altamonte Springs. Among Embassy Suites' standard guest service programs are complimentary newspaper and full breakfast each morning, complimentary open bar reception each evening, private suites, restaurants on each property, complimentary parking, wheelchair accommodations, express checkout, valet and room service, guest laundry, and conference facilities.

Embassy Suites are designed for comfort and convenience. Most are located near major roadways for easy access to airports, businesses, and area attractions. The hotels feature gardens and atria, incorporating a Florida-friendly environment with tall palm trees and indoor fountains and ponds.

RESORT LUXURY

The Embassy Suites Resort at Lake Buena Vista offers 280 two-room suites, including 232 atrium suites

and 48 lanai suites. The six-story main building with adjoining five-story lanai is owned and managed by Promus Hotels, headquartered in Memphis. Located on a 10-acre site directly adjacent to the Walt Disney World Resort inside Lake Buena Vista, the hotel provides free scheduled transportation to and from the theme parks, making it convenient for vacationers eager to tour area attractions. Additionally, the shops and restaurants of the Walt Disney World Village are nearby.

The Embassy Suites Resort also features family-sized suites that comfortably sleep four to six people, with separate bedroom and living room, pullout sofa bed, two telephones, two television remotes, voice mail messaging, and a dining table. Suites include a separate living room with amenities that include a wet bar, coffeemaker, cable television, videocassette player, and computer modem hookup.

For recreation, the resort offers guests their choice of a heated free-form swimming pool, indoor exercise center, tennis, volleyball, or a two-thirds-mile fitness course. For relaxation, the property features saunas and a whirlpool. A children's

program, Crazy Cat Kid's Club, offers an array of activities, games, and snacks.

The Embassy Suites Resort at Lake Buena Vista also features four dining options, more than 7,200 square feet of meeting space, and a 3,078-square-foot ballroom for those grand Florida nights.

EMBASSY SUITES ORLANDO SOUTH

Rich in elegance, the Embassy Suites Orlando South combines the style and charm of the Florida tropics with the sophistication of a contemporary city. Located less than one mile from the Orlando/Orange County Convention Center,

the Embassy Suites Orlando South is ideal for convention planners and business travelers. The hotel is also located in close proximity to all area attractions, golf courses, and Florida's famous white sand beaches, which makes the Embassy a smart choice for families.

All of the guest rooms at the Embassy Suites Orlando South overlook an eight-story atrium filled with native plants and beautiful waterfalls. With 244 guest suites, visitors can select from king suites, double suites, nonsmoking suites, executive conference suites, and a presidential suite. The hotel also features two specially designed suites for physically challenged guests.

Each suite includes such amenities as a microwave, coffeemaker, refrigerator, and separate living room. Telephones in each suite are equipped with voice mail systems and computer dataports.

Dining and entertainment are available at the Embassy Suites'

Sedona Café, which features a casual menu with more than a dozen wines offered by the glass. The 100-seat lounge serves specialty drinks indoors or on the outdoor patio.

For families traveling with small children, the Embassy Suites Orlando South offers a children's swimming pool and a family fun center game room.

EMBASSY SUITES ORLANDO NORTH

Conveniently located at the intersection of Interstate 4 and Highway 436 in Altamonte Springs, the Embassy Suites Orlando North is just six miles from downtown Orlando. The 277-suite hotel is uniquely positioned for business travelers, with easy access to such central business districts as Maitland Center and Heathrow's International Business Complex.

The Embassy Suites Orlando North offers facilities traditionally associated with a high-end busi-

ness hotel, such as banquet rooms, expansive lobby areas, and more than 7,000 square feet of meeting space. Each guest suite is elegantly decorated and includes a separate living room and a wet bar.

Guests of the Embassy Suites Orlando North can enjoy shopping at the nearby Altamonte Mall, one of the state's largest shopping centers. While Embassy Suites serves a unique blend of steak and seafood entrées in its grill restaurant, guests are a short drive to dozens of area restaurants specializing in everything from quick and easy fast food to elegant gourmet dining. Complimentary transportation is provided by Embassy Suites to locations within a five-mile radius of the hotel.

Catering to business travelers, conventioneers, and vacationing families, the three Embassy Suites locations in Orlando are proud to offer the best in service and amenities, and are equipped to meet the unique needs of all of its guests.

CLOCKWISE FROM TOP LEFT: THE EMBASSY SUITES RESORT AT LAKE BUENA VISTA FEATURES FAMILY-SIZED SUITES THAT COMFORTABLY SLEEP FOUR TO SIX PEOPLE, WITH SEPARATE BEDROOM AND LIVING ROOM, PULLOUT SOFA BED, TWO TELEPHONES, TWO TELEVISION REMOTES, VOICE MAIL MESSAGING, AND A DINING TABLE.

MANY OF THE GUEST ROOMS AT THE EMBASSY SUITES ORLANDO SOUTH OVERLOOK AN EIGHT-STORY ATRIUM FILLED WITH NATIVE PLANTS AND BEAUTIFUL WATERFALLS.

LOCATED ON A 10-ACRE SITE DIRECTLY ADJACENT TO THE WALT DISNEY WORLD RESORT, THE EMBASSY SUITES RESORT AT LAKE BUENA VISTA PROVIDES FREE SCHEDULED TRANSPORTATION TO AND FROM THE THEME PARKS, MAKING IT CONVENIENT FOR VACATIONERS EAGER TO TOUR AREA ATTRACTIONS.

RICH IN ELEGANCE, THE EMBASSY SUITES ORLANDO SOUTH COMBINES THE STYLE AND CHARM OF THE FLORIDA TROPICS WITH THE SOPHISTICATION OF A CONTEMPORARY CITY.

THE SOFTWARE SUPPORT DIVISION OF MATRIXX MARKETING INC. (MATRIXX-SSD) is headquartered in Heathrow, Florida. MATRIXX-SSD is considered a quality leader for outsourced technical support, delivering highly effective solutions to computer users nationwide. These solutions include support for off-the-shelf personal computing software; hardware; peripheral devices, such as printers and modems; and advanced

networking equipment to business professionals and consumers via the telephone—24 hours a day, seven days a week, 365 days a year. MATRIXX-SSD handles approximately 3.5 million technical support calls per year and has three major call centers that are located in Heathrow, Houston, and Salt Lake City.

MATRIXX Marketing Inc. is a wholly owned subsidiary of Cincinnati Bell (NYSE: CSN) and is the world leader in providing outsourced customer management solutions that increase sales, im-

prove customer service, and lower operating costs. As a single-source provider, MATRIXX combines the people, knowledge, and technology to create dedicated customer service and sales coverage programs, and then complements these programs with telephone marketing campaigns, skilled market research fulfillment services, database expertise, and interactive technology.

MATRIXX-SSD's innovative approach to outsourced technical support services truly differentiates the company within the industry. The MATRIXX-SSD approach

combines advanced computer telephony integration (CTI) technology with computer hardware and software expertise and a three-tiered quality assurance process to deliver highly effective technical support solutions to the users of computer technology.

TECHNOLOGY

MATRIXX-SSD developed a de-escalation system to route support calls to the most knowledgeable customer support representative (CSR) available first, based upon the caller's need. This innovative

LEFT: MATRIXX-SSD's FIRST-CALL RESOLUTION RATE IS APPROXIMATELY 93 PERCENT—13 POINTS ABOVE THE INDUSTRY AVERAGE OF 80 PERCENT.

RIGHT: MATRIXX-SSD's FRIENDLY, HIGHLY SKILLED CUSTOMER SERVICE REPRESENTATIVES PROVIDE SUPPORT FOR MORE THAN 400 OFF-THE-SHELF SOFTWARE PACKAGES.

NASH BAKER

method is directly contrary to the standard industry practice of routing calls to the lowest-level person first and then escalating the caller to a more knowledgeable representative, if necessary. Using MATRIXX-SSD's approach, callers receive problem resolution more than 93 percent of the time during their first call.

EXPERTISE

MATRIXX-SSD has strategically located its call center facilities in major metropolitan areas that are rich with academic resources and provide qualified technical support candidates. Access to these resources gives MATRIXX-SSD a competitive advantage.

MATRIXX-SSD provides a growth environment for its employees with career paths in both advanced technology and management through ongoing training and the company's organizational need for multiple levels of management. The best and brightest experts stay with MATRIXX-SSD because of its unique business culture, making the company's turnover rate among the lowest in the industry.

QUALITY ASSURANCE

MATRIXX-SSD's strong company culture focuses on quality. The quality of the services provided by the company is tracked back to each CSR via quality surveys and call monitoring. CSRs are compensated based upon their ability to provide high-quality solutions effectively and efficiently. This unique culture provides a win-win situation for both employees and customers. Employees work within a positive and rewarding environment—a factor that constantly drives MATRIXX-SSD customer service to new levels.

Due to this unique approach to outsourced technical support services, the division has earned the industry's prestigious *Service*

News' Harold H. Short Jr. Innovations in Service Award for having the most innovative software support system. The division also has received the ALEX Award, presented by Audiotex News in honor of Alexander Graham Bell.

MATRIXX-SSD won the ALEX award in the Best Consumer and Business Communications, Assistance, and Payments Application category.

MATRIXX-SSD prides itself on providing tomorrow's solutions today. Its outsourcing support allows businesses to focus on strategic goals and core businesses, increase profitability through decreased support overhead, and increase productivity as downtime and learning curves decrease. It also offers individuals and businesses in-house expertise and centralized support services, enhanced service offerings without additional overhead, and complete and timely reporting.

From a passing fad to an essential business-building tool, MATRIXX-SSD has become a vital member of the computer industry. And it promises to maintain this position for years to come.

TOP: MATRIXX-SSD's STATE-OF-THE-ART CALL CENTERS HANDLE 3.5 MILLION TECHNICAL SUPPORT CALLS PER YEAR.

BOTTOM: A MATRIXX-SSD NETWORK ENGINEER MONITORS THE INTEGRATED VOICE RESPONSE (IVR) SYSTEM.

A S A $270 MILLION NATIONAL OPERATION, ORLANDO'S SIGNATURE FLIGHT Support at Signature Plaza is one of the country's top aviation support service providers. The company today operates in more than 22 states, as well as in Zurich. Its 40 divisions develop, implement, integrate, and market service to the general aviation industry. Signature also provides support to airline operations at dozens of national airports.

SIGNATURE FLIGHT SUPPORT IS THE WORLD'S LARGEST NETWORK OF AVIATION FLIGHT SUPPORT OPERATIONS, WITH MORE THAN 50 YEARS OF EXPERIENCE IN GENERAL AVIATION AT THE NATION'S LARGEST METROPOLITAN AIRPORTS (LEFT).

A GENERAL AVIATION AIRCRAFT IS FUELED BY A SIGNATURE FLIGHT SUPPORT FUEL TRUCK AND RECEIVES SIGNATURE'S COMPLIMENTARY CABIN CLEANING SERVICE (RIGHT).

Signature Flight Support is the world's largest network of aviation flight support operations, with more than 50 years of experience in general aviation at the nation's largest metropolitan airports. A Delaware-based company, Signature is owned by BBA Group, PLC, a publicly held corporation that is traded on the London Exchange. BBA has annual sales of approximately $2 billion, and its core businesses are friction materials, specialty electrical, nonwoven textiles, and aviation products and service.

ON LAND AND IN THE AIR

Signature Flight Support offers a wide range of specialized aviation services to its customers. One of the key components of Signature Flight Support's operation is fuel services. Signature sells and distributes more than 72 million gallons of general aviation fuel annually, providing aviation clients with the highest level of fuel quality. Signature maintains operations at many leading airport destinations, including Boston's Logan, Chicago's O'Hare, New York's LaGuardia, and Washington, D.C.'s Dulles and National airports, as well as terminals in Anchorage and Zurich.

Signature is a recognized leader in the aviation support services industry in commercial airline ground handling and fueling, general aviation technical services, and general aviation fueling. From Anchorage to Honolulu, Austin to Milwaukee, and Nashville to Orlando, Signature's more than 4,200 employees are

committed to providing the highest level of service support in the aviation industry. Signature's employees have been consistently recognized and voted best flight support operation by *Professional Pilot* magazine's annual survey.

FROM SOUP TO NUTS AND BOLTS

Signature works at many of the nation's top airports to provide first-class flight support services. The company offers a type of "welcome wagon" service to arriving aircraft at every Signature facility. Due to the on-call schedules of flight crews, specifically designed assistance concerning transportation and hotel accommodations is also provided. Signature reserves cars and vans for crew transportation to and from airports during overnight stays, and provides crews with hotel reservations, city maps, and a national travel service guide. The guide features detailed airport information; facts on a city's aver-

ARCH PHOTO EDUARD HUEBER

age climate; suggestions for local shopping, dining, and entertainment; and a list of all available Signature services. These include weather and flight-planning services, aircraft towing, aircraft deicing, catering, health clubs, recreational programs, crew refreshments, faxing and copy center services, and information on local museums, tourist attractions, limousine services, and more.

Signature also offers Tour de Signature, a complimentary bicycle program. At many of the airports served by a Signature location, bicycles are made available to pilots, flight attendants, and others who wish to sightsee via bicycle or continue their personal exercise programs. Participants also are provided with safety helmets, water bottles, and route maps for their cycling pleasure.

Back at the airport, Signature also provides general aviation aircraft with the 10-point Gold CAP Service. With pilot approval, the service is complimentary to all aircraft, and includes carpet cleaning, seat belt folding, galley cleaning, trash removal, lavatory cleaning, interior and exterior window cleaning, and more.

TRAINED TO BE THE BEST

Providing the highest quality in the aviation industry is the goal of Signature Flight Support. The cornerstone of its success is the commitment and professionalism of its workforce. To encourage companywide success and consistency, Signature has developed one of the industry's top training programs for employees, known as the Professional Service Training (PST) program. Through this program, employees enhance their technical and customer service skills, and help the company and its clients maintain compliance with the regulations and safety procedures recommended by the Federal Aviation Administration, the Environmental Protection Agency, and Signature's own high professional standards. Signature's training programs involve employees in state-of-the-art technical training designed to provide service beyond customers' expectations while at the same time ensuring safety and compliance with federal, state, and local regulations.

Signature provides flight support services to the nation's leading airports, airline companies, and general aviation aircraft operators. The company plays an active role in the aviation industry through board memberships, committee involvement, and hands-on volunteer efforts. Many of Signature's employees belong to the nation's top professional associations and industry-related organizations, including the National Business Aviation Association (NBAA), American Association of Airport Executives (AAAE), Airports Council International (ACI), and National Air Transport Association (NATA).

Whether providing vital maintenance services to aircraft between flights or providing its customers with bicycles for personal exercise while on the ground, Signature Flight Support strives to cover the full gamut of its customers' needs. Through the efforts of a highly skilled staff that has received much favorable recognition within the aviation industry, Signature Flight Support will continue to be an indispensable ally to aircraft operators, airports, airlines, and the customers it serves.

SIGNATURE FLIGHT SUPPORT'S MORE THAN 4,200 EMPLOYEES NATIONWIDE ADD TO THE STRENGTH OF THE INDUSTRY'S NUMBER ONE FLIGHT SUPPORT OPERATION (LEFT).

A GENERAL AVIATION PILOT IS GREETED BY A SIGNATURE FLIGHT SUPPORT REPRESENTATIVE (RIGHT).

Fidelity National Title Insurance Company

WITH ORIGINS THAT CAN BE TRACED BACK NEARLY 150 YEARS, Fidelity National Title Insurance Company, through its family of underwriters, has become one of the nation's premier title insurance companies. In 1992, Fidelity National Title opened its Orlando district office, adding to its string of successful service centers, located throughout the United States and including Puerto Rico,

the Bahamas, and the Virgin Islands. By nurturing quality and attending to customer needs, Fidelity National Title has created a strong entrepreneurial spirit that has helped fuel the company's rapid growth.

"Fidelity National Title is built upon the efforts of the most dedicated and focused employee group in the industry," says President Patrick F. Stone. "Our productivity is the envy of our competitors, and our service levels set the standard by which others are measured. While our diligent pursuit of productivity and service borders on dogma, the net result is profitability through client retention.

"From entry level to top management, we are still the most flexible, proactive organization in the industry," Stone continues. "No company providing our depth and breadth of products and services can take action as quickly, or be as innovative, as Fidelity National Title. Success is the direct reflection of customer satisfaction. Having extolled our virtues, it would be a tragic mistake to rest on our laurels. We can continue to set the standard by being an action-oriented, customer-intimate, nonbureaucratic, entrepreneurial, employee-owned company."

Committed to Customer Satisfaction

Fidelity National Title employees are committed to providing customers with a level of satisfaction that is unparalleled in the title insurance industry. In Orlando, 55 Fidelity representatives issue title insurance and perform other title-related services for thousands of area clients. Title insurance differs from other

types of insurance in that it relates to past events that affect the title to a property at the time of closing, and not to unforeseen future events.

The quality of customer service and the level of employee loyalty and commitment at Fidelity National Title, its parent company Fidelity National Financial, and its family of underwriters—including American Title Insurance Company—are enhanced by its employee stock ownership. Stock ownership serves as a motivational force for employees who recognize that the company's success is dependent upon their individual efforts and contributions. The program is credited with helping the company grow from its ranking of 48th in 1981 to become the nation's fourth-largest title insurance underwriter.

While other title insurance companies struggled for survival during an industry dip between 1987 and 1991, Fidelity National Title was the only title insurance company

to report consecutive profits from its operations during that time. Moody's Investors Service found Fidelity National Title's investment portfolio had a higher percentage of cash and investment-grade fixed maturities than the portfolios of any leading title insurance company in the United States. Moody's findings showed Fidelity's ratio of liquid assets to paid losses exceeded all others, and that the company had the most years of claims payments in reserves of all eight leading national title insurance firms.

Setting the standard is all part of the Fidelity National Title Insurance Company philosophy. "At Fidelity, we offer our client a real and meaningful customization of products and services," says Lyvonne Hatton, vice president and Central Florida district manager. "With a passion for seeking solutions and an expertise that drives performance, our goal is to secure long-term business relationships."

TOP: RICHARD AUSTIN, VICE PRESIDENT AND STATE AGENCY MANAGER (LEFT), AND LYVONNE HATTON, VICE PRESIDENT AND CENTRAL FLORIDA DISTRICT MANAGER, DISCUSS BUSINESS MATTERS OF FIDELITY NATIONAL TITLE INSURANCE COMPANY.

BOTTOM: "AT FIDELITY, WE OFFER OUR CLIENT A REAL AND MEANINGFUL CUSTOMIZATION OF PRODUCTS AND SERVICES," SAYS HATTON.

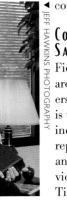

JEFF HAWKINS PHOTOGRAPHY

Splendid China

A s one of Central Florida's newest attractions, Splendid China has been described as a miniature journey through 5,000 years of Chinese history and culture. Replicas highlighting China's most scenic landmarks and historical sites are featured throughout the showcase. More than 10,000 miles of China's vast beauty have been condensed into a picturesque walking tour. From the ancient stones of the Great Wall to the 35-foot re-creation of the 1,200-year-old *Grand Buddha* statue, each exhibit has been meticulously constructed in miniature to represent its original counterpart in China.

Cultural Exchange

The making of Splendid China has been called a labor of love for both Chinese and American workers. Covering 76 acres, the $100 million Splendid China is modeled after the original Splendid China theme park, which opened in 1989 in Shenzhen, China, near Hong Kong. Built by the Overseas Enterprise of China Travel Service (Holdings) Hong Kong Limited, Florida's Splendid China was designed to tell the story of the Chinese people and to promote interest in Chinese culture. It has also served to enhance international relations between the United States and China. As the first tourism project of its size and nature ever built outside China, the attraction exemplifies economic and technical cooperation between the United States and China.

"Our new park is the external symbol of our friendship," says Ma Chi Man, chairman of Splendid China and vice president of China Travel Service Ltd. in Hong Kong. "It will also help to enhance cultural exchange as well as tourism development in our two countries."

Something for Everyone

From its newly designed Chinatown—filled with authentic shops, vendors, collectibles, artifacts, foods, and street entertainers—to theater shows with more than 100 performers, Splendid China combines education with entertainment for a unique travel experience. The park is an inspiration to one's senses with its serene plant and flower gardens. Suzhou Garden is a 65,000-square-foot plaza displaying the sights, sounds, and aromas of a centuries-old Chinese commercial street. There is a children's amusement park featuring Chinese legends and craft demonstrations for all ages.

Splendid China's 1,000-seat amphitheater features a variety of original Chinese entertainment, including folk dancers and singers, acrobatic performers, actors, musicians, magicians, and martial artists who have arrived directly from China to perform for thousands of area visitors.

For those intrigued by Chinese art and architecture, there is much to see throughout the park. Guests are greeted by the largest traditional Chinese-style decorated archway— 44 feet high and 82 feet wide— ever built outside of China. There are temples, towers, palaces, grotto murals, wooden pagodas, and stone arch bridges. Among the rare works of art featured are more than 30,000 tiny, handmade figurines and life-size figures. The pieces, including replicas of the famed terra cotta warriors, populate the park to illustrate the lives and customs of the Chinese people.

The park also features bookshops, herb shops, and apparel stores. Fast-food restaurants offer traditional fare as well as such Chinese delicacies as octopus flakes and stewed bamboo.

Evenings at Splendid China are filled with an array of colorful performances, including the *Mysterious Kingdom of the Orient*, featuring the best Chinese acrobats and dancers, and the *Magical Snow Tiger Adventure*, which allows audience members to pet the Florida panther, sit beside a beautiful snow tiger or 750-pound lion, and touch a variety of animals, many of which are endangered species.

Brilliantly lit lanterns line the theme park's walkways, waterscapes, and gardens. Specially designed lighting systems illuminate exhibit areas to enhance the authentic storytelling settings. Splendid China offers educational and recreational fun for all ages, spanning centuries to bring harmony between American and Chinese cultures.

CLOCKWISE FROM TOP LEFT: SPLENDID CHINA ALLOWS VISITORS TO VIEW REPLICAS THAT HIGHLIGHT SOME OF CHINA'S MOST SCENIC LANDMARKS, SUCH AS THE GREAT WALL.

SPLENDID CHINA PRESENTS AN ARRAY OF COLORFUL PERFORMANCES AND EXOTIC ANIMAL ENCOUNTERS AT THE *Magical Snow Tiger Adventure*.

THE *Mysterious Kingdom of the Orient* FEATURES THE BEST CHINESE ACROBATS AND DANCERS.

PHOTOGRAPHERS

WILLIAM E. BARKSDALE is a Memphis-based, independent agricultural photojournalist who has photographed and written about Memphis-area agriculture for nearly four decades. He contributes to numerous farm magazines, and his photography is used in marketing communications by many firms providing input to the farm market. A native of Fort Smith, Arkansas, Barksdale earned a bachelor of science in agriculture from the University of Arkansas. His images also appeared Towery Publishing's *Memphis: New Visions, New Horizons.*

GARY BENDER has lived in West Virginia and Tennessee and specializes in wedding photography. He spent four years in the U.S. Marines, and 12 as an air traffic controller. Bender currently resides in Christmas, Florida.

BOB BRAUN is a freelance photographer specializing in corporate, industrial, architectural, and resort photography for brochures, annual reports, and editorial works. A graduate of Brooks Institute of Photography in Santa Barbara, Braun has won numerous industry awards, and his images have appeared in such publications as *Architectural Digest, Better Homes & Gardens,* and *Orlando Magazine.* Braun's clients have included Kodak, Choice Hotels, Best Western International, and Chemlawn.

EVERETT & SOULÉ is owned by Skip Everett and Anne Soulé, who for the past 15 years have specialized in architectural, residential, commercial, and interior/exterior photography. Prior to that, the two worked in the advertising industry, photographing for various corporate clients. Everett and Soulé have traveled the country, documenting the professional rodeo circuit and other elements of western culture. Currently, they are at work on a book of photographs documenting their 1995 bicycle trek from San Diego to Orlando.

CHARLENE FARIS, a native of Fleming County, Kentucky, is the owner and operator of Charlene Faris Photos. Specializing in travel, historic, and inspirational photography, Faris has won numerous awards, including several honors from the National League of American Pen Women art shows. She was a 1994 Pulitzer Prize nominee for wedding photos of Lyle Lovett and Julia Roberts, which have now been published in more than 20 nations. Faris also completed an art project for the Hoosier Salon with a grant from the Indiana Arts Commission and the National Endowment for the Arts. Faris' images have appeared in several Towery publications.

WILLIAM T. GRIFFIN, originally from Montgomery, Alabama, has lived in the Orlando area since 1961. He specializes in wedding and commercial product photography, as well as oil portraits and paintings, and his images have been displayed at Epcot in the Kodak pavilion. A World War II veteran, Griffin now enjoys making furniture and building radio-controlled model airplanes.

C. JORDAN HARRIS is a freelance photographer specializing in editorial, corporate, and documentary photography. A graduate of Southeastern Photographic Studies in Daytona Beach, Harris travels to the Dominican Republic annually to work on his long-range project, a book of photographs documenting his travels.

JONATHAN M. HAYT is a self-employed sports photographer, working for the Tampa Bay Lightning as team photographer. Hayt also photographs for Pinnacle Brands trading cards, the NBA, and the NFL. A native of San Diego, Hayt graduated from the University of Idaho with a bachelor's degree in architecture, and gained considerable experience working for eight years as a lighting technician for *Sports Illustrated.* His images also appeared in Towery's *Treasures on Tampa Bay: Tampa, St. Petersburg, Clearwater.*

HILLSTROM STOCK PHOTO, established in 1967, is a full-service stock photography based in Chicago. Its files include images of architecture, agriculture backgrounds, classic autos, gardens, and high-risk adventure/sports.

TOM HURST, a native of Ohio, specializes in editorial photography for such corporate clients as AT&T, Lucent Technologies, Nickelodeon Studios, and the Kansas City Royals. A recipient of the Florida Golden Image Award for black-and-white still photography, Hurst enjoys the excitement of location shoots for his various clients. His images have appeared in numerous national publications, including *USA Today, People,* the *Saturday Evening Post,* and the *New York Times.*

ALAN C. KNAPP is originally from North Point, Long Island, and has lived in the Orlando area since 1986. His specialties include stock, travel, and sports photography. With degrees from Furman University and the University of Central Florida, Knapp also studied commercial photography at Mid-Florida Technical Institute.

BUD LEE studied at Columbia University School of Fine Arts in New York and the National Academy of Fine Arts before moving to the Orlando area about 20 years ago. A self-employed photojournalist, Lee was named *Life* magazine's News Photographer of the Year in 1967 and received the Military Photographer of the Year award in 1966. He founded both the Florida Photographers Workshop and the Iowa Photographers Workshop. Lee's work can be seen in *Esquire, Life, Travel and Leisure, Rolling Stone,* the *Washington Post,* the *New York Times,* and *Treasures on Tampa Bay: Tampa, St. Petersburg, Clearwater.*

JAMES LEMASS studied art in his native Ireland before moving to Cambridge, Massachusetts, in 1987. His areas of specialty include people and travel photography, and his work can be seen in publications by Aer Lingus, British

Airways, and USAir, as well as the Nynex Yellow Pages. Lemass has also worked for the Massachusetts Office of Travel and Tourism, and his photographs have appeared in three other Towery publications—*New York: Metropolis of the American Dream; Treasures on Tampa Bay: Tampa, St. Petersburg, Clearwater;* and *Washington: City on a Hill.*

JAMES PHILLIPS had intended to make a career in museology, having received an anthropology degree from the University of South Florida, as well as specialized training from the Smithsonian Institute in Washington, D.C., and the Florida State Museum in Gainesville. As a student of photography only in his spare time, Phillips won the grand prize in the 32nd Annual Suncoast Photography Competition, the first major photography contest he had entered. Since then, he has won numerous awards for his work. In 1988, Phillips left the museum field altogether and began a new career as a freelance commercial photographer, specializing in Florida nature and scenic stock images. His photographs have appeared in calendars, posters, magazines, and books, including *Treasures on Tampa Bay: Tampa, St. Petersburg, Clearwater.*

JOHN B. RANDLE, a native of Toronto, moved to the Orlando area in 1988. A graduate of the University of Illinois, he owns Randle Communications, Inc., which specializes in graphic design, business-to-business print communications, and corporate logos and photography. His clients include AAA, Pfizer Pharmaceuticals, Centex Homes, and Omega Medical Imaging. Randle is the recipient of 32 international graphic design awards for television and publication design from the Broadcast Designers Association.

BRITT RUNION is a freelance photographer specializing in advertising, corporate, and editorial photography. His clients include Texaco, Target, Harcourt Brace & Company, and Sheraton Hotels, for whom he spent six months in South America on photo shoots. A former chief photographer for Sea World in Orlando, Runion is the recipient of several Addy awards, and his images have appeared in *PC Week, Inc.,* and *Money* magazines.

DOUG SCALETTA, originally from Frederick, Maryland, holds a bachelor of visual arts in photography from the University of Maryland. A freelance photographer, he specializes in advertising and commercial photography for clients such as Sprint, Columbia Healthcare, and Grand Cypress Resorts. Scaletta has received numerous awards, including gold (1994) and silver (1995) medals from Creative Club Orlando.

DOUG SEIBERT is the owner of Orlando-based Esquire Photographers Inc., which specializes in commercial and aerial photography. Currently, Seibert lives in downtown Orlando with his wife and four cats.

TOM TILL is a widely published freelance photographer from Moab, Utah. A graduate of Iowa State University, he specializes in landscape, nature, and historical photography, and has photographed these subjects worldwide. Till has been the sole photographer for 17 books and was honored with the Guilfoyle/NANPA award for landscape photography in 1995.

JOHN UNRUE, a native of Michigan, has lived in Winter Park since 1984. A freelance photographer, he has extensive experience in aerial photography and, as an avid golfer, a special interest in golf courses. The recipient of numerous awards from Kodak, Unrue has worked with such clients as Hitachi, Penzoil, Shell Oil, and Disney.

BEN VAN HOOK is a freelance photographer for national magazines, as well as a contract photographer with New York City-based Black Star. Originally from Lexington, Kentucky, Van Hook was the corecipient of the 1989 Pulitzer Prize for Photography and has been named Kentucky Photographer of the Year three times. His images have appeared in publications including *Sports Illustrated, National Geographic, Fortune, Newsweek,* and *Life,* as well as on the cover of *A Day in the Life of the National Hockey League.* Van Hook and his wife live in Orlando.

STEVE VAUGHN is a familiar name to outdoor festival followers throughout Florida; he won first place in photography at the 1995 Winter Park Sidewalk Art Festival and was chosen as poster artist for the 1996 Winter Park Autumn Art Festival. A graduate of the University of Florida, Vaughn specializes in panoramic images, and his work is included in numerous private and corporate collections. He maintains a file of about 500 photographs from throughout Florida, which includes panoramics of all major Florida cities. Prior to launching his career as a fine art photographer, Vaughn spent 25 years with the *Orlando Sentinel*, serving as managing editor from 1979 to 1980 and as executive editor from 1980 to 1992.

Other photographers and organizations that contributed to *Orlando: The City Beautiful* are Randy Belice, Andrew Bernstein, Nathaniel Butler, Glenn James, Bobby Jenkins, Fernando Medina, NBA Photos, and the Orange County Historical Museum.

▲ BEN VAN HOOK

ORLANDO'S OWN *Lady Liberty* IS ONE OF THE CITY'S MOST BELOVED LANDMARKS. A MINIATURE REPLICA OF THE ELLIS ISLAND ORIGINAL, THE PATRIOTIC STATUE GREETS TRAVELERS TO LAKE IVANHOE.

INDEX OF PROFILES

cocktails
STYLE RECIPES

cocktails
STYLE RECIPES

photography DAVID MATHESON

styling GEORGE DOLESE

text NORMAN KOLPAS

executive editor CLAY IDE

a toast – to the perfect cocktail

When it comes to entertaining, style is in the details. A well-mixed drink not only makes guests feel welcome, it's also the ultimate way to set the mood for a festive gathering. And like the best parties, the most memorable cocktails are a balance of tradition and originality.

That's why we're pleased to bring you this collection of classic drinks and new variations on old favorites. The recipes have been organized to help you choose the right drinks for any occasion, from an intimate fireside gathering to a backyard barbecue. Throughout, you'll find easy tips and tricks to serve drinks with an extra touch of style that will help you make them – and the event – uniquely your own.

THE POTTERY BARN DESIGN TEAM

POTTERY BARN

President Laura Alber
Executive Vice President Nancy Green
Senior Vice President, Creative Services Clay Ide
Senior Vice President, Design Celia Tejada
Print Production Julia Buelow Gilbert
Editor Samantha Moss
Photo Coordinator, Special Projects Laura Thomas

WELDON OWEN

Chief Executive Officer John Owen
President & Chief Operating Officer Terry Newell
Chief Financial Officer Christine E. Munson
Vice President, Publisher Roger Shaw
Vice President, International Sales Stuart Laurence
Creative Director Gaye Allen

Senior Art Director Emma Boys
Project Editor Peter Cieply
Designers Briar Levit, Shadin Saah
Photo Coordinator Meghan Hildebrand
Production Director Chris Hemesath
Color Manager Teri Bell

Cocktails Style Recipes was conceived and produced by
Weldon Owen Inc.
814 Montgomery Street, San Francisco, CA 94133
in collaboration with Pottery Barn
3250 Van Ness Avenue, San Francisco, CA 94109

Set in Praxis EF™ and Formata™

Color separations by Bright Arts Graphics Singapore (Pte.) Ltd.
Printed in Singapore by Tien Wah Press (Pte.) Ltd.

A WELDON OWEN PRODUCTION

First printed 2005
10 9 8 7 6 5 4 3 2 1

Library of Congress Cataloging-in-Publication Data is available.
ISBN 1-7408-9540-1

Photographs: margarita (page 1); kir framboise royale, bellini bella,
berry merry Christmas (from left, page 2); pousse-café (page 5);
choco-mintini (right); dirty martini, vesper, green apple martini,
red vesper (from left, pages 22–23); Manhattan (page 25); frozen
mojito, mojito (pages 48–49); blue Hawaiian (page 51); white
Russian (pages 74–75); cognac and brandy (page 77).

contents

AND ACCESSORIES FOR MASTERFUL MIXOLOGY. FROM CHOOSING

THIS IS YOUR QUICK GUIDE TO **bar** essentials

REDISCOVER ONE OF THE CLASSIC PLEASURES OF ENTERTAINING: SERVING DRINKS FROM YOUR OWN HOME BAR

Hospitality often begins with the simple act of offering guests something to drink when they arrive at your home. No gesture puts people at ease more quickly, providing the pleasure of refreshment and the promise of spirited festivity and lively conversation.

Setting up a bar is easy, whether your home already has one built in or you use a sideboard, counter, cocktail table, or service cart. The following pages outline the basics of preparing your bar, from choosing mixing tools and glassware to selecting accessories and creating garnishes. You don't need a fully stocked bar to prepare most cocktails, however. Make entertaining simple and fun by setting up your bar to serve a smaller selection of drinks, whether our classic cocktails and new twists on old favorites, or your own inspired variations. Your hospitality will be all the more memorable for it.

TAILOR YOUR HOME BAR TO THE STYLE OF THE OCCASION AND THE DRINK MENU THAT YOU'VE CHOSEN FOR IT

When you entertain with drinks, the first step to ensure success is to gear the party to the occasion. Are you hosting casually elegant cocktails before the theater, or throwing a relaxed poolside party? An after-dinner gathering beside the fireplace calls for a different selection of drinks than a barbecue on the patio. With that in mind, we've organized the recipes in this book by the style of occasion to which they're best suited.

Once you've settled on your choices, compile two lists: one with all the ingredients you'll need for the drinks, the other with the mixing tools, accessories, and glassware you'll need to prepare them. Check off the items you already have, and shop in advance for those you still need. Then, before guests arrive, arrange your ingredients and equipment in the bar area, setting them out, as space allows, in a logical and attractive arrangement that suits the order of preparation.

A home wet bar stands ready to prepare an array of classic and contemporary cocktails, from martinis to refreshing blended drinks.

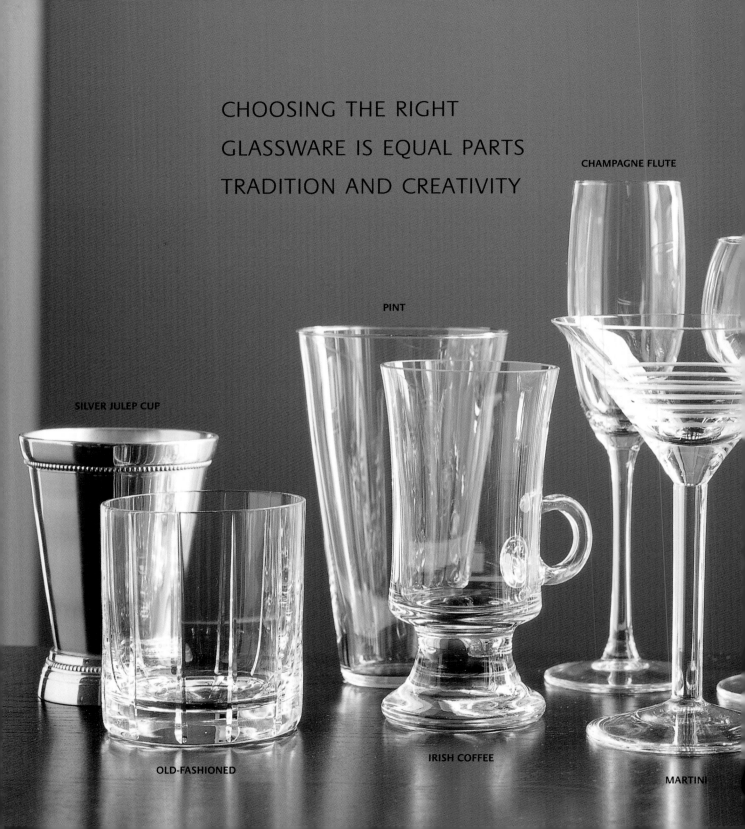

CHOOSING THE RIGHT
GLASSWARE IS EQUAL PARTS
TRADITION AND CREATIVITY

CHAMPAGNE FLUTE

PINT

SILVER JULEP CUP

OLD-FASHIONED

IRISH COFFEE

MARTINI

Never let the lack of a specific glass keep you from making a cocktail. You can always get creative, as long as the glass you choose is generally appropriate for the drink. Long stems let you hold a chilled drink without warming it; sturdy glasses stand up to muddling. Tradition calls for specific glasses to be used for drinks like juleps or old-fashioneds, but don't be afraid to break the rules.

WINE GLASS

COLLINS

POUSSE-CAFÉ

HIGHBALL

MARGARITA

DOUBLE OLD-FASHIONED

BASIC TOOLS FOR PREPARING DRINKS CAN BE AS STYLISH AND BEAUTIFUL AS THEY ARE USEFUL AND FUNCTIONAL

Designed to tailor form to function, the mixing tools you assemble can bring visual style to a home bar. Cocktail shakers feature snug caps with built-in strainers, letting you quickly combine and chill liquids with ice before trickling them into glasses. Mixing glasses and slender bar spoons can be used to stir drinks gently before pouring, and calibrated shot glasses and beakers help you measure potions with precision.

Smaller bar tools fulfill still more specific tasks, including spouts to make pouring from bottles easier; muddlers to crush sugar and seasonings in the bottom of a glass; reamers to extract juice from citrus halves; zesters, peelers, and paring knives to cut garnishes; and scoops or tongs for ice. Many implements may also be found in antique shops, giving you further opportunities to buy tools that are uniquely beautiful.

All the basics: bottle with pouring spout, large and small cocktail shakers, mixing glass, shot glass, and martini pitcher (opposite, clockwise from back); assorted bar tools (left, top); muddler (left, middle); ice bucket and tongs (left, bottom)

ACCESSORIES GIVE YOUR
PRESENTATION AN AIR OF
OCCASION AND YOUR
DRINKS A SENSE OF STYLE

Cocktail accessories serve practical purposes, of course. Coasters and cocktail napkins prevent furniture surfaces from being marred. Small dishes and bowls hold classic complements to many cocktails, like olives or nuts (and an extra bowl provides a place to deposit olive pits). Swizzle sticks let guests re-stir drinks as ice melts. Cocktail picks make it possible to pluck olives and other garnishes from a glass.

Beyond these utilitarian roles, however, your choice of accessories adds to the atmosphere of an occasion. Coasters may be elegant silver, crafted stone, rustic cork, or many other materials. Cocktail picks needn't be standard wood; look for reusable stainless steel ones, or spear olives with playful cocktail umbrellas. There's even the opportunity to create your own original accessories – gluing objects to the ends of swizzle sticks, for example, to make them distinctive.

Cocktail accessories add style: small bowls and reusable picks for garnishes (opposite); swizzle sticks topped with seashells (left, top); a variety of coasters (left, middle); and chocolate-dipped candy cane swizzle sticks (left, bottom).

WHEN HOSTING SPECIAL
GATHERINGS, SMALL DETAILS
LIKE GARNISHES CAN MAKE
A BIG IMPRESSION

Oftentimes, a celery stalk or an olive on a toothpick suffices
as a cocktail's finishing touch. With a little additional effort,
however, you can achieve eye-catching, casually stylish effects
with the drinks that you serve — final flourishes that add both
visual appeal and flavor enhancement.

Instead of one piece of fruit, for example, stack thin slices of
several kinds with complementary colors and flavors. When
fresh cherries are in season, use them instead of bottled
maraschino cherries. Look for ideas for unique swizzle sticks
like vanilla beans, licorice twists, or beef jerky. Look, too, for
ways to vary the ingredients that sometimes coat the rims of
glasses, adding flavorful embellishments like chili powder or
minced herbs to the salt or crushed candy or grated chocolate
to the sugar, to complement a drink's taste and hue.

Garnishes can be simple and still be dramatic: lemon twists and slices give
margarita setups fresh appeal (opposite); strawberry and lime slices decorate
a blended strawberry margarita (right, top); lemon zests float in champagne
cocktails (right, middle); olives and lemon zests are classic martini garnishes.

EASY RECIPES AND STYLISH SERVING IDEAS. WE'LL SHOW YOU

MARYS, AND MANY MORE   classic cocktails

CLASSIC COCKTAILS GIVE GATHERINGS
A SENSE OF SOPHISTICATED GAIETY
AND ADD GLAMOUR TO ANY SETTING

"Cocktails at six." So begins many a classic dinner invitation, conjuring images of spirited gatherings full of witty conversation and convivial mingling before moving on to "dinner at eight."

The word "cocktail," which originally referred to a mixed-breed horse with a docked tail, was first fancifully used around the beginning of the 19th century to describe mixed drinks that combine one or more spirits, water, sugar, and a dash of bitters – a formula that endures today in drinks like the classic Manhattan (opposite and page 37). Down through the decades, creative bartenders and at-home hosts have broadened that definition to include drinks as varied as the dry martini and its many offspring (pages 26–31), the fruity cosmopolitan family (pages 32–35), and various bloody Marys (pages 44-47). Diverse as they may be, any of these cocktails can help start an evening in style.

martini

ALTHOUGH VODKA OFTEN STARS IN TODAY'S MARTINIS, THE TRUE
CLASSIC GETS ITS BRACING TASTE FROM JUNIPER-SCENTED GIN, PLUS
A HINT OF DRY VERMOUTH – EVEN IF ONLY A DROP.

serve in style

- Complement the pristine elegance of a classic martini by presenting it on a tray made of silver or other lustrous metal.
- Allow guests to choose their own garnish. In addition to olives stuffed with red pimiento, serve those filled with almond, lemon peel, or onion, or offer whole caperberries. Olives stuffed with anchovies, garlic, or jalapeño chiles provide guests with stronger-flavored alternatives.

1 tablespoon dry vermouth • 3 oz (90 ml) gin •
1 green cocktail olive, for garnish

- Put a martini glass in the freezer, or fill it with ice and water.
- Pour the vermouth into a cocktail shaker or mixing glass; swirl it around to coat the sides of the shaker, then pour it out. (If you prefer a "wetter" martini, leave some of the vermouth in.)
- Fill the cocktail shaker or mixing glass two-thirds full of ice cubes. Pour in the gin. Close the shaker and shake vigorously, or stir in the mixing glass with a bar spoon, for 15–20 seconds.
- Remove the martini glass from the freezer or empty out the ice and water, shaking out any remaining drops. Strain the drink into the chilled glass. Spear the olive on a cocktail pick or toothpick, place it in the glass, and serve immediately.

vesper

1½ oz (45 ml) vodka • 1½ oz (45 ml) gin • 1 oz (30 ml) Lillet Blanc • 1 strip lemon zest, 3 inches (7.5 cm) long

- Chill a martini glass in the freezer, or fill it with ice and water and set it aside to cool.

- Pour the vodka, gin, and Lillet Blanc into a cocktail shaker or mixing glass filled two-thirds with ice. Close and shake the shaker, or stir in the mixing glass with a bar spoon, for 15–20 seconds.

- Remove the martini glass from the freezer, or empty out the ice and water, shaking out any drops. Strain the drink into the chilled glass. Hold the lemon zest strip over the drink and twist its ends in opposite directions to release its oils before dropping it into the glass and serving.

dirty martini

3 oz (90 ml) gin or vodka • 1–2 teaspoons juice from green cocktail olives • 1 teaspoon dry vermouth • 3 green cocktail olives, for garnish

- Chill a martini glass as above. Fill a mixing glass or cocktail shaker two-thirds full of ice. Add the gin or vodka, olive juice, and vermouth. Stir, or close the shaker and shake, for 15–20 seconds.

- Strain the drink into the chilled empty glass. Spear the olives on a cocktail pick or toothpick, place in the glass, and serve immediately.

red vesper

1½ oz (45 ml) vodka • 1½ oz (45 ml) gin • 1 oz (30 ml) Lillet Rouge • 1–3 fresh red raspberries, for garnish

- Chill a martini glass as described at left.

- Follow the instructions for the Vesper at left, substituting Lillet Rouge for the Lillet Blanc in the same proportions.

- Strain the red Vesper into the chilled glass. Spear the raspberries on a cocktail pick, place the pick in the glass, and serve.

martini tips

- The Vesper was James Bond's drink of choice. Look for a paperback copy of Ian Fleming's *Casino Royale*, in which Bond names this martini after his love interest, Vesper Lynd. Photocopy the page on which he orders the drink, and cut the copies for use as tongue-in-cheek coasters.
- For a special presentation, chill a small individual carafe or pitcher along with the martini glass. Mix a double batch of the cocktail, pour the extra into the carafe, and serve it alongside the drink, set into a small bowl of crushed ice to keep it chilled.
- For a modern slant, look for stemless martini glasses that nestle in their own small bowls of crushed ice.

melonball martini

2 oz (60 ml) melon liqueur • 1 oz (30 ml) vanilla vodka • 1 tablespoon lemon juice • 3 balls ripe honeydew melon, cut with a melon baller, for garnish

● Chill a martini glass in the freezer, or fill it with ice and water and set it aside to cool.

● Fill a mixing glass or cocktail shaker about two-thirds full with ice cubes. Pour in the melon liqueur, vanilla vodka, and lemon juice. Stir with a bar spoon in the mixing glass, or cover the shaker and shake it, for 15–20 seconds.

● Remove the martini glass from the freezer, or empty out the ice and water, flicking out any last drops. Strain the drink into the chilled glass. Spear the melon balls on a cocktail pick or toothpick, place the pick in the glass, and serve immediately.

green apple martini

2 oz (60 ml) apple vodka • 1 oz (30 ml) sour apple schnapps • 1 tablespoon bottled sweetened lime juice (such as Rose's) • 3 thin wedges green apple, rubbed with 1 teaspoon lemon juice, for garnish

● Chill a martini glass as above. Fill a mixing glass or cocktail shaker two-thirds full of ice. Pour in the apple vodka, schnapps, and sweetened lime juice. Stir the drink in the mixing glass with a bar spoon, or close the shaker and shake, for 15–20 seconds. Strain the drink into the empty chilled glass.

● Garnish the glass with the apple wedges by spearing them with a cocktail pick or toothpick and fanning them out slightly, halfway down the pick. Place the pick in the drink and serve immediately.

choco-mintini

6 peppermint-stick candies, crushed • 1 tablespoon chocolate shavings • 1 tablespoon light corn syrup • 1 oz (30 ml) vanilla vodka • 2 oz (60 ml) white crème de cacao • 1 oz (30 ml) peppermint schnapps • peppermint sticks dipped in chocolate, for garnish

● Mix the crushed peppermint candies and chocolate shavings, and pour the mixture onto a shallow plate slightly larger than the rim of the martini glass. Pour the corn syrup onto another shallow plate and use it to moisten the martini glass rim; then immediately invert the rim into the crushed candy, turning it until the rim is evenly coated. Chill thoroughly, upright, in the freezer.

● Pour the vanilla vodka, crème de cacao, and peppermint schnapps into a mixing glass or cocktail shaker filled two-thirds full with ice. Stir in the mixing glass with a bar spoon, or close the shaker and shake vigorously, for 15–20 seconds.

● Remove the martini glass from the freezer. Strain the drink into the chilled glass. Insert the chocolate-dipped candy cane, leaning it along the side of the glass. Serve immediately.

cosmopolitan

SINCE ITS RISE TO WIDESPREAD POPULARITY IN THE MID-1990s,
THE "COSMO" HAS BECOME A COCKTAIL STANDARD, WITH ITS
PERFECTLY REFRESHING BALANCE OF TART AND SWEET FLAVORS.

2 oz (60 ml) lemon vodka • 1 oz (30 ml) cranberry juice cocktail •
1 tablespoon Cointreau • 1 tablespoon fresh lime juice • 2 frozen
cranberries and 1 strip lime zest, 3 inches (7.5 cm) long, for garnish

- Chill a cocktail glass in the freezer or by filling it with ice
cubes and cold water and setting it aside to cool.

- Fill a cocktail shaker about two-thirds full with ice cubes. Pour
in the vodka, cranberry juice, Cointreau, and lime juice. Close the
shaker and shake vigorously for 15–20 seconds. (Note: this drink
is best shaken, not stirred in a mixing glass.)

- Remove the glass from the freezer or empty out the ice and
water, shaking out any remaining drops. Strain the liquid into the
chilled glass. Spear two frozen cranberries on a cocktail pick and
loosely wrap with lime zest, and serve alongside or in the drink.

a cosmopolitan approach

- For an elegant and personal
touch, present each individual
cocktail on its own small serving
tray, which can double as a
coaster for the drink.

- For dramatic effect, use a
large tray to carry drinks, still in
their shakers, and glasses to
wherever guests have gathered,
and decant and garnish the
cosmopolitans in front of them.

tropicosmo

2 oz (60 ml) pineapple-flavored vodka • 1½ oz (45 ml) pineapple juice • 1 tablespoon passion fruit–flavored liqueur • 1 tablespoon bottled sweetened lime juice (such as Rose's) • 3 fresh pineapple wedges, for garnish

• Chill a cocktail glass in the freezer or by filling it with ice and cold water and setting it aside to cool.

• Fill a cocktail shaker two-thirds full with ice cubes. Pour in the pineapple-flavored vodka, pineapple juice, passion fruit–flavored liqueur, and sweetened lime juice. Close the shaker and shake vigorously for 15–20 seconds.

• Remove the cocktail glass from the freezer or empty out the ice and water, shaking out any remaining drops. Strain the drink into the chilled glass. Spear the pineapple wedges on a cocktail pick, or cut small holes in them and thread the wedges onto a bendable straw. Serve immediately.

mediterranean

2 oz (60 ml) orange- or mandarin-flavored vodka • 1½ oz (45 ml) bottled pomegranate juice • 1 tablespoon fresh lemon juice • 1 tablespoon limoncello (Italian lemon-flavored liqueur) • 1 strip each lemon and orange zest, 3 inches (7.5 cm) long, for garnish

• Chill a cocktail glass as above. Pour the vodka, pomegranate juice, lemon juice, and limoncello into a cocktail shaker filled two-thirds with ice. Close the shaker and shake for 15–20 seconds.

• Strain the drink into the empty chilled glass. Twist together or tie the lemon and orange zest strips, and garnish the drink by draping the tied zests on the edge of the glass. Serve immediately.

citropolitan

Granulated sugar and grated lemon zest, for coating rim • 1 fresh lemon wedge, for coating rim • 2 oz (60 ml) lemon-flavored vodka • 1 oz (30 ml) triple sec or Cointreau • 1 oz (30 ml) fresh lemon juice • 1 tablespoon bottled sweetened lime juice (such as Rose's) • 1 strip lemon zest, 3 inches (7.5 cm) long, and 1 sour lemon hard candy, for garnish

• Pour a layer of sugar and grated lemon zest onto a plate slightly larger than the rim of a cocktail glass. Moisten the rim of the glass generously with the lemon wedge; then invert the rim into the lemon-sugar mixture, turning it until the rim is evenly coated. Chill, upright, in the freezer.

• Fill a cocktail shaker two-thirds full with ice cubes. Pour in the lemon-flavored vodka, triple sec or Cointreau, and lemon and lime juice. Close the shaker and shake vigorously for 15–20 seconds.

• Remove the cocktail glass from the freezer and strain the drink into the chilled glass. Hold the lemon zest strip over the cocktail and twist in opposite directions to release its oils before dropping it into the drink. Place the sour lemon hard candy in the glass and serve immediately.

manhattan

2½ oz (75 ml) whiskey (preferably bourbon or rye) • 1½ tablespoons sweet vermouth • 2 dashes Angostura bitters • 1 small strip fresh orange peel • 1 maraschino cherry with stem, for garnish

- Chill a cocktail glass in the freezer.

- Fill a cocktail shaker two-thirds full with ice cubes. Pour in the whiskey and sweet vermouth; add the bitters. Close the shaker and shake vigorously for 15–20 seconds. Strain the drink into the chilled glass. Twist the orange peel between your fingers to release its oils, and rub the orange part around the rim of the glass; discard the peel. Garnish with the cherry and serve.

metropolitan flair

- Add a sense of club-room sophistication by presenting the Manhattan to your guest on a leather coaster.
- To spark conversation, pick up copies of your favorite New York City newspaper and leave them folded on the cocktail table.

SOME COCKTAILS JUST CAN'T BE IMPROVED UPON. THE MANHATTAN HAS BEEN A CLASSIC SINCE THE LATE 19TH CENTURY, AND THOUGH SOURS MAY BE MADE WITH OTHER LIQUORS, WHISKEY IS THE DEFINITIVE CHOICE.

whisky sour

2 ounces (60 ml) Canadian blended whisky • 1½ tablespoons fresh lemon juice • 1½ teaspoons superfine sugar • 1 thin slice fresh orange, seeded, for garnish • 1 maraschino cherry with stem, for garnish

- Chill a sour glass or other cocktail glass in the freezer.

- Fill a cocktail shaker two-thirds full with ice cubes. Pour in the whisky and lemon juice and add the sugar. Close the shaker and shake vigorously for 15–20 seconds.

- Remove the sour glass from the freezer. Strain the drink into the chilled glass. Twist the orange slice to release some of its juice, and add it and the cherry to the glass. Serve immediately.

sour garnishes

- Use a cocktail pick to skewer the orange slice and cherry together, for easier removal.
- For a more exotic effect, in place of the orange and cherry, substitute a whole fresh kumquat on a toothpick or cocktail stick; kumquats are edible, peel and all.

tom collins

2 oz (60 ml) gin • 1 oz (30 ml) fresh lemon juice • 2 teaspoons superfine sugar • 4–6 oz (120–180 ml) club soda • 1 orange wedge and 1 maraschino cherry, for garnish

- Fill a cocktail shaker two-thirds full with ice cubes. Add the gin, lemon juice, and sugar. Close the cocktail shaker and shake vigorously for 15–20 seconds.

- Fill a Collins glass with ice cubes. Strain the cocktail into the glass. Pour in the club soda to taste, and stir briefly with a swizzle stick. Garnish with the orange wedge, squeezing it slightly, and the cherry. Serve immediately.

tall and cool

- For the traditional presentation, use one of the tall, narrow, straight-sided glasses specifically known as a "Collins glass."
- A Collins simply doesn't seem complete without a swizzle stick. Clear sticks are classic, but many options are available.

LEGEND HAS IT THAT THE LEMON-SCENTED TOM COLLINS WAS INVENTED IN LONDON AND NAMED FOR THE BARTENDER WHO CREATED IT, AND THE SIDECAR IN PARIS, TO WARM A MOTORCYCLING WWI CAPTAIN.

sidecar

granulated sugar and 1 lemon wedge, for coating rim • 2 oz (60 ml) brandy • 1 oz (30 ml) triple sec • 1 oz (30 ml) fresh lemon juice

- Pour a layer of sugar onto a plate slightly larger than the rim of a cocktail glass. Squeezing the lemon wedge between your fingers, use it to moisten the rim of the glass generously; then immediately invert the rim into the granulated sugar, turning it until the rim is evenly coated. Chill thoroughly, upright, in the freezer.

- Fill a cocktail shaker two-thirds full with ice. Add the brandy, triple sec, and lemon juice. Cover and shake for 15–20 seconds. Strain the cocktail into the glass and serve.

creative color

- For a more colorful rim coating, mix the granulated sugar with some finely grated lemon zest.
- After moistening the glass's rim with lemon juice, coat only half of it with sugar or sugar and lemon zest, giving your guest the option of sweet or tangy sips.

mint julep

THE SIGNATURE DRINK OF THE KENTUCKY DERBY IS TRADITIONALLY
SERVED IN A SILVER JULEP CUP, THE EXTERIOR OF WHICH DEVELOPS
AN ENTICING LAYER OF FROST WHEN THE COCKTAIL IS MIXED.

derby chic

- Wrap a silver julep cup for decorative effect. Use a wide grosgrain ribbon to tie a bow, or double it to form a "ribbon cozy" that protects hands from the cold surface of the cup. Using a ribbon with wire reinforcement allows you to create a decorative bow that will retain its shape.
- Stylish stainless-steel or other metal cups are also available.

1 or 2 sugar cubes • 4 large fresh mint leaves • 3 oz (90 ml) bourbon • 3 large mint sprigs, for garnish

- Put 1 or 2 sugar cubes and the mint leaves in the bottom of a silver julep cup or a highball or old-fashioned glass. With a muddler, muddle the sugar cubes and mint, crushing them together until the mint leaves are fragrant.

- Fill the julep cup or the glass with crushed ice.

- Pour in the bourbon. Stir well with a bar spoon or a swizzle stick to thoroughly combine the sugar, mint, and bourbon; if using a julep cup, stir until a thin film of frost forms on the outside. Garnish with mint sprigs, crushing them slightly before setting them atop the drink, and serve immediately.

cozy julep

4 large sprigs fresh mint • 1 sugar cube • 3 oz (90 ml) Southern Comfort • 1 lemon slice, for garnish

● Put three mint sprigs and the sugar cube in the bottom of a julep cup or a highball or double old-fashioned glass. With a muddler, firmly but gently pound and grind the mint sprigs and sugar together until the mint is partially crushed.

● Fill the cup or glass with crushed ice. Pour in the Southern Comfort and stir well with a bar spoon or swizzle stick; if using a julep cup, stir until a film of frost forms on the outside. Garnish with the lemon slice and remaining mint sprig and serve.

sparkling lemonade julep

1 large sprig fresh mint • 1 tablespoon superfine sugar • 2 oz (60 ml) lemon juice • 1½ oz (45 ml) bourbon • 4 oz (120 ml) club soda • 1 slice lemon, seeded, for garnish

● In the bottom of a sturdy highball glass, firmly but gently pound and grind the mint sprig, sugar, and lemon juice with a muddler until the sugar is dissolved. Stir in the bourbon.

● Fill the glass loosely with ice cubes. Pour in the club soda. Stir well with a bar spoon. Garnish with the lemon slice on top, or, cut a slit in the slice from the center to the edge halfway across, slip it onto the edge of the glass, and serve.

peach julep

3 large sprigs fresh mint • 3 oz (90 ml) peach brandy • 2 drops Angostura bitters • 1 wedge ripe fresh peach, for garnish

● Place the mint sprigs in the bottom of a julep cup or a highball or old-fashioned glass. With a muddler, firmly but gently pound the mint sprigs until they are partially crushed and aromatic.

● Fill the cup or glass with ice. Add the peach brandy and bitters and stir with a bar spoon for 15–20 seconds or, if using a julep cup, until a film of frost forms on the outside. Garnish with the peach slice, placing it on top of the ice, and serve.

southern style

● Add a touch of the Old South by placing a glossy magnolia leaf or other large plant leaf beneath each drink.

● For a more minty-tasting julep, steep the fresh herbs in the spirit for several hours before mixing.

● Make a mint simple syrup for use in juleps or other drinks. Simmer together a bunch of cleaned mint leaves (about 1½ oz/45 g), 1 cup of sugar (250 g), and 2 cups of water (500 ml) in a small saucepan for about five minutes. Before use, cool and remove mint.

bloody mary

AN AMERICAN FAVORITE, THIS DRINK WAS INVENTED AT HARRY'S NEW YORK BAR IN PARIS IN THE 1920s. MANY BARTENDERS HAVE SIGNATURE WAYS TO ADD AN EXTRA JOLT, SUCH AS THE GRATED HORSERADISH IN THIS RECIPE.

extra zing

- Add excitement to the flavor and appearance by sprinkling freshly ground pepper (shown above) or fresh chiles into the ice cube tray before freezing cubes.
- Coat the rims of the glasses by moistening them with fresh lime juice and rolling them in a mixture of salt and mild or medium-hot chili powder.

2 oz (60 ml) vodka • 4 oz (120 ml) high-quality canned or bottled tomato juice • 1½ tablespoons fresh lime juice • ¼ teaspoon prepared horseradish • ¼ teaspoon Worcestershire sauce • ¼ teaspoon hot pepper sauce (such as Tabasco) • ¼ teaspoon freshly ground black pepper • ⅛ teaspoon celery salt • 1 celery stalk, for garnish

- Fill a cocktail shaker two-thirds full with ice cubes. Add the vodka, tomato juice, lime juice, horseradish, Worcestershire sauce, hot pepper sauce, black pepper, and celery salt.

- Cover the cocktail shaker and shake for 15–20 seconds. Place the celery stalk in a pint or double old-fashioned glass and fill it with ice cubes. Strain the cocktail into the glass and serve.

- The spiciness of this cocktail is easy to control. For a hotter drink, use pepper-flavored vodka or more hot pepper sauce; for more zing but a gentler heat, increase the amount of horseradish.

blushing mary

1 cup (250 ml) high-quality canned or bottled tomato juice • 1½ oz (45 ml) hot chili pepper vodka • 1 oz (30 ml) fresh lime juice • ¼ teaspoon Worcestershire sauce • ⅛ teaspoon freshly ground white pepper • ⅛ teaspoon salt • ½ lime slice and 1 cherry tomato, for garnish

● An hour before serving time, line a fine-mesh sieve or a large, clean coffee-filter cone with a paper coffee filter, and set it over a mixing glass. Pour the tomato juice into the filter and let it drain until all that remains is a thick paste of tomato solids. There should be about 5 oz (150 ml) of translucent red tomato "water" in the glass. (If you're planning to serve several drinks, adjust the amount of juice that you filter accordingly.)

● Chill a martini glass in the freezer or by filling it with ice and cold water and setting it aside.

● Fill a cocktail shaker two-thirds full with ice cubes. Add 4 oz (120 ml) of the tomato water, along with the pepper vodka, lime juice, Worcestershire sauce, white pepper, and salt. Cover and shake vigorously for 15–20 seconds.

● Remove the martini glass from the freezer, or empty out the ice and water, shaking out any remaining drops. Strain the drink into the glass. With a cocktail pick, spear the lime slice and the tomato, and place the garnish in the drink, leaning it against the rim of the glass. Serve immediately.

bloody bull

2 oz (60 ml) vodka • 3 oz (90 ml) canned beef broth • 2 oz (60 ml) high-quality canned or bottled tomato juice • 1 tablespoon fresh lemon juice • ¼ teaspoon Worcestershire sauce • ⅛ teaspoon hot pepper sauce (such as Tabasco) • ⅛ teaspoon freshly ground black pepper • ⅛ teaspoon celery salt • 1 lemon wedge, for garnish • 1 stick beef jerky, for garnish (optional)

● Fill a cocktail shaker two-thirds full with ice cubes. Add the vodka, beef broth, tomato juice, lemon juice, Worcestershire sauce, hot pepper sauce, black pepper, and celery salt.

● Shake for 15–20 seconds. Fill an iced tea or pint glass with ice cubes. Strain the cocktail into the glass. Garnish with the lemon wedge and, if you like, the beef jerky. Serve immediately.

michelada

6 oz (180 ml) lager-style Mexican beer (such as Corona or Pacifico) • ½ fresh lime • hot pepper sauce (such as Tabasco) • 4 oz (120 ml) high-quality canned or bottled tomato juice • ⅛ teaspoon salt

● Fill a large iced tea or pint glass with ice cubes. Slowly pour in the beer. When the foam subsides, squeeze in the lime, dropping it into the glass, and add several drops of hot pepper sauce to taste.

● Slowly pour in the tomato juice. Add the salt and stir briefly and gently with a swizzle stick or bar spoon before serving.

WHEN THE SUN IS SHINING AND THE HEAT IS ON, NOTHING

THEN ADD FRUIT OR JUICES — PLUS A TOUCH OF IMAGINATION —

SATISFIES THIRST LIKE DRINKS THAT BEGIN WITH ICE AND SPIRITS,

TO CREATE PERFECT quenching refreshers

NO MATTER WHAT THIRST-QUENCHING REFRESHER YOU PLAN TO SERVE, ONE INGREDIENT IS ESSENTIAL: LOTS OF ICE

"Breaking the ice" is a perfect metaphor for getting a party rolling. Not only does it evoke images of clear sailing ahead but, especially when the weather is hot, it also holds out the hope of well-chilled drinks.

Always keep plenty of ice on hand when you plan to serve any of the drinks in this chapter. Some, such as margaritas (pages 52–55) and the blue Hawaiian (opposite and page 57), are most commonly served on the rocks. Blended drinks require a generous amount of ice per serving to produce a thick, shiver-inducing slush; and champagne or sparkling wine used for champagne cocktails (pages 70–73) is quickly and effectively chilled in a bucket filled with ice. So check your freezer's ice maker to see that it's turned on and filled to capacity, and be prepared to supplement your supply with a trip to the market.

margarita

SINCE AT LEAST THE 1940S, MARGARITAS AND PARTIES HAVE BEEN INSEPARABLE, ESPECIALLY AT POOLSIDE OR PATIO GATHERINGS. THE SWEET-CITRUS MIX IS A COOL FOIL FOR THE WARMTH OF TEQUILA.

coarse salt and 1 lime wedge, for coating rim (optional) • 2 oz (60 ml) tequila (use a top-shelf brand for best taste) • 1½ oz (45 ml) Cointreau or Grand Marnier • 1 oz (30 ml) fresh lime juice • 1 slice lime, for garnish

● Pour a shallow layer of salt onto a plate slightly larger than the rim of a cocktail or old-fashioned glass. Lightly squeeze the lime wedge and use it to moisten the rim of the glass. Invert the glass into the salt to coat the rim. Using a scoop or tongs, fill the glass with ice cubes, taking care not to disturb the salt rim.

● Fill a cocktail shaker two-thirds full with ice cubes. Add the tequila, Cointreau or Grand Marnier, and lime juice. Cover and shake vigorously for 15–20 seconds. Strain the cocktail into the ice-filled, salt-rimmed glass and serve immediately. As with many cocktails, margaritas may also be served "up." Simply strain the drink into a chilled martini glass and garnish with lime.

summer splash

● Instead of using coasters, look for glasses that fit into their own basket-weave holders that also keep hands from feeling chilled.

● Garnish the cocktails with a decorative lime "pinwheel." Cut a thin slice of lime, then make a slit halfway across its diameter, from the center to one side. Pass a cocktail umbrella or pick through one corner, then twist the other corner down and pass the pick through it.

blended mango margarita

coarse salt and 1 lime wedge, for coating rim (optional) • 2 oz (60 ml) tequila • 1 oz (30 ml) bottled sweetened lime juice (such as Rose's) • 1 medium ripe mango, peeled, flesh cut from pit, and 3 thin wedges saved for garnish • 1 cup (250 ml) ice cubes

● If you enjoy a salt-crusted rim, pour a shallow layer of salt onto a plate slightly larger than the rim of a margarita or old-fashioned glass. Lightly squeeze the lime wedge and moisten the rim of the glass with it. Invert the glass into the salt to coat the rim. Put the glass in the freezer to chill.

● Put the tequila, sweetened lime juice, mango flesh, and ice cubes into the jar of a bar blender. Cover and blend until smooth, about 30 seconds.

● Pour the cocktail into the chilled glass. Spear the mango wedges on a cocktail pick and place it in the glass, leaning it against the rim, and serve.

flavor twists

● Many fruits work well for margaritas. Besides the ones here, possibilities include banana, blueberry, cranberry, papaya, passion fruit, peach, pineapple, and raspberry.

● For a more complex flavor, use a *reposado* (briefly aged) or *añejo* (aged for a year or more) tequila.

blended strawberry margarita

2 oz (60 ml) tequila • 1 oz (30 ml) bottled sweetened lime juice • 1 cup (250 ml) fresh or frozen strawberries • 1 cup (250 ml) ice cubes • 2–3 teaspoons superfine sugar • fresh strawberry and lime slices, for garnish

● Place a margarita glass in the freezer to chill. If you like a salt-crusted rim, follow the instructions at left before chilling the glass.

● Combine the tequila, sweetened lime juice, strawberries, ice cubes, and sugar in the blender. Cover and blend for about 30 seconds.

● Pour the cocktail into the chilled glass. With a cocktail pick, spear three strawberry slices, with two small lime slices alternated between them, and garnish the drink. Serve immediately.

blended citrus margarita

2 oz (60 ml) tequila • 1½ oz (45 ml) triple sec or Cointreau • 1 tablespoon fresh lemon juice • 1 table-spoon fresh lime juice • 1 cup (250 ml) ice cubes • 1 each lemon, lime, and orange slice, for garnish

● Chill a margarita or cocktail glass and salt the rim if desired. Blend the tequila, triple sec or Cointreau, lemon and lime juice, and ice in a blender, as above, for about 30 seconds. Pour the drink into the chilled glass. Slightly fold and then spear the three citrus slices with a cocktail pick and lay the garnish across the top of the glass.

mai tai

1 oz (30 ml) golden rum • 1 oz (30 ml) white rum • 1 oz (30 ml)
triple sec • 1 oz (30 ml) fresh lime juice • 1 oz (30 ml) orgeat syrup
(see Glossary, page 93) • 1½ teaspoons superfine sugar • 1 oz (30 ml)
dark rum • 1 maraschino cherry and one sprig fresh mint, for garnish

- Fill a cocktail shaker two-thirds full with ice cubes. Add the
golden and white rum, triple sec, lime juice, orgeat, and sugar.
Cover and shake for 15–20 seconds.

- Fill a double old-fashioned glass nearly full with crushed ice.
Strain the drink into the glass. Pour the dark rum in, floating it
on the surface. Garnish with the cherry and mint sprig, and serve.

perfect pairings

- Make a frozen mai tai by
blending all the ingredients
except the dark rum together
with one cup of ice, then float
the dark rum on top.

- Serve a bowl of almonds
alongside the drink, to pick up
the flavor of the orgeat syrup.

ORIGINALLY CREATED AT TRADER VIC'S RESTAURANT, THE MAI TAI IS A
TROPICAL CLASSIC THAT STILL PACKS A PUNCH. THE BLUE HAWAIIAN'S
AZURE COLOR CONJURES THE WATERS OF ITS NAMESAKE ISLANDS.

blue hawaiian

1 oz (30 ml) light rum • 1 oz (30 ml) blue curaçao • 2 oz (60 ml)
pineapple juice • 1 tablespoon superfine sugar • 1 tablespoon lemon
juice • 1 tablespoon fresh lime juice • 1 oz (30 ml) cream of coconut
(optional) • 1 maraschino cherry and 1 pineapple wedge, for garnish

- Put the light rum, blue curaçao, pineapple juice, sugar, lemon
and lime juice, and cream of coconut (if using) into a cocktail
shaker filled two-thirds full of ice, and shake for 15–20 seconds.

- Fill a tall highball or Collins glass with ice cubes. Strain the
cocktail into the glass. Garnish with the maraschino cherry and
and pineapple wedge, and serve immediately.

tropical touches

- You can create decorative
wraps for drinks that not only
enhance their presentation but
also make cold drinks more
comfortable to hold. Here, a
coconut bark strip is tied with
natural raffia and a ti plant leaf
is tied with green raffia.

sangria

SPAIN'S FAMED RED-WINE PUNCH GETS ITS PLEASANT SWEETNESS FROM FRESH FRUIT AND A TOUCH OF SUGAR. SPLASHES OF BRANDY AND ORANGE-FLAVORED LIQUEUR ADD A DISARMING KICK.

2 oz (60 ml) brandy • 2 oz (60 ml) orange-flavored liqueur (such as Cointreau or Grand Marnier) • 4 tablespoons superfine sugar • 1 (750-ml) bottle dry red wine, preferably Spanish • 1 cup (250 ml) orange juice • 1 oz (30 ml) lemon juice • 1 orange, thinly sliced and seeded • 1 lemon, thinly sliced and seeded • 2 cups (500 ml) club soda

● In a large nonreactive punch bowl or pitcher (made of a material that does not react to acids, such as glass, stainless steel, or enameled metal), stir together the brandy, orange liqueur, and sugar until the sugar dissolves. Stir in the wine, orange juice, lemon juice, and fruit slices. Though the sangria may be served right away, it's better to cover and refrigerate it for 2–4 hours.

● Just before serving, pour in the club soda and stir briefly. Fill old-fashioned, highball, or wine glasses with ice cubes. Pour or ladle the sangria, with the fruit slices, into the glasses and serve.

fresh tips

● Hand-painted tiles from Spain or Mexico make perfect coasters for this Latin libation.

● Many drinks use citrus slices as a garnish. A simple way to make them more stylish is to fold two or more slices together, then spear them on a cocktail pick.

● If you don't have a punch bowl to mix the sangria, try using a large, sturdy hurricane lantern or vase instead.

one To offer a choice of sangrias, assemble ingredients from several recipes (see pages 59 and 63): red and white wines, fresh fruit, spirits, juices, sparkling beverages, and sugar.

two Mix the sangrias in separate containers, following the recipes. Depending upon the size and length of the party, keep extra ingredients on hand to replenish each sangria.

three Before serving, label each choice of sangria by tying a ribbon with an identifying tag around the punch bowl or pitcher. Assemble glasses and coasters.

four Make extra fruit garnishes by spearing fruit slices on cocktail picks. Before serving, stir the soda into the sangria. Fill the glasses with ice, ladle in the sangria, and garnish.

fruity sangria blanca

4 oz (120 ml) Cointreau or triple sec • 2 tablespoons superfine sugar • 1 (750-ml) bottle dry white wine, preferably Spanish • ½ cup (125 ml) fresh orange juice • 1 oz (30 ml) lemon juice • 2 ripe peaches, halved, pitted, and thinly sliced • 2 ripe plums, halved, pitted, and thinly sliced • 1 lemon, thinly sliced and seeded • ½ pound (250 g) fresh cherries, pitted • 1¾ cups (355 ml) lemon-lime soda

● In a large nonreactive pitcher or punch bowl (glass, stainless steel, or enameled metal), stir together the Cointreau or triple sec and sugar until the sugar dissolves. Stir in the wine, orange juice, lemon juice, and fruit slices. Hold each cherry over the pitcher or bowl, squeeze gently to release some of its juice, and drop it into the liquid. If time allows, cover and refrigerate the sangria for 2–4 hours, although you may serve it right away.

● Just before serving, stir in the lemon-lime soda. Fill glasses with ice cubes. Ladle the sangria, with the fruit slices, into the glasses and serve.

tropical sangria mexicana

2 oz (60 ml) tequila • 2 oz (60 ml) triple sec or Cointreau • 6 tablespoons superfine sugar • 1 (750-ml) bottle dry red wine • 1 cup (250 ml) pineapple juice • 2 oz (60 ml) fresh lime juice • 1 small, ripe pineapple, peeled, cored, and sliced into rings • 1 small ripe mango, peeled, pitted, and cubed • 2 limes, thinly sliced and seeded • 2 cups (500 ml) club soda

● In a large nonreactive pitcher or punch bowl, stir together the tequila, triple sec or Cointreau, and sugar until the sugar dissolves. Stir in the wine, pineapple juice, lime juice, pineapple, mango, and lime slices. If time allows, cover and refrigerate for 2–4 hours, although you may serve it right away.

● Before serving, stir in the club soda. Fill large wine glasses with ice cubes. Ladle the sangria, with the fruit slices, into the glasses and serve.

sangria de cava

4 oz (120 ml) framboise (raspberry liqueur) • 1 oz (30 ml) fresh lemon juice • 2 tablespoons superfine sugar • ½ pound (250 g) ripe strawberries, stemmed and sliced • ½ pound (250 g) ripe raspberries or blackberries • ½ pound (250 g) ripe blueberries • 1 lemon, thinly sliced and seeded • 1½ cups (375 ml) cranberry juice cocktail • 1 (750-ml) bottle Cava (Spanish sparkling wine) or other sparkling wine

● In a large nonreactive pitcher or punch bowl, stir together the framboise, lemon juice, and sugar until the sugar dissolves. Stir in the strawberries, raspberries, blueberries, and lemon slices, then stir in the cranberry juice cocktail. Cover and refrigerate for 2–4 hours, stirring occasionally.

● Ladle the fruit mixture into glasses until about halfway full, making sure to include a mix of fruit in each glass. Add several ice cubes, then pour in the Cava to fill the glass. Serve immediately.

tequila sunrise

3 ounces (90 ml) white tequila • 6 ounces (180 ml) fresh orange juice • 2–3 teaspoons grenadine • 1 orange wedge, raw sugar, and grated orange zest, for coating rim (optional)

● Fill a tall highball or Collins glass with ice cubes. Pour in the tequila, then the orange juice. Drizzle in the grenadine to taste, allowing it to settle to the bottom of the glass, and serve.

● For a festive sugared rim, pour a layer of raw sugar and grated orange zest onto a plate that's larger than the glass rim. Moisten the rim with an orange wedge, then press it into the sugar mix.

seaside style

● For a presentation that evokes days at the beach, line a serving tray with a layer of coarse sand and nestle the drinks into it.

● Take the style one step further by gluing small seashells to the tops of cocktail picks.

POMEGRANATE-FLAVORED GRENADINE SYRUP SWIRLS DOWN INTO THE CLASSIC TEQUILA SUNRISE, EVOKING A MORNING SKY. PLANTER'S PUNCH IS A COOL FAVORITE THAT ORIGINATED WITH JAMAICAN PLANTERS.

planter's punch

2 oz (60 ml) dark rum • 2 oz (60 ml) pineapple juice • 1 oz (30 ml) grapefruit juice • 1 oz (30 ml) fresh lime juice • 1 tablespoon superfine sugar • 2 oz (60 ml) club soda • 1 fresh pineapple wedge, for garnish

● Fill a cocktail shaker about two-thirds full with ice cubes. Add the rum, pineapple juice, grapefruit juice, lime juice, and superfine sugar. Shake vigorously for 15–20 seconds.

● Fill a tall highball or Collins glass with ice cubes. Strain the cocktail mixture into the glass. Pour in the club soda to top off, and stir briefly with a bar spoon or swizzle stick. Garnish with the pineapple wedge and serve immediately.

punch it up

● To serve tropical drinks like planter's punch, shop antique stores or yard sales for retro-style Polynesian-themed glassware.

● You might also serve tropical drinks in small pineapples (hollowed out with a melon baller) or in split coconut shells.

mojito

THIS CUBAN CLASSIC IS SAID TO HAVE BEEN A FAVORITE OF ERNEST
HEMINGWAY. IT HAS JUST THE RIGHT BALANCE OF MINT, LIME, RUM,
AND SUGAR TO CHASE THIRST AWAY ON A SULTRY SUMMER'S DAY.

2 or 3 sugar cubes • ¼ cup (10 g) fresh mint leaves • 1½ tablespoons
fresh lime juice • 2 oz (60 ml) light rum • 3 oz (90 ml) club soda •
1 lime wedge and 1 sprig fresh mint, for garnish

● In the bottom of a sturdy tall highball or pint glass, muddle
the sugar cubes, mint leaves, and lime juice together with a
muddler, pounding firmly but gently and grinding the ingredients
together until the sugar cubes are crushed and partially dissolved.

● Fill the glass with ice cubes. Add the rum, then pour in the
soda. Stir well with a bar spoon or swizzle stick. Garnish with
the lime wedge and mint sprig and serve immediately.

● For an unusual, spicy version, try substituting fresh basil
leaves for the mint, and lemon for the lime.

fresh frozen

● To make a blended version
(left, opposite page) muddle the
sugar, mint, and lime juice in a
glass. Add the rum, and steep for
two hours. Put a glassful of ice
cubes into a blender; pour in the
rum mixture through a fine-mesh
sieve. Add another ¼ cup (10 g)
of fresh mint leaves along
with the club soda. Cover
and blend until smooth.

sake mojito

2 sugar cubes • ¼ cup (10 g) fresh mint leaves • 1 oz (30 ml) fresh lime juice • 3 oz (90 ml) sake • 2 oz (60 ml) club soda • 1 lemon slice and fresh mint, for garnish

● Put the sugar cubes, mint leaves, and lime juice in the bottom of a sturdy highball glass. With a muddler, firmly but gently pound and grind the ingredients together until the sugar cubes are crushed and partially dissolved.

● Fill the glass with ice cubes. Add the sake, then pour in the soda. Stir well with a swizzle stick or bar spoon. Garnish with the lemon slice folded on a cocktail pick and the mint sprig, and serve.

make it special

● Add creative details geared toward the drinks you're serving. For the sake mojito, use origami paper to make coasters, or wrap the drinks in the paper and tie them with a bit of palm twine or raffia. A coco-limon mojito can be enhanced with the addition of a coconut rim: dip the rim of the glass in light corn syrup, then into a plate of shaved coconut.

● Like many spirits, rum is now available in a wide variety of flavors, making it easy to create new variations of the classic mojito. You can also experiment with additions of fresh fruit such as raspberries.

coco-limon mojito

1 or 2 sugar cubes • ¼ cup (10 g) fresh mint leaves • 1 tablespoon fresh lemon juice • 2 oz (60 ml) coconut-flavored rum • 3 oz (90 ml) lemon-flavored soda • 1 strip lemon zest, 3 inches (7.5 cm) long, for garnish

● In the bottom of a highball glass, combine the sugar cube(s), mint leaves, and lemon juice. Firmly but gently pound and grind the ingredients together with a muddler, until the sugar is crushed and partially dissolved.

● Fill the glass with ice. Add the coconut-flavored rum, then pour in the lemon soda. Stir well with a bar spoon or swizzle stick. Garnish with the lemon zest, skewered on a cocktail pick, and fresh mint.

ginger twilight mojito

2 or 3 sugar cubes • 1 slice fresh ginger, about ¼ inch (6 mm) thick and 1 inch (2.5 cm) in diameter • 1 tablespoon fresh lime juice • 2 oz (60 ml) spiced rum • 3 oz (90 ml) club soda • 2 slices crystallized ginger, for garnish

● Muddle the sugar cubes, fresh ginger, and lime juice in a highball or old-fashioned glass as with the previous mojitos.

● Fill the glass with ice cubes. Add the spiced rum, then pour in the soda. Stir well with a bar spoon or swizzle stick. Spear two slices of crystallized ginger on a cocktail pick and place it in the drink, resting it along the side of the glass.

champagne cocktail

THIS PARAGON OF SIMPLE ELEGANCE DATES TO THE MID-19TH CENTURY.
A BITTERS-SOAKED SUGAR CUBE AND A TWIST OF LEMON ZEST GIVE A
DIGNIFIED LIFT TO EVEN THE MOST HUMBLE SPARKLER.

1 sugar cube • 2 or 3 drops Angostura bitters • 5 oz (150 ml)
well-chilled champagne or sparkling wine • 1 strip lemon zest,
3 inches (7.5 cm) long, for garnish

- Place the sugar cube on a small plate and carefully drip the
bitters onto the cube. Put the sugar cube in a champagne flute.

- Slowly pour the champagne into the glass. Hold the lemon
zest strip over the glass, and twist it in opposite directions to
release its oils before dropping it into the glass.

- For added drama, pour the champagne into the flutes first.
Prepare the sugar cubes beforehand by dropping the bitters onto
them, and let each guest drop a cube into a glass before toasting.

a votre santé

- Make it easy for guests to
keep track of glasses by attaching
small initialed tags (available at
stationery stores) to the stems.

- Turn this cocktail into a version
of a "French 75": mix 1 oz (30 ml)
cognac with 1 tablespoon lemon
juice and add it to the flute
before adding the sugar cube.

kir framboise royale

4 oz (120 ml) well-chilled champagne or other sparkling wine • 1 tablespoon framboise (raspberry liqueur) • 1 tablespoon crème de cassis • fresh raspberries, for garnish

● Chill a champagne flute in the freezer. Pour in the champagne, then add the framboise and crème de cassis. Garnish with the raspberries.

---

champagne service

● Champagne should always be served in long-stemmed flutes or tulip-shaped glasses, which enhance the rise of bubbles to the crown and concentrate the aromas.

● Use caution when opening champagne and sparkling wines. It's wise to keep a finger or thumb on the cork as you undo the cage, to prevent the cork from bursting out.

● Though popping the cork may seem festive, it dissipates some of the bubbles and affects the wine's taste. The bottle should "sigh," not pop. Hold the cork and turn the bottle (rather than turning the cork), dislodging the cork as gently as you possibly can.

---

bellini bella

1½ oz (45 ml) well-chilled peach nectar • 1 teaspoon lemon juice • 1 tablespoon peach schnapps • 4 oz (120 ml) well-chilled prosecco or other sparkling wine • 1 thin wedge fresh peach, for garnish

● Chill a champagne flute in the freezer.

● In a small measuring cup, stir together the peach nectar, lemon juice, and peach schnapps.

● Just before serving, pour the peach nectar mixture into the chilled flute. Slowly pour in the prosecco. Stir gently with a swizzle stick or bar spoon, garnish with the peach wedge, and serve.

berry merry christmas

1 sugar cube • 2 drops orange or Angostura bitters • 4 oz (120 ml) well-chilled champagne or sparkling wine • 1 oz (30 ml) well-chilled cranberry juice cocktail • fresh or frozen cranberries, for garnish

● Chill a champagne flute in the freezer.

● Put the sugar cube on a small plate. Gently shake the drops of bitters onto the sugar cube.

● Pour the champagne into the chilled flute. Add the cranberry juice. Drop the sugar cube into the glass, garnish with a few cranberries, and serve.

SOME DRINKS ARE DESIGNED TO BE SLOWLY SIPPED AND SAVORED.

LAYERED LIQUEURS, AND SPIRIT-FORTIFIED COFFEES SATISFY AFTER-DINNER

BLACK RUSSIANS, BRANDY ALEXANDERS, CLASSIC FRENCH-STYLE

CRAVINGS FOR DECADENT rich indulgences

CAP OFF A MEMORABLE OCCASION BY SERVING DRINKS THAT INVITE GUESTS TO LINGER A LITTLE WHILE LONGER

"How about a nightcap?" That time-honored offer signals a congenial and cozy transition towards evening's end, and perfectly captures the way that drinks can conclude a party in soothing style.

Some people like to transform spirited liquids into a form of dessert, adding cream to vodka and coffee liqueur to make a white Russian (page 81), for example, or layering liqueurs with complementary flavors and colors to make a classic French-style pousse-café (page 85). Other recipes, by contrast, add spirits and spices to coffee to make intensely flavorful concoctions that are best appreciated in small, slow sips. Both approaches offer an ideal way to prolong the pleasures of good company, whether you're seated around the dinner table, on the terrace, in the living room, or beside the fireplace.

eggnog

THIS TRADITIONAL HOLIDAY TREAT CAN BE SERVED HOT OR COLD.
INSPIRED BY A POTTERY BARN FAMILY RECIPE, THIS OLD-FASHIONED
EGGNOG NICELY BALANCES RICHNESS, SWEETNESS, SPICE, AND SPIRITS.

6 eggs • ¾ cup (180 ml) sugar • 2 cups (500 ml) milk • 2 cups (500 ml) brandy • ⅔ cup (160 ml) Jamaican rum • ¼ cup (60 ml) Grand Marnier or Cointreau • 1 teaspoon vanilla extract • 2 cups (500 ml) heavy cream, chilled • freshly grated nutmeg, for garnish

● Put the eggs and sugar in a pot and whisk briefly until smooth. Put the pot over the lowest possible heat and whisk continuously, just until the eggs are warmed, 3–5 minutes, taking care not to let them curdle. Still whisking, add the milk, brandy, rum, Grand Marnier, vanilla, and half of the cream. Raise the heat slightly and cook, stirring frequently, until hot but not boiling, 8–10 minutes.

● Remove from the heat. Whisk in the remaining cream. Pour into a heatproof punch bowl. Serve warm, or cover and transfer to the refrigerator to chill. Before serving, lightly dust the surface with nutmeg; ladle into glass mugs, and dust with more nutmeg.

make merry

● To give your presentation a quiet elegance, place the punch bowl on a silver platter and arrange cut-glass ornaments around its base.

● Chocolatey peppermint bark extends the holiday theme.

● New heat-resistant double-walled glasses (opposite page) give hot drinks contemporary style and may be used with cold drinks as well.

black russian

2 oz (60 ml) vodka • 1–1 ½ oz (30–45 ml) coffee-flavored liqueur
(such as Kahlúa or Tía Maria)

- Fill an old-fashioned glass with ice cubes. Pour in the vodka.
Add coffee liqueur to taste, using less if you prefer a drier cocktail,
more if you like it sweeter. Stir briefly with a bar spoon or
swizzle stick. Serve immediately.

- For a variation on the classic, you might substitute other spirits
for the vodka; using Irish whiskey instead yields a "black Irish"; a
"blackjack" is made with Jack Daniels bourbon instead of vodka.

sweet inspiration

- Serve drinks on individual trays accompanied by chocolate-covered espresso beans.
- For a frappé-style black Russian, serve the drink over crushed ice instead of ice cubes, or blend it in a blender.

POPULAR SINCE THE 1960s, THE SOPHISTICATED "RUSSIANS" PAIR
WELL WITH STRONG COFFEE. SUBSTITUTE DIFFERENT SPIRITS TO LEND
ADDED INTRIGUE TO THESE CROWD-PLEASING CLASSIC DRINKS.

white russian

2 oz (60 ml) vodka • 1 oz (30 ml) coffee-flavored liqueur (such as
Kahlúa or Tía Maria) • 1 oz (30 ml) heavy cream

- Fill an old-fashioned glass with ice cubes. Pour in the vodka,
add the coffee liqueur, and stir briefly with a bar spoon or swizzle
stick. Drizzle in the cream, shaking the glass slightly to swirl it in.

- For variations on the white Russian, add a splash of soda to
temper the sweetness; substitute orange-flavored vodka for the
plain vodka; substitute dark crème de cacao for the Kahlúa to create
a "brown Russian"; or substitute Irish cream liqueur for the cream.

make mine vanilla

- Instead of a swizzle stick, use a vanilla bean to swirl the cream into the drink.
- For more vanilla flavor, substitute a vanilla-flavored vodka for the plain vodka in the drink recipe.

brandy alexander

SIP AFTER SIP, THIS LONGTIME AFTER-DINNER FAVORITE CAPTURES THE APPEAL OF A CREAMY CHOCOLATE TRUFFLE, WITH THE ADDED WARMTH OF BRANDY AND THE SILKY RICHNESS OF CRÈME DE CACAO.

sugar and spice

● To make chocolate shavings, draw a swivel-bladed vegetable peeler along the edge of a room-temperature chocolate bar

● For a "brandy Alejandro," substitute Mexican brandy and mix ground cinnamon with the cocoa powder for dusting.

● A set of glasses in a rainbow of different colors adds variety to pale-hued drinks – and helps guests identify which is theirs.

2 oz (60 ml) brandy • 1 oz (30 ml) dark crème de cacao • 1 oz (30 ml) heavy cream • cocoa powder and fresh chocolate shavings, for garnish

● Chill a martini or other cocktail glass in the freezer or by filling it with ice cubes and water and setting it aside to chill.

● Put the brandy, crème de cacao, and cream in a cocktail shaker two-thirds filled with ice cubes. Shake for 15–20 seconds.

● Remove the glass from the freezer or empty out the ice cubes and water, shaking out any drops. Strain the drink into the chilled glass. Sprinkle lightly with a little cocoa powder and some chocolate shavings to garnish, and serve. For a less sweet garnish, dust the top of the drink with a sprinkle of grated nutmeg.

● For an updated take on this classic, substitute vanilla-flavored vodka for the brandy and light crème de cacao for dark.

pousse-café

FRENCH FOR "COFFEE-PUSHER," THE POUSSE-CAFÉ HAS BEEN MAKING
AFTER-DINNER COFFEE A PLEASURE SINCE THE MID-19TH CENTURY.
CAREFUL LAYERING OF THE LIQUEURS GIVES THE BEST EFFECT.

1½ tablespoons grenadine, chilled • 1½ tablespoons green
crème de menthe, chilled • 1½ tablespoons light rum, chilled

- Pour the grenadine into a pousse-café glass or other tall,
narrow liqueur glass.

- Hold the back of a slender teaspoon with its tip just above
the surface of the grenadine. Slowly trickle the crème de menthe
down the back of the spoon so that it floats on top of the
grenadine (see step-by-step photos on the following pages).

- Rinse the spoon, then, using the same technique, layer the
light rum to float on top of the crème de menthe. Take care not
to disturb the glass as you serve; it is meant to be sipped in layers.

- This recipe is easily adapted to use your favorite liqueurs,
but always layer the liqueurs in order of their density.

custom options

- Create your own favorites
by selecting other spirits or
liqueurs with complementary
flavors, such as crème de cassis,
white crème de menthe, and blue
curaçao, or Kahlúa, Irish cream,
and Frangelico.

- Put the liqueurs you'll be
using into the freezer for one
hour before you're ready to serve
them to thicken them slightly.

one Assemble the liquids for the pousse-café. For easy pouring and attractive tableside presentation, prepare a clean bottle for each, labeling it with a decorative tag.

two Insert a clean funnel into the neck of a bottle. Pour the liqueur from its container into the funnel to fill the new bottle. Chill the filled bottles before using.

three Insert a pouring spout with a narrow nozzle into the neck of each bottle. Place a pousse-café glass on an individual serving tray. Carefully pour in the first liquid.

four Hold the tip of a bar spoon close to but not touching the surface of the liquid. Drizzle the next liquid down the back of the spoon's bowl. Repeat with the final liqueur.

rich indulgences **87**

irish coffee

THIS AFTER-DINNER FAVORITE WAS FIRST SERVED AT IRELAND'S SHANNON AIRPORT IN THE 1940s AND QUICKLY CAUGHT ON, ESPECIALLY IN AMERICA. HIGH-QUALITY WHISKEY AND STRONG COFFEE ENSURE SUCCESS.

delicious style

- To add a touch of Ireland's favorite color, drizzle a little green crème de menthe over the whipped cream before serving.

- To make the presentation more special, brew a pot of strong coffee in a cafetière and present the cafetière, shot glasses or cordial glasses full of Irish whiskey, and a bowl of lightly whipped cream on a tray, and let guests make their own drinks.

2 oz (60 ml) Irish whiskey • 1–1½ teaspoons superfine sugar • 6 oz (180 ml) hot, strong freshly brewed coffee • 2 heaping tablespoons lightly whipped chilled heavy cream

- Heat an Irish-coffee mug, stemmed goblet, or snifter by pouring boiling water into it and setting it aside for a moment to heat, then emptying the water, shaking out any remaining drops.

- Put the whiskey, along with sugar to taste, in the mug, goblet, or snifter and stir with a bar spoon until the sugar dissolves.

- Pour in the coffee and stir briefly. Spoon the whipped cream on top and serve immediately. (Note: the cream should be whipped only until it just begins to thicken.)

- Traditionalists insist that you not stir the coffee after adding the cream. The coffee is meant to be sipped though the cream.

mocha brûlot royale

1 cup (250 ml) brandy • 1 tablespoon sugar • 6 whole cloves • 4 strips orange zest, 3 inches (7.5 cm) long, cut with a swivel-bladed vegetable peeler • 2 cinnamon sticks, broken in half • 2 oz (60 ml) dark crème de cacao • 3 cups (750 ml) strong black freshly brewed coffee • 4 oz (120 ml) lightly whipped heavy cream • cinnamon sticks and shaved chocolate, for garnish

● Combine the brandy, sugar, cloves, orange zest, and cinnamon sticks in a nonreactive saucepan. Heat over medium-high heat, stirring occasionally, just until the mixture begins to simmer. Remove the pan from the heat to an open area on the kitchen counter or near the sink.

● Strike a long wooden match and slowly and very carefully bring the flame near the surface of the liquid to ignite the brandy's fumes. Let the brandy flame for about 30 seconds. Then, cover the pan to extinguish the flames. Uncover and stir in the crème de cacao. Ladle the mixture into 4 glasses or mugs. Add the coffee and top with whipped cream. Garnish with cinnamon sticks and sprinkles of freshly shaved chocolate. Serves 4.

cafe à la russe

2 oz (60 ml) vodka • 2 oz (60 ml) freshly brewed espresso-strength coffee • 1–1½ teaspoons superfine sugar • 1 tablespoon heavy cream • 3 chocolate-covered coffee beans and ground cinnamon, for garnish

● Fill a cocktail shaker two-thirds full with ice cubes. Add the vodka, coffee, sugar to taste, and cream. Shake vigorously for 15–20 seconds.

● Fill a tall old-fashioned or pint glass with ice cubes. Strain the drink into the glass. Garnish the froth on top with the chocolate-covered espresso beans and a dusting of cinnamon, and serve.

jamaican coffee frappé

2 oz (60 ml) dark spiced rum • 1–1½ teaspoons superfine sugar • 6 oz (180 ml) strong black coffee, preferably Jamaican Blue Mountain, cooled • 1 oz (30 ml) chilled heavy cream • 1 cup (250 ml) ice cubes

● Put the rum, sugar, coffee, cream, and ice cubes into the jar of a bar blender. Cover and blend until well mixed and smooth, about 30 seconds. Pour into a chilled glass, and garnish with a little whipped cream, if desired.

wrap it up

● You can easily create drink "cozies" like the ones shown here, to make hot or cold drinks more comfortable to hold. Simply cut squares of felt about 6 x 6 inches (15 x 15 cm). Place a glass on top of each fabric square, lift up the corners, and tie each glass with a thin leather lace. Tie beads to the ends of the laces.

GLOSSARY

Aperitif A term for any spirit-based drink sipped before dining with the purpose of stimulating the appetite.

Bar spoon A long, slender spoon used to stir cocktails and other mixed drinks.

Beer This popular beverage is made by fermenting mashed cooked grains and hops. Lager-style beers are the familiar pale golden beers popular in America.

Bitters Distilled from secret formulas of botanical ingredients, these highly concentrated alcoholic elixirs – of which the most familiar brands are Angostura and Peychaud – are used just a few drops at a time to add a hint of flavor to mixed drinks.

Boston shaker A type of cocktail shaker consisting of one tall, sturdy glass with straight, sloping sides and a similar metal container that is inverted snugly over it, forming a tight seal while liquid ingredients and ice are agitated. Those drinks that are stirred rather than shaken may be mixed with a bar spoon in the glass portion.

Bourbon From Kentucky and other parts of the American South, this type of whiskey is distilled from a mash of fermented grains and must contain at least 51 percent corn, combined with malted barley and rye or wheat, producing a full-bodied flavor.

Brandy Any strong spirit distilled from fermented fruit juice, of which the most common source is wine made from grapes. Other brandies may be made from such fruits as peaches, raspberries, cherries, or apples; but when the term "brandy" is used alone, it refers always to grape brandy.

Cava A term referring to the sparkling wine produced primarily in northeastern Spain, made from a blend of seven grapes, including Chardonnay and Pinot Noir, that gives it a rich, fruity, yet dry character.

Champagne Although this term is misused to refer to any sparkling wine, it specifically designates those carefully produced, complex sparkling wines made according to tradition (and law) in the northeastern French region of the same name.

Cocktail Any mixed drink that is shaken or stirred and then poured or strained into a cocktail glass.

Cocktail shaker Any of a variety of sturdy watertight containers used to mix drink ingredients while quickly chilling them with ice cubes. While the Boston shaker variety is made up of two glasses, those referred to as "cocktail shakers" generally are composed of a glass or metal beaker atop which sits a snug metal top with a built-in strainer covered with a cap.

Coffee-flavored liqueur Coffee beans or brewed coffee is featured as the flavoring ingredient in a wide range of popular sweet liqueurs such as Kahlúa and Tía Maria.

Cognac A type of well-aged wine-based brandy produced in the Cognac region of southwestern France, prized for its purity and mellowness of flavor.

Cordial A sweet alcoholic beverage, also generally referred to as a liqueur, based on a spirit, a sweetener, and one or more complementary flavorings. See also "Liqueur."

Curaçao Originally made with fruit from the Caribbean island of the same name (still used in some premium brands), this liqueur is intensely flavored with the essence of orange peel. It is available in a clear colorless "white" version as well as in colored forms, including orange, green, brown, and blue.

Dash A drink ingredient measurement equivalent to $\frac{1}{8}$ teaspoon, named for the rapid wrist motion used to dispense such bottled flavoring agents as bitters, hot pepper sauce, or Worcestershire sauce.

Digestif Refers to beverages, often spirit-based, sipped after a meal to aid the digestive process.

Garnish Any fruit or vegetable – including sweet maraschino or fresh cherries, orange slices or wedges, whole strawberries, mint sprigs, celery stalks, and pickled olives or cocktail onions – added to a drink just before serving, not only to enhance its visual appeal, but also sometimes to provide a pleasurable nibble.

Gin A clear spirit distilled from a grain mash, flavored with botanical ingredients that always include juniper berries, which give it a clean, bracing flavor.

Grenadine A deep blush-colored syrup for coloring and flavoring drinks, sometimes made with pomegranate juice.

Hawthorn strainer A kind of strainer for shaken or stirred drinks, characterized by a flat, circular piece of screen with a metal spring coil around its rim that holds it snugly in place over a mixing glass.

Highball A simple mixed drink that usually consists of just two ingredients, a spirit and a mixer, poured directly into a tall highball glass filled with ice.

Hot pepper sauce Any of a wide variety of different commercially bottled condiments made from hot red chili peppers, of which the most widely known brand is Tabasco.

Jigger A liquid measurement equivalent to 1½ ounces (45 ml), as well as a small vessel used to measure that amount when mixing drinks.

Lager See beer, lager-style.

Lillet A French brand of aperitif made from Bordeaux wine fortified with Armagnac and a proprietary blend of herbs, spices, and fruits. Lillet is available in *blanc* (white) and *rouge* (red), each with its own flavors.

Lime juice, bottled sweetened A popular source of citrusy tang and sweetness for mixed drinks. The most commonly available brand is Rose's.

Limoncello An Italian digestif produced along the Amalfi Coast, made by steeping lemon peels in clear spirits, sweetening with sugar, and diluting with water.

Liqueur Also referred to as a cordial, this sweetened spirit may be flavored with fruits, nuts, herbs, spices, or other botanical essences, either singly or in combination, to produce an intensely flavored liquid that may be sipped on its own as an after-dinner drink or used to flavor mixed drinks

Maraschino cherry Frequently used as a garnish for drinks, often with its stem still attached, this bottled pitted red cherry has been steeped and dyed in a flavored sugar syrup. Red maraschino cherries are slightly flavored with almond, green ones with mint.

Melon liqueur A bright neon-green liqueur flavored with honeydew melon, most commonly known by the Japanese brand name Midori.

Mixed drink Any drink made with two or more liquid ingredients, at least one of which includes alcohol. The cocktail and the highball are the two most common subcategories.

Mixer Any nonalcoholic liquid that is combined with an alcoholic liquid to make a mixed drink. Included in this category are sodas such as cola, lemon-lime soda, ginger ale, and flavorless club soda; fruit juices; and tomato juice.

Mixing glass The tall, sloping-sided glass portion of a Boston shaker.

Muddling The process of mashing together sugar cubes or granulated sugar with aromatic or flavorful ingredients such as fresh mint, fruit, or bitters to combine and release their flavors before ice and liquids are added. The long, narrow pestle known as a "muddler" is the most convenient tool for the job, although the back of a sturdy spoon may also be used.

Orange-flavored liqueur Orange is a very popular liqueur flavor, with numerous brands available and sometimes referred to categorically by the term "triple sec" or Curaçao. Two of the most popular brands of orange-flavored liqueur are Cointreau and Grand Marnier, both of which have been produced in France since the 19th century.

Orgeat A sweet, thick, milky-hued syrup made with almonds and either rose water or orange-flower water, used to flavor and sweeten mixed drinks. If you can't find orgeat, substitute one of the clear bottled almond-flavored syrups now widely available for flavoring coffee.

Prosecco An aromatic, fruity, light sparkling wine produced in northeastern Italy from a grape variety of the same name.

Rum A spirit of the Caribbean and South America, distilled from molasses or sugar-cane juice. White or light rum has been filtered to remove all traces of color. Golden and dark rums may get their colors and additional flavor from the omission of that final filtration, from aging in oak casks, or from the addition of caramel. Many distillers now also market flavored rums.

Rye A type of whiskey made from a fermented grain mash that includes at least 51 percent rye grains, generally aged in new charred oak barrels.

Sake A Japanese wine, generally dry, made from rice and water, with a mellow flavor and lingering sweetness. Traditionally sipped cool or warm, sake has also found favor as a mixed drink ingredient.

Schnapps A German term that technically refers to a clear brandy or eau-de-vie based on fruit or some other botanical ingredient. The word "schnapps" is also used to refer to a commercially bottled sweetened brandy similar to a liqueur, such as peppermint or peach schnapps.

Scotch Another term for whisky produced in Scotland. Among the most popular Scotches are "single-malt" varieties, made by individual distilleries from their own malted barley mashes then aged in oak barrels for three years (or many more) before finally being bottled without blending. Single-malt Scotch should be savored on its own, never used as part of a mixed drink.

Shot A single, neat portion of a spirit, equivalent to 1½ oz (45 ml), generally measured in a measuring glass of the same name. Note, however, that not all glasses sold as shot glasses may be precise, and some hold as much as 2 oz (60 ml).

Southern Comfort A brand of fruit-flavored liqueur made by steeping peaches and other ingredients in a base of Bourbon.

Sparkling wine A generic term referring to any wine that contains small bubbles of carbon dioxide gas. Usually, this is produced by a secondary fermentation of the wine that occurs within the bottle, a process referred to as "méthode champenoise," a reference to the classic method developed in the Champagne region of France.

Sugar, superfine, A form of white sugar, widely available in food stores, that has been finely ground to help it dissolve quickly and thoroughly in liquids, making it a convenient way to sweeten mixed drinks.

Swizzle stick A slender rod that may be used either to mix a drink in a pitcher or glass before serving or to stir it between sips. Swizzle sticks may range from fanciful disposable plastic varieties to reusable glass or metal sticks of various decorative designs.

Tequila A liquor made in the Tequila region of Mexico, fermented and distilled from the steam-roasted and mashed hearts of the blue agave plant. Tequila *blanco*, known in English as "white" or "silver" tequila, is a sparkling-clear unaged spirit with a bright, slightly peppery flavor. Gold tequila contains a percentage of two-month-old aged tequila and may also include caramel or other flavoring agents to enhance its smoothness. Tequila *reposado*, literally "rested," has been aged in oak for a minimum of two months, yielding a smoother, rounder flavor. Tequila *añejo*, or "aged," has spent at least one year (and often many more) in oak barrels, giving it a dark color and a rich, round flavor.

Vermouth A white wine that has been slightly fortified with additional alcohol and given subtle aromas from blends of botanical ingredients. Available in both dry and sweet forms, vermouth is most often used in small amounts as a modifier for drinks based on other spirits.

Vodka A clear, relatively flavorless spirit distilled from a fermented mash of grains or vegetables such as potatoes. Look also for a wide range of vodkas now available flavored with essences of fruits and spices.

Whisk(e)y A spirit distilled from a fermented mash of grains and aged in wooden casks, resulting in an amber color and a rich, round flavor. The spelling "whisky" refers specifically to those products made and bottled in either Scotland or Canada, while "whiskey" designates those produced in Ireland or the United States.

Zest The outermost, brightly colored layer of a citrus fruit's peel, full of flavorful essential oils. When a recipe calls for zest, remove it with a special zesting tool, a sharp paring knife, or a swivel-bladed vegetable peeler, taking care to leave behind the spongy, bitter-tasting layer of pith beneath it.

INDEX

ACKNOWLEDGMENTS

Author Norman Kolpas would like to thank Katie and Jake for their support during the production of this book.

Weldon Owen would like to thank the photography and editorial teams, and acknowledge the following people and organizations:

Copy Editor
Sharron Wood

Indexer
Ken DellaPenta

Associate Stylist
Elisabet der Nederlanden

Photography Assistant
Tom Hood

Lead Merchandise Coordinator
Mario Serafin

Merchandise Coordinator
Peter Jewett

Assistance, advice, or support
Birdman, Inc., Sarah Putman Clegg, Elizabeth Dougherty, the Griggs family, Kass Kapsiak (Catering by Kass), Charlie Path, Sara Terrien, and the Pottery Barn product development team and staff at the Pottery Barn Store, Corte Madera, California.